FOR THE LOVE
OF ANTHONY

FOR THE LOVE OF ANTHONY

A MOTHER'S SEARCH FOR PEACE AFTER THE LONDON BOMBINGS

MARIE FATAYI-WILLIAMS

HODDER &
STOUGHTON

British Library Cataloguing in Publication Data
A record for this book is available from the British Library

ISBN-10: 0 340 91018 6
ISBN-13: 978 0 340 91018 4

Typeset in Goudy by Avon DataSet Ltd,
Bidford on Avon, Warwickshire

Printed and bound in Great Britain by
Clays Ltd, St Ives plc

The paper used in this book is a natural recyclable product
made from wood grown in sustainable forests.
The hard coverboard is recycled.

Hodder & Stoughton
A Division of Hodder Headline Ltd
338 Euston Road
London NW1 3BH
www.madaboutbooks.com

For the love of all grieving mothers and families of the London 7/7 attack . . . and for the love of all innocent casualties of war and terror, the world over.

ACKNOWLEDGEMENTS

This is one of the most difficult things of all to write. I hardly know where to start, because of the outpouring of love and support I have received from good and loving people the world over. In your prayers and phone calls, personal visits, e-mails, letters, cards, condolence messages and in many other ways, you have provided support and strength to me and my family.

It would be impossible to thank each one of you by name but I want you to know that you are very special to me and my prayers are with you and yours always.

To all the lovely parishioners of the Church of the Assumption Falomo – lagos, The past and present Parish Priests and their assistants as well as the Priests who celebrated the July 30th memorial service; to all the wonderful parishioners and Priests of the Sacred Heart Church, Mill Hill and St Phillips at Church End, Finchley; to his Eminence Cardinal Cormac Murphy O'Connor, Bishop Alan Hopes, the con-celebrating priests as well as all who attended the funeral mass of July 23rd, Monsignor Langham and the clergy of Westminster Cathedral; to the Monastic community of the Tyburn nuns at Hyde Park, London, and the Mother Abbess and community of the Ave Mother of the Church Monastery Lekki, Lagos; to Professor D. Noibi, the Chief Imam of the Muslim Association of Nigeria (United Kingdom), and the Chief Imam of the Anwar-Ul-Islam in Lagos; to all of Anthony's ever-loving friends, as well as those of my two daughters and their cousins; to all the members, and Matrons of the Guild of

Immaculate Conception, the Confraternity of Christian Mothers, Sacred Heart of Jesus and the Immaculate Heart of Mary Association, St Rita's devotees, Young Catholic professionals, the Divine Mercy prayer group, the Board of Lectors, and St Anthony's Guild; to all the members of St Teresa's College Old Girls Association, London and Lagos branches and in particular class of 67; to my course mates at the University of Ife; to Alan's and my professional colleagues everywhere; to the two family liaison officers to members of the press; to all the Patrons and Trustees of the Anthony Fatayi-Williams Foundation; to my and Alan's immediate and extended Families – the Ikimi family of Igueben LGA of Edo state and Issa Williams family of Lagos state and all their wonderful friends; to my editor and researcher Christopher Stevens, to my friend Sade Marriott the facilitator and to my ever-thoughtful agent Heather Holden-Brown who made this book possible . . . my deep thanks and love to you all.

THE SPEECH IN TAVISTOCK SQUARE

On Monday 11 July 2005, in the wake of the London bombings, Marie Fatayi-Williams delivered this momentous speech in Tavistock Square, London:

This is Anthony, Anthony Fatayi-Williams, twenty-six years old. He's missing and we fear that he was in the bus explosion . . . on Thursday. We don't know. We do know from the witnesses that he left the Northern line in Euston. We know he made a call to his office at Amec at 9.41 from the NW1 area to say he could not make it by Tube but he would find alternative means to work. Since then he has not made any contact with any single person.

Now New York, now Madrid, now London. There has been widespread slaughter of innocent people. There have been streams of tears, innocent tears. There have been rivers of blood, innocent blood. Death in the morning, people going to find their livelihood; death in the noontime on the highways and streets.

They are not warriors. Which cause has been served? Certainly not the cause of God, not the cause of Allah because God Almighty only gives life and is full of mercy. Anyone who has been misled, or is being misled to believe that by killing innocent people he or she is serving God should think again because it's not true. Terrorism is not the way, terrorism is not the way. It doesn't beget peace. We can't deliver peace by terrorism, never can we deliver peace by killing people. Throughout history, those people who have changed the world have done so without violence; they have won people to their cause through peaceful protest. Nelson Mandela, Martin Luther King, Mahatma Gandhi: their discipline, their self-sacrifice, their conviction made people turn towards them, to follow them. What inspiration can senseless slaughter provide? Death and destruction of young people in their prime as well as the old and helpless can never be the foundations for building society.

My son Anthony is my first son, my only son, the head of my family. In African society, we hold on to sons. He has dreams and hopes and I, his mother, must fight to protect them. This is now the fifth day, five days on, and we are waiting to know what happened to him and I, his mother, need to know what happened to Anthony. His young sisters need to know what happened, his uncles and aunties need to know what happened to Anthony, his father needs to know what happened to Anthony. Millions of my friends back home in Nigeria need to know what happened to Anthony. His friends surrounding me here, who have put this together, need to know what has happened to Anthony. I need to know, I want to protect him. I'm his mother, I will fight till I die to protect him. To protect his values and to protect his memory.

Innocent blood will always cry to God Almighty for reparation. How much blood must be spilled? How many tears shall we cry? How many mothers' hearts must be maimed? My heart is maimed. I pray I will see my son, Anthony. Why? I need to know, Anthony needs to know, Anthony needs to know, so do many others, unaccounted-for, innocent victims: they need to know.

It's time to stop and think. We cannot live in fear because we are surrounded by hatred. Look around us today. Anthony is a Nigerian, born in London, working in London; he is a world citizen. Here today we have Christians, Muslims, Jews, Sikhs, Hindus, all of us united in love for Anthony. Hatred begets only hatred. It is time to stop this vicious cycle of killing. We must all stand together, for our common humanity. I need to know what happened to my Anthony. He's the love of my life. My first son, my first son, twenty-six. He tells me one day, 'Mummy, I don't want to die, I don't want to die. I want to live, I want to take care of you, I will do great things for you, I will look after you, you will see what I will achieve for you. I will make you happy.' And he was making me happy. I am proud of him, I am still very proud of him but I need to know where he is, I need to know what happened to him. I grieve, I am sad, I am distraught, I am destroyed.

He didn't do anything to anybody, he loved everybody so much. If what I hear is true, even when he came out of the Underground he was directing people to take buses, to be sure that they were OK. Then he called his office at the same time to tell them he was running late. He was a multi-purpose person, trying to save people, trying to call his office, trying to meet his appointments. What did he then do to deserve this? Where is he, someone tell me, where is he?

1

Thursday 7 July 2005. None of us knows what a new day will bring.

I thought I knew, that morning, because for more than a week I had been praying for my family. Today was to be the climax of nine days of prayers which I had been praying for all my extended family, and especially for my children. Most especially, for my only son, Anthony, a young man blessed with many friends and a loving nature. Today was a day for giving thanks.

So I thought, when I awoke.

The day dawned to the crowing of the cockerel that runs about our garden in Lagos. I swung my legs out of bed, chuckled as the cockerel gave another raucous squawk, and knelt to begin my prayers. I don't know how long I lingered there, head bowed and eyes closed, the rub of my rosary beads against my fingertips being the only physical sensation in my world. I only know that when I stood up, my heart felt clean and light, as if I had bathed in a pool of mountain water.

During those nine days of prayer, which are called a novena, my thoughts had been fiercely focused on my family: my husband, Alan; our daughters, Lauretta and Aisha; my four sisters and two brothers, and their children too. I had prayed passionately for my family to grow in spirit as their health and happiness flourished. Most of all, my prayers were for my beloved Anthony, my golden boy, who was twenty-six years old and working hard to build up his career in London. His ambition was some day to bring his expertise to bear in Nigeria's oil and gas industry.

Anthony had always been my 'gift of gold'. His fair skin and sparkling eyes made me the envy of other mothers when he was a child, and now that he was a man he was no less beautiful.

I was still smiling and floating as I opened the front door, a few minutes after nine o'clock. I called out a goodbye to my daughters, who barely a week earlier had been seen off from Heathrow by their brother. I was on my way to do a few things before going to our parish church, where there would be a Mass shortly after midday. It would be a wonderful way to complete my nine days' prayers. This was a wonderful time in my life. I had no way of knowing that those seconds were the very last of an era.

With my hand on the open door I glanced around the apartment. My eye fell on the television. Something within me said, 'Why don't you watch the morning news before you go out?'

I hesitated. I knew the voice well – a priest once described it to me as 'the still, small voice'. When I try to explain it to my friends, I call it my 'mystery voice', as if it belonged to an actor, off-screen, commenting on the events in the reels of my life. But I know what it truly is: this is the voice that I speak with in my most heartfelt prayers, both my deepest self and my God within me. And when it makes a suggestion, I would always do well to listen.

But what kind of frivolous suggestion was this? To watch the television, when I was on my way out of the door and ultimately to church?

'Some silly ideas you have, Marie!' I said out loud.

'Why don't you watch the morning news?' the voice repeated. Persistent, insistent.

'Because I watched the news last night. I sat up late, and went to bed long after I should have done. And now I'm on my way out of the door, like a few million others. There can't be so much that has happened since I switched off.'

'Then you needn't do more than glance at the headlines,' my inner voice said. So reasonable, and so utterly unreasonable at the same time.

'No!' I retorted. 'I feel great. I feel clean. I feel at peace, and the news will spoil that feeling. I don't want to know that there's been a plane crash in Afghanistan or a hurricane in Mexico or a currency collapse in the South Sea islands. It will contaminate my mood. The news will tell me unwelcome things and sad things, and it will force them into my head with graphic detail, and that will spoil things. I shall become upset. So no. I don't want to see the news, thank you. I won't listen to you.'

And with that, I marched over to the television set and switched it on.

It was a compulsion. My inner voice had ceased to argue with my conscious mind – it simply took control of my limbs instead.

The first image I saw as the picture settled was a screaming red banner: 'Breaking News'. Trailing across the bottom of the screen, in white letters, the ticker-tape reported several explosions on the Underground in London.

I froze. Anthony was in London. The newsreader's voice said the name of the stations, but I was transfixed by the words on the scrolling headline. The newsreader said the cause of the explosions was unknown. There was some suggestion that the blasts had been caused by power surges on the electric rails. Then the stations came up: King's Cross, Edgware Road, Aldgate. King's Cross was the biggest terminal that Anthony would pass through on his Tube train to the City, heading for Old Street on the Northern Line.

But I was being a fool, I told myself. I was a fool to switch on the television in the first place, and I was a fool to imagine my son might be involved in this bizarre, fuzzy news event, just because he happened to commute through a Tube station that had been named as one of three affected. King's Cross was a huge tangle of intersecting railways, both above and below ground. It was as confused as a bowl of noodles. And so was I, if I was going to start leaping to panicky conclusions every time I heard King's Cross station mentioned on the television.

The newsreader said it appeared that the King's Cross explosion had occurred on the Northern Line.

Anthony travels on the Northern Line, I found myself thinking.

All right, there was an easy way to check this. I could call him. He was 3,000 miles away, but as close as my telephone. I snatched it up and pressed the speed-dial that instantly connected me to his mobile. It rang; I waited impatiently to hear his voice. Something good was going to come of this silly fright – I would hear my son's voice. Perhaps that was what my nagging inner monologue had been driving at: I should speak with Anthony before I set out. We hadn't talked since the afternoon before, and then only briefly, for I had called at an inconvenient moment. In fact, I had called in the middle of an important oil seminar, and Anthony had been able to do no more than whisper, 'Mummy, I'll call you back.'

The dialtone switched to voicemail. I was invited to leave a message. I rang off, a little frustrated but no more alarmed than I had been twenty seconds earlier. Anthony often didn't answer his phone on the first try. I had chided him about it, and he had explained there might be many reasons he couldn't answer his phone instantly. He might be on the line to someone else, the phone could be buried under documents in his briefcase, he might be talking face-to-face with someone important, or he might be in a spot where there was no signal.

The likeliest explanation was that he was already at work, writing up his report on the previous day's seminar. He would very likely be on the phone to a superior. But I knew I wouldn't be happy till I had heard him tell me to stop fussing about him, so I flicked through the phone's memory to find his office number. It wasn't there. That was a sensible precaution – to help me resist the temptation of phoning my boy too often when he was busy at work. But I knew where I could find the number instantly – Anthony's sister Lauretta had it on her phone, and she was upstairs. She and her sister, Aisha, both went to schools and colleges in England, but at this time they were home in Nigeria for a holiday.

I was calling my daughter's name before I had even moved from where I was standing.

My tone must have carried real urgency, because Lauretta answered instantly: 'Mummy, what is it? What's up, what's wrong?'

'Nothing's wrong. I just need to call Anthony. But there's nothing the matter, stop making a fuss and tell me his number please.'

'Why are you like this if there's nothing the matter?'

'Go and watch the news and then you'll see,' I snapped.

I regretted being so brusque with my sweet-tempered girl a moment later, when she turned her face to mine. I explained what I had seen on the television. 'The Northern Line is Anthony's route to his office, isn't it? But he must be fine, Mummy. He'll already be at work. Quick, call him, call him.'

She read out her brother's number, and a few moments later I heard the female receptionist announce the name of his company. As calmly as I could, I asked to be put through to Anthony Fatayi-Williams's number. 'Transferring you now,' she said, and after a few rings the automated recording cut in, stating in robotic tones that the person at that extension was not available to answer the phone.

I stared at the television. All that I could glean was that three stations had been affected by blasts of an unknown nature. The newsreaders seemed to intimate that these might be bomb-blasts, simply by skirting around the word so carefully. I thought of the terrible events of September the

11th, and how the newsreaders had avoided for several minutes the suggestion that the planes could have been directed into the towers by terrorists, even after the second impact.

At that moment I began to pray, and I must have been speaking aloud because Lauretta looked over at me. 'Please let me hear from my son that he is safe. Keep him safe. Let it be that he was nowhere near the places where there have been these accidents or disasters or whatever they are. Let today be the day he has overslept, and let him have got no further out of his front door than you have allowed me to go today.'

But I knew Anthony would not have overslept, today of all days. The oil and gas seminar scheduled for the previous day, 6 July, had been intensely important to him. He was ambitious, hard-working and focused, and today he would have got up early to ensure he was as perfectly dressed and groomed as ever. Anthony took great pains over his appearance: he believed a man's outer layer revealed his inner self. His excitement over the seminar had infected me, and when I had called the previous afternoon it was to find out if any of his fellow delegates were friends of our family. If there was any networking to be done, any friendly word that Alan or I could offer, we wouldn't hesitate. Our son's career was paramount.

He had not been able to call me back that afternoon, and the telephone had been silent all evening too. 'Come on, Anthony,' I murmured, 'you owe me a phone call. I need to hear you.'

My inner voice chimed in with a nugget of ancient wisdom: God helps those who help themselves. If I needed to hear my son's voice, I should not be afraid to take positive action. I dialled his mobile again, and prayed he would answer: 'Please God, not voicemail, please Anthony, please, my Sonny-Boy, please pick up the phone.'

Voicemail again. Oh no, why was that? This time, I steeled myself to leave a message. I wanted very much to warn him, to do anything I could to keep him safe, and if this was the only way I had of reaching him, then I must use it. 'Anthony, this is Mummy. I have just watched Sky News and there seems to be something going on in London, an explosion in the Underground – they say it's a power surge, or whatever. Do be careful. I am rather worried. Please call me as soon as you get this message to assure me that you are fine. Anthony, *please, please* call me, or call Lauretta, or do something, just to let me know that you are all right, because we are worried. I am worried. I love you.'

There was no reason to believe that everything was not OK, and in fact my Sonny-Boy was still alive when I left that message. We did not know his fate for many days, but it appeared from the timings, when we compared the record of that phone call to the events in London, that the bomb on the Number 30 bus had not exploded when I left that first plea on his voicemail.

Immediately, I called his office again, and this time I was put through to a woman who said they had heard from Anthony. Thank God! The relief was wonderful. I could hardly hear what she said to me, my heart was thumping so loudly in my ears, but I thanked her again and again, and lay back as if I'd run twenty miles, panting and gasping. I caught Lauretta's arm and told her, 'A lady at the office says Anthony called to say he would be late getting in because of delays on the Underground.'

It made perfect sense. When Anthony was suddenly plunged into a commuter maelstrom, his first thoughts would hardly be to call me: 'Hello, Mummy, bit of a delay on the trains this morning, but don't worry if they say anything about it on the news because I'm fine.' No, his overwhelming priority would be to get word to his bosses, especially on a day when he had such an important report to deliver. I imagined he had probably been slaving away on the wording for half the night – how infuriating for him to face railway chaos that morning. He had doubtless been on the phone

7

when I first called him. That explained why I'd only got his voicemail.

I tried to think what else the woman at his office had told me. Something about background noise – such a hubbub that she could barely make out his words. And she hadn't known which station he was calling from. I felt reassured, but far from comfortable.

Why had I got Anthony's voicemail a second time? Why hadn't he called me back yet? I tried to imagine what he might be doing. Then I had it: he'd be calling a friend, to give vent to a bit of frustration. Important seminar, burning the midnight oil, vital report, rush-hour madness – Anthony would not be suffering in silence. He would call someone to let off steam. And the friend he'd call would almost certainly be his great buddy Amrit Walia.

I dialled Amrit's number and he answered immediately. 'Have you heard from Anthony?' I demanded. 'There have been these explosions – has he been in touch with you? I can't reach him!'

Amrit calmed me down. He had been Anthony's closest friend for a long time and he always called me Auntie. For a moment I thought he was telling me the words I was desperate to hear: 'Auntie, Anthony phoned me this morning.'

'When? When was this?'

'Some time after eight, some time before eight-thirty. Usually when he calls that early, he is either waiting at the bus stop or he's on the railway platform, waiting for his train.'

'So he was on his way to work? I knew he didn't oversleep. He never does when something is pressing so much on his mind. Have you tried to call him since nine o'clock?'

Amrit measured his words carefully. I believe he was already anxious for his friend, though not nearly as far advanced into panic as I was becoming. 'Auntie,' he said, 'I saw the news of the problems on the Tube, and I tried his number, but I couldn't get through. Probably the whole world is trying to phone into that part of London right now and all the lines are busy. That makes sense, doesn't it? So I'll keep trying to get through, and you keep trying, and one of us will reach Anthony very soon.'

'The moment you speak to him, you must call me. Promise me, Amrit.'

'Of course I promise you, Auntie.'

As I ended the call I realised that Anthony's father might not even be aware of the explosions. He was at his clinic, and a busy doctor would not be looking at the television news every five minutes. I told myself he would want to be informed, but really what I wanted was to hear his grave, reassuring manner, setting the world to rights with a reasonable word. Naturally there was not a tremor of anxiety in his voice when he took my call. London was a big place, he said, and Anthony was well able to take care of himself.

That should have been enough to settle my nerves, but I couldn't help myself: I dialled Anthony's number again, praying desperately that he would answer. When he did not, I laid my hands across my lap and studied my fingers. I had turned to the television and the telephone, and these manmade contraptions had increased my anxieties. I had asked my daughter, my son's friend and my husband for reassurance, and they had tried to give it, but I felt far from calm. I was going to do what I had planned to do from the start: go to church. In fact, I was going to readjust my programme and go to church straightaway.

2

The interior of the Church of the Assumption was cool and tranquil. This was my parish church, in Falomo, Ikoyi, on Lagos island, about eight minutes' drive from my home. I entered it determined that God would take care of my worries for me. But I also left my mobile phone on, for the first time in my life, buried deep in my handbag, so that Anthony would be able to leave a message for me.

As I arrived at church I spoke to a friend, Lilian, another parishioner who prayed regularly and devotedly, and who also had children in London. She hadn't heard about the chaos in London, and immediately slipped outside to speak with her daughter. It seemed she had no difficulty getting through on the phone, for she soon returned with the news that her children were safe and that the explosions were now confirmed as bomb-blasts.

It was almost half-past twelve, and the church had filled for the Mass. The lector's seat was empty and I looked around for whoever was due to take that day's reading. When I saw no sign of anyone, I began to make my way to the lector's seat, since I am also one of the readers at the church. As I walked past the pews, the mysterious voice stirred deep within me: 'When the names are read out for the Mass intentions, the special prayers of the day, be sure that Anthony's name and all your family's are among them.'

I stopped and shook my head to drive away my thoughts. Why, I wondered, why should such a notion occur to me at this moment? As I turned the idea over in my mind, I saw Chris, the day's lector, and before I knew what I was doing I was at his side, whispering urgently: 'Please check the list of Mass intentions and if our names are not there, do add them – especially my children, Anthony and his sisters.'

Chris smiled and nodded at me. Nothing could be more natural than my request. Lectors hear it made every day. But to my utter amazement, when Chris stood at the ambo, or pulpit, he called Anthony's name first. Then he named me and my family separately.

I wanted to jump up and shout, 'I didn't ask you to do that! I didn't say you should separate Anthony from his family and his mother! What made you say it that way?' I must have been staring at Chris, for he caught my eye as if to say: 'There. Isn't that what you wanted?'

I tried to reassure myself that he had simply misunderstood my request, or that perhaps he'd thought of Anthony, 3,000 miles from home, and symbolically named him apart from the rest of the Fatayi-Williams clan. But a memory flashed through my mind, and I remembered how just such an innocuous moment had prefigured a family tragedy once before.

I was a young woman, visiting Paris with my friends, on a trip away from Nigeria without my family to protect me. I had promised my father that I would return safely to him, but it never occurred to me to ask whether he would remain safe and well while I was away.

Sitting at a café with friends, I reminisced as I poured the tea from a silver pot. And as I watched the milk swirl, I remarked: 'My father never joked when he had his morning or evening tea. Far too serious a business. In fact, he used to say the first cup of tea of the day should always be drunk black.'

And my blood suddenly ran cold.

Just chit-chat. Nothing but the nonsense we talk when certain things take us back to lovely moments, and we're young without a care in our heads. But why had I spoken of my father in the past tense? Why had I talked of him as though he were dead?

'Of course,' I said aloud to my friends, 'my father is still alive.' To my mystery voice, I added: 'I'm only talking in the past tense because, well – everything that has happened is in the past, isn't it? It's just a grammatical way of speaking. It doesn't signify anything.'

My friends, puzzled, allowed me to change the subject. I quickly introduced another anecdote about my father, and this time I was careful to use the present tense. But the small, quiet voice within me chimed up and warned: 'You're trying to unsay something that you've already said. And that is not possible.'

All that day I composed little prayers in my head for my father, so far away in Africa. When the phone call came, it was barely any surprise at all: I was to cut short my visit and return to Benin City in Edo state. I was told my father was seriously ill in hospital, asking for me. After my plane touched down in Nigeria, I learned that in fact he was already dead. He might even have passed away at the moment I was at the café, speaking of him.

I will always believe that somehow, telepathically, he reached out to me and tried to let me know that he needed to see me.

It is almost impossible to interpret these flashes of intuition. So often they are telling us awful truths that we would do anything not to hear. But when I heard Chris read my son's name singly, in isolation from his family, I remembered that curious turn of events in Paris and a cold hand clutched at my heart.

The Mass started and I prayed as I had never prayed before for Anthony. All the time, my conscious, rational, reasonable mind kept trying to drown the terrors of my intuition. Anthony had not been on any of the Tube trains when the bombs exploded. He had emerged from the Underground.

He had called his office. I should be rejoicing – and at the same time I should be praying for all those who had not been so lucky during the terrible rush-hour events in London. I poured all my fears and wild worries into my prayers, and when I finished I felt drained but cleansed.

My daughters and my friend joined me and I led us all in prayers for everyone in London: 'Dear God, please take control of our lives and lead us out of the darkness to safety.' I tried to imagine what it could be like to be on an Underground train when a bomb went off – the isolation, the confusion and the claustrophobia.

As we walked up the aisle, I reached into my bag and, without glancing at it, handed my phone to Lauretta. 'Go and see what messages your brother has left,' I told her, and held back, not wanting to go outside. Despite all my prayers, I was still anxious: but I was sure there would be a message from Anthony and I just needed Lauretta to tell it to me with a smile.

When I came out of the church, it was clear that Lauretta was desperate to give me good news. She hero-worshipped her brother, and he guarded her jealously, calling her 'Lolsy-bubs'. Now Lolsy-bubs was clasping my telephone and she hugged me as she explained that there was a message from her father: Alan had spoken to a woman at Anthony's office who had taken a call from our son sometime well after 9 a.m.

Bitter disappointment jabbed and pierced me, making it hard to breathe. 'No,' I said, 'we already knew that. I also called his office and they told me he had come out of the Underground and was seeking an alternative means of transport. They said they didn't know exactly where he was. And nor do I.'

I stood still outside the church. My mind raced. I stared at the phone. I willed it to ring. 'This is becoming a very long day,' I said aloud, without humour. But that was scarcely the half of it: I was enduring what would become the longest day and the most hellish night of my life.

Now the cycle began again of dialtones that went through to voicemail and desperate questions that, like the phone calls, were never answered. I am an active woman, and I needed to act. I dialled Anthony's mobile number, and then his home. The mobile invited me to leave a message – it was the last thing I wanted to do, but soon even that small comfort was to be denied me. 'You should have called me already, Sonny-Boy,' I chided. 'Please, please, we are troubled, we know there has been a bomb in London. Just call me, call home, call Mummy. I hope you are safe, keep safe.'

Immediately after that I called Amrit again: 'Have you heard from Anthony?' He said, 'Auntie, don't worry, don't worry,' and I became impatient with him: 'You told me the lines are down and that's why I'm getting his voicemail, but how come I'm getting you on the phone? If I am able to get you, I should be able to get him.'

Amrit tried to soothe me: 'My area is different,' he claimed. 'Where the whole thing is happening, central London, the telephone lines are down. If not, Anthony would have called me myself by now. He is the sort of person who would call us to make sure that we are OK.'

It was true: Anthony would certainly have called me and Amrit. The awful question was: why hadn't he? Was the whole of central London suffering a communication breakdown?

Later that day my husband would have a different explanation for Anthony's silence: 'Marie, you know Anthony, he would be helping people. He has his first-aider's certificate, after all, and if there are injuries among the victims he will be doing everything he can to save lives. That is important work, and I can tell you it is overwhelming – the mind has no space to think of anything but the essential tasks, from one moment to the next. He would not think for an instant about phoning us. There is more important work for him to do.' That was the doctor in my husband talking of course. He never stops being a doctor, even when he is asleep. He knew how he would react in the aftermath of a terrorist attack, and he believed, rightly, that Anthony would act the same way, because he was a very giving person.

I understood what he was saying, and yet my spirit could not fully grasp it. The doubts were gnawing me too hard to be ignored. 'He should know that we are worried,' I insisted.

Alan took my hands. 'Marie,' he promised, 'he'll call. He must be helping. He always wants to give a hand.'

I dropped the girls off at the house and called my sister Roseline. Anthony's pet name for her was Antroza, but the rest of us call her Rosa. She had seen the news and had already called me to find out if Anthony was safe. Rosa was as confident as Alan, Amrit and Lauretta that my Sonny-Boy would be fine. Like the others, she had her own, unfailing logic. 'Marie, it's OK,' she insisted. 'You know Anthony, he'll keep safe.' And I knew what she meant, because my son was nobody's fool. He knew how to look after himself, a big, strong fellow who worked out regularly in the gym. He wasn't going to stumble into any trouble, even if central London had become a bit lawless amid the communications chaos. I imagined traffic jams and accidents, bad temper spilling on to the streets. But even in my worst imaginings, I couldn't see Anthony being drawn into an altercation.

All these confident people, showing me clear-cut reasons why I should stop worrying, ought to have dispelled my panic. Instead, they stoked it. They all had different ways to prove why Anthony must be safe – but they couldn't all be right. And if one of them was wrong, why shouldn't they all be wrong?

I decided I would call him, and call him, and call him, until he answered. I was about to dial his very dear friend Nike, when my phone rang – and it was Nike herself. My heart leapt: I thought she was going to tell me he had surfaced. But then I could hear something in her voice, in her greeting, that dashed my hopes.

I asked if she had heard from Anthony, and she sighed:

'Oh Auntie, I was hoping, I was thinking that maybe you . . .'

I said, 'No, I haven't heard from him: I would have called you, and if you can call me and I can call you, why can't we reach him?' Nike said the lines were all down, and I snapped, 'Your line is up! How come I can speak to you?'

Like Amrit, she had an answer: 'I am outside the city, but in central London the lines are all down. Don't worry, don't worry, don't worry. Someone will find him, I'm sure. Maybe he is helping out, or maybe he is walking, he is just walking along and here we are worrying. That's probably it – he's walking to work now because there's no transport.'

I said, 'Nike, don't give me that stuff. If he is walking, there are phones. Even if the mobile phones are down, there are call boxes. He can go to a phone and, if not call me, call one of you. Call yourself, call Amrit, call anybody.'

Nike just kept saying, 'Don't worry, don't worry,' as if I could do anything else.

I took up Nike's mantra: 'Don't worry,' I told myself. 'It's like everybody says – Anthony likes to help. Maybe he is helping others. And he will not have time to think of his mother or to call her.' But that stirred sadness and even anger within me, because I felt he should at least think of me and realise that we would all be worried sick.

That's the thing about Anthony, I thought, he will always put others first. Why can't he just put me first? Call me and let me know that he's fine. See what he's doing to me? Well, if I call his phone again I am not going to leave any more messages on the voicemail, because really I don't like it. And that was so prophetic, for by the time I called his phone again the message box was full, because all his friends were calling him. So when I tried to leave a message, I got this cold, heartless message: no more room. Voicemail full.

Why couldn't he collect his messages? Was the mobile network really so damaged? Or had he perhaps lost his phone in the chaos? Was it perhaps lying in some corner, ringing and ringing? I knew he hadn't left it at home, because Amrit had spoken to him before the bombing, and he had called his office afterwards.

The worst possibility was that the phone was fine. It wasn't lost and the networks were carrying calls. But something had happened to Anthony and he couldn't use his phone. Maybe he was injured. Maybe he had suffered a bang on the head, in a car accident or a crowd mêlée. Maybe he was lying on a pavement or a stretcher, conscious but with no memory of who he was or what he was supposed to be doing. Concussed, confused, frightened.

'No,' I told myself. 'This is a test. They've told you he's come out of the Underground, they've told you he's called his office, they've told you the times of these other explosions. You've been to Mass, you've prayed, you've done everything – why are you so worried? Put on a brave face.

When eventually I got home, I sat by the television for hours. I saw there had been a fourth explosion, on a bus, but to me it didn't mean anything because there was no way Anthony was on a bus. There was no bus service running from his flat to his office. And I knew Anthony went by train. He might have taken a bus as far as the Tube station, but he didn't like them: he said trains were faster.

By the time early evening came, the news hadn't changed, and now my sister Teresa in Abuja, and Grace in Ibadan, as well as my brothers Ben and Tom, called and admitted to me: 'We have been calling Anthony's number and we can't get him.'

I kept that brave face and said, 'Yeah, that's Anthony for you – he's putting us on edge because we need him to call us and he's busy helping other people. I've called his friends umpteen times, and all of them say they'll call me the moment they hear anything.'

And as we were talking, two of my friends walked in, one of them Betty, a magazine publisher. They were yet unaware of the London explosions. Immediately they saw me they could tell I was troubled and fighting back anxiety, but I insisted, 'Oh no, no, no, it's nothing.' I was trying to keep as quiet and calm as possible, even as more friends called round and the talk turned to the London bombings. I didn't contribute much, and it didn't seem to cross my friends' minds that I had a son in that city. My thoughts were only half focused on what they were saying, and my eyes kept straying to the telephone, waiting for it to ring.

3

I'm writing this on Valentine's Day. It is seven months and seven days since my son was killed, and recalling the events of that awful day and night are almost too much to bear, almost too much to tell. I think of that moment when the phone rang, when I was so desperate for news, when I was surrounded by friends yet feeling so alone, and it seems as though that instant has been repeating itself endlessly, for seven months and seven days.

Whenever the phone rings, whenever I see a young man in the crowd who has Anthony's build or Anthony's smart clothes, whenever I hear a door open or catch a movement from the corner of my eye, my heart lurches. I know I can never see him or speak with him again physically in this life, but my heart still expects it. My heart is maimed, and it does not understand.

Today has been a day of agonies, and also of a miracle. There was one special letter that Anthony wrote to me, which I very much wanted to put in this book. I remembered I'd had it a few months earlier, but now I could not find it. I told everyone I had lost it, and I was so upset. Believe it or not, it has turned up, mysteriously and miraculously, today, on Valentine's Day.

This morning, feeling very sad and full of pain, I prayed in front of my little altar where I have placed Anthony's photograph. I shed a tear; I talked to him and I said, 'This time last year I was in London and you sent me a huge bouquet of flowers.'

On that day, he really surprised me! The doorbell rang and I opened it to a huge vase crammed with roses and greenery. I said, 'Wow, from who?' And the card said, 'For my mummy, with all my love. Anthony.' He had ordered it through a florist from work.

He called me later and said, 'Hi, Mummy, are you having a nice Valentine's Day?'

I said, 'Yes! You made my day!'

I could hear a smile in his voice as he said, 'Yeah, yeah, I love you lots, I hope you're happy, I really do.'

I said, 'Me too.'

When he came home, he warned me, 'I'm taking my girlfriend out tonight – I know you understand I can't spend Valentine's Day with you.'

I said, 'But you've done it already, because you sent me this huge bouquet. So off you go, enjoy your dinner.'

That was how it was last year, so this year I felt so sad. I was in agony. Can you imagine if anyone had told me that that was the last Valentine's Day he would ever phone me or tell me he loved me? I would have said, 'It can't be true . . .'

About an hour after I had steadied my emotions, I was sitting at my computer. Anthony's picture is beside that too. I had decided I had to do some work. There were books and paper bags scattered all around the table and the computer, and I have never let that sort of clutter bother me. There were so many things on the floor that I had simply put down and left there. But something inside me prompted, 'Why don't you take a look around here?'

I said, 'Look for what? I'm not searching for anything in particular at the moment. There are old things down there, new things, what could I possibly want from this lot? But actually I think I do need to tidy this corner a little bit . . .'

So I just kept removing things, saying to myself, 'Oh, this old thing, I'll put this here. I'll put that there.' There is solace in small tasks. And as I moved three little bags, there at the bottom was one more, an airline bag, the kind of plastic carrier that you use to carry all the free bits and pieces they load you with.

I picked it up, thinking, what's this bag doing here? What could be in it? I looked into it and there were a couple of books and some papers. The first book I pulled out of this bag was a spiritual book. It was one of the books that I have bought for comfort during the time that I have been grieving. I'd read it and put it away, and I couldn't for the life of me think where I'd put it, because someone had given me another book and I'd started reading that.

I just took this book out of that bag, opened it, and from the page I flicked open, Anthony's letter fell out.

I took the letter and my eyes filled with tears. I held it to me and said, 'Oh! On Valentine's Day, you showed me this book and you gave me this letter to calm my heart. Oh, how I have been searching for it. Oh my Anthony, you have reached out to me today with love even from beyond.'

I read the letter again and again, and at the end it says, 'Love you lots, Mummy, Anthony xx'. So a little smile came back to my face, after everything that had happened that day. I got down on my knees and just said, 'Thank you.'

Anthony wrote this letter after we had a small, silly disagreement. It was the end of the Christmas holidays last year, and I had suggested he was going out a little too much. He was a young man, full of energy, and it was right that he should enjoy being with his friends, but I am his mother and it was right also that I should issue a word of caution. Like me – too much like me – Anthony could be headstrong, and we had argued: not nastily, but the discussion ended without resolution. He had turned away and gone to his room.

A day or two later, this is what he wrote to me:

Dear Mummy,
Firstly I would like to apologise for my actions of late.

23

That is to say, if I have offended you or taken you for granted, either by commission or omission, I am really and truly very sorry.

I love you very much, and it is not intentional that I have not spent as much time with you as I would like to. I have thankfully realised this myself and will make amends.

Mummy, I prayed before I wrote this note. Prayed that I would wake up and we would be happy with each other, as we have been, and to keep getting along as is God's blessing to us this year and hopefully for the rest of our years. I pray for your blessings in my life and in anything that I do or am involved in, and I fully put my life in the hands of the Lord and know firmly that He will not see harm or evil or bad befall me. I hope to make you more and more proud as time goes on. Please let us not begin to allow things to make a rift in our own newfound closeness, lest it start to divide us and as such make us weaker.

I will not be going clubbing for the rest of the holiday if it makes you upset. Please don't be angry with me. I love you very much.

Anthony xxx

When I first read those words I wept, and every time I re-read them I weep. I am weeping now.

'I fully put my life in the hands of the Lord and know firmly that He will not see harm or evil or bad befall me.' Why did my son write those words? Surely he had no premonition of his own death, because he lived every moment of his life so fully. Yet it is almost as if that letter was written to be a comfort to me in the days after he died.

'He will not see harm or evil or bad befall me . . .' That sentence had been ringing in my head, and I clung to its promise as the phone shrilled in my home that July evening of 2005. I was so flustered as I seized the handset. All my efforts to preserve an outward show of calm were shattered. But it was not Anthony; that could not be. Amrit was calling, Anthony's friend. Of course my friends could see how quickly I jumped.

As I started to talk to Amrit, he responded with question after question. Suddenly his own poise and rational calm were shredded too. He wanted all the answers that none of us could have unless Anthony made contact: 'But you think he was walking? He had left the Tube when he called his office – do you think he was on foot? How far had he come? And you think he might have set out to walk home? All the way to Hendon? Even if he did, he would have reached the house by now, he would have talked to you, he would have called you.'

Our situation was reversed, and now it was me telling Amrit to calm down, not to worry. My son's friend took a breath that I could hear down the line all the way from London, and the effort he required to place his emotions in a clamp was so intense I could almost touch it. 'All of Anthony's friends have been talking together, all day,' he said, 'and we think, even if he was hurt . . . well, don't worry, Auntie – even if the worst comes to the worst, if he's hurt he's in hospital. We can check every hospital, we can find him.'

I was horrified. I said, 'You mean now we are talking of checking every hospital? Why do you say that?'

Amrit backtracked: 'Well, maybe he has gone there to help with the wounded.'

'No,' I told him, 'don't try to tell me that. I know what you really mean. OK, Amrit, let's do this, let's start checking the hospitals. Can you begin to organise that? Because from where I am, in Lagos, it's impossible. I wish more than I can say that I was in London at this moment.'

'Don't worry, Auntie. Really, don't worry.' It was clear that Amrit, in his anxiety, had said far more than he intended. 'I was just calling to find out if Anthony had been in touch yet, because we all feel certain that he'll call you first. Even if he doesn't call us, he would call home. Anyhow . . .' and he was suddenly lost for words. He wanted to reassure me and reassure himself, but the words to do that have never been thought of. 'We'll keep in touch, Auntie,' he ended.

In the course of that call, all my friends suddenly realised that something was odd. They had talked of the bombing, but it had occurred to no one to fear for Anthony. He simply wasn't the kind of man to stir your fears. When there is a storm at sea, you fear for the ships, but you never imagine the rocks could be washed away. And Anthony was a rock.

My voice sounded strange as I gave words to this imposs-ible fear: 'Actually, we haven't heard from Anthony . . .'

There was a silence, no one said very much, and then suddenly they were all talking at once: 'Don't worry, you know Anthony, he'll call, he's a young man, he knows his way around, he is probably working with people, giving all sorts of excuses to himself for not calling.'

It is at times like these that the world lets you fool yourself.

I kept saying to myself and to my friends that Anthony was all right, because I knew he'd come out of the train station. The bus I had ruled out – completely. There was absolutely no reason why he would catch that bus.

So I tried to phone his office again. I called Amec a third time, and I pleaded with them: 'Tell me precisely what he told you when he called. I don't have a clue why he hasn't got through to you by five o'clock.' But they had seen and heard nothing more.

I said to myself, 'Well, this can't go on all night. Anthony has to call me before the night sets in because I will not be able to take this. I can't.' My heart was full. My mind was racing a mile a minute. Again and again in front of my friends, I muttered, 'No, no, no, no, no.'

My younger daughter came down and I was so desperate to hear good news that I practically commanded her to bring me word of my son: 'He *must* call you! You always talk to each other.'

Lauretta so wanted to help me. 'I've been calling his mobile as well,' she said, 'and it's not even taking any more messages.'

We tried calling the landline as well, but that was going to BT Answer, the messages service. Every time I left the same plea: 'Anthony, it's Mummy again, *please, please, please* call me. I'm at the end of my tether. Please, Sonny-Boy, call me.'

As the evening lengthened, my friends left. And I sat there, unable to move away from the phone, exhausted from hearing nothing and being able to do nothing. My sister Rosa came over, and later my brother Ben. Ben and Anthony shared a gift for dressing well, and some of Anthony's favourite shirts and jackets were gifts from his uncle. They had both come over to encourage me and to sit with me while I rested, but I told them, 'I'm just going to wait here by the phone till we find him.'

Ben sounded confident as he reassured me: 'Anthony's fine, we'll find him, there's no doubt he's OK.' Meanwhile, out of my earshot, everybody in my family was on their mobile, desperately ringing round, trying to make some sense of what had happened to him.

Alan arrived home around this time. Naturally I looked to my husband for news, and he sought to ease my fears by seeming relaxed and unconcerned: 'Oh, he'll call, he'll call.'

I simply said 'All right' – what else was there to say? I had to have faith, and that meant I had to keep believing exactly what Alan was saying: that Anthony would call.

Eventually my sister left, insisting that I was to call her when I heard from Anthony, however late it was. My plea to her was just the same: if he calls at any time of the night, tell me immediately.

When Rosa and Ben had gone, my daughter Aisha came and sat next to me. She has a congenital learning difficulty, and there is no pretence with her: when she is concerned, she shows it. Her question was direct: 'Mummy, what of Anthony?'

Aisha and Anthony adored each other. I said, 'Anthony, well – we're waiting for him to call. There's been a bomb in London but we know that he's fine.'

She said, 'OK.' Her faith in the truth of what I told her was absolute. I wanted to have faith as great as that. And then she added, 'I just wish he would call.'

I held her close and said, 'I wish so too.'

Lauretta didn't say a word throughout the evening. As far as she was concerned, Anthony was all right but he should call, because she'd been calling him all day.

I stopped watching the news, because it was the same thing over and over. I held on to my beads and I prayed the rosary, again and again. When Lauretta spoke at last, it was to tell me, 'Mummy, it is almost midnight.'

'Well,' I said, 'go to sleep.' And then I softened my tone and added, 'And I'll sleep too. That's the best thing to do.'

But where was the sleep to come from? I hadn't heard from Anthony; how could I sleep? The girls went off to their rooms and I stayed quietly on the settee. Time passed, and Lauretta came down to ask, 'Mummy, when are you going to bed?'

I realised that, as long as I was fretting wide-eyed by the phone, my daughters would not sleep a wink either. For their sakes, I said: 'OK, I'm going to bed. You guys sleep.' So I lay down, and I put my mobile by my pillow.

A burning sensation was growing in my chest. It began to feel as if my heart was outside my body. I tried to close my eyes, but they kept springing open, as I constantly checked that the mobile had a signal. The time on its monitor said 2 a.m. As I clutched it, I thought, oh no, this is becoming more difficult. Anthony, call me, I pleaded.

I was hot, I was cold, my heart was racing, my limbs were fidgeting. I was thinking of the last thing he said to me: 'Mummy, I'll call you back.'

'Oh no, no, no,' I kept telling myself, 'he's not dead, Anthony is not dead.' And then some gnawing doubt in me said, 'Maybe, what if it wasn't him who called the office;

what if he was in the train?' I simply wasn't thinking of the bus. 'What if he is so badly injured he cannot call us? What if he comes out totally maimed? What will become of his young life? But it's so unlikely, in a city of so many millions. I know that he was one of those countless people who were commuting on the Northern Line this morning, and I know too that he came out of the Underground station and was able to call the office. Even though he was on a train, he was not in one of those fatal coaches.'

But something tried to make me picture him maimed. And I said, 'No no, I can't picture Anthony maimed, I can't. It is too tragic, too difficult.' And then something said, 'What if he's dead?'

I cried out, 'Don't use that word. He can't die. Lord, I prayed for life for Anthony.'

And the mysterious voice inside me answered, 'Remember: "Courage, there is a purpose for this." '

My heart felt as though it was going to pop out of my chest; it was beating as though it was going to burst through. So I had to lie completely flat. I threw away the pillows and I lay on the mattress, face down, and I said, 'My heart is going to burst but I can't afford for it to do that, no, no. What if Anthony wakes up and I am not here – no, no, no, no, no.' So I lay very flat, and pressed my chest hard down on the mattress. And I took deep breaths, and more deep breaths, and I said, 'Please Lord, calm my soul, please.'

The phone didn't ring. So I said, 'OK, I am going to call the flat; let it be that Anthony will pick up the phone, because by now, even if he has been helping people and he has been lost, and he has been walking round feeling upset, even if he has been hitting things and feeling anger, he has had time enough to walk home now. Even if he was going to walk to the other side of the country, he would have reached there by now. By now he ought to be in the flat to receive this call, or with one of his friends, whichever friend he has decided to go to.'

So I picked up the phone. I phoned his mobile, just on the off chance, but as soon as it went to voicemail I didn't want to hear any more, so I cut it off. Then I called the flat.

The call went through to BT Answer. I jumped up, crying out, 'No, no, no, no,' and I ran to the bathroom, because I was physically incapable of staying still any longer.

At that moment it seemed that my mystery voice took on a different air and whispered something that sounded like, 'He is alive. Fear not.'

I splashed water on my face and stared at my reflection, dripping with tears and tap-water. If I could not find the strength to continue through that dark and evil night, I was going to fall apart completely. But where was I going to find that strength?

Anthony would not fall apart. In any situation where circumstances were against him, he had the resolve to draw a line and say, 'Beyond this point there can be no weakness.' Since he was a small child, he had possessed this rigid determination.

I remembered an incident from his childhood. It is funny how on looking back you can actually see the adult character of a man: it is already manifest in the young child. Anthony was about three years old, and Alan, my sisters Grace and Teresa and I had taken him on an outing to the seaside, to Brighton. This was before Aisha had even been thought of, and Anthony was our only child. That made him even more special, more protected and fully showered with love.

The family was returning to London by train and there we were in this old-fashioned compartment, all seated happily on one side. In came another family – a mother and a young daughter about Anthony's age, seated across from us. After a while, Anthony decided to jump down from his seat and hopped on to the seat by the window opposite. He was wearing his favourite pair of sunglasses that had teeny crystals in a heart-shape stuck on the lenses. Sitting down, he crossed his legs and engagingly peered out the window.

The little girl jumped down and made a beeline for Anthony. We all watched in silence as she pointed a chubby index finger at him and muttered some inaudible words before going back to her seat. Anthony kept peering out the window. The little girl jumped down again and poked Anthony; this time he turned and smiled. She pointed her chubby finger at him again, muttering something that perhaps was her own way of saying he should leave that seat and go back to his own family.

Her mother looked at me somewhat nervously but with a smile, so I smiled back and just looked on. I said to Teresa, 'It looks like Anthony has met his match!' After all, he was always the one running around the house, poking people and getting everyone to do his bidding.

This little girl provoked Anthony again, and her mother called her nervously to sit down. At that point, it was as if the pool of patience had run dry. Anthony got down from his seat, stood straight in front of the little girl, eyeball to shaded eyeball, and shakily pointed his own chubby little index finger.

'Ify, ify, ify, you do dat again,' he declared, 'I boot you up.' And he jumped back to his seat again and peered out the window as if nothing had happened.

A palpable silence filled the coach. The tough little girl huddled close to her mum, almost to the point of disappearing into her armpit. And then, suddenly, there were smiles and laughter all round.

By the time the family got off the train, Anthony and the little girl had ended up sharing the seat, messing around with a game of solitaire. Teresa, the girl's mum and I were talking and laughing as if we'd all been on the day-trip together, and it ended up with happy waves and goodbyes.

Anthony could always bring different people together, even at the strangest of times and in the strangest of ways. No wonder his belief as a young man was that there is always something good in everybody and every situation. You just have to seek it out.

31

4

In the bathroom, a sound brought me out of my reverie, and my heart started racing again. I saw Aisha standing in her nightdress, looking sad and forlorn, and I realised that she too could not sleep.

'I am waiting for my brother,' she said.

We sat together, and I held her hand. My mind began to wander again, away from terrible thoughts of what might have happened to my son, and towards comforting thoughts of his spiritual strength. I needed some of that now. 'Mummy,' he would tell me, 'you have to accept people as they are. There is something good in everybody. Something good in everything. You just have to look for it and you'll find it.'

I remembered walking with him in London, a year or two earlier, through an underpass. I was a step or two ahead of him, and when I glanced around he wasn't there. A flicker of alarm passed through me.

'Anthony, where are you?' He reappeared with a hurried step. 'What were you doing?'

He said, 'Oh Mummy, I just had to, I was searching for some coins to give to that man.'

'Which man?

'The beggar back there. You went past him.'

'What of it?' I asked.

'Aren't you always telling me to practise what we preach?'

I regarded my son sternly. 'Are you giving me a lecture?' I demanded.

'No, no, I just thought we could have dropped something in his bowl. So I did.'

'Fine,' I said. 'Now he'll go and spend it on drink.'

'Mummy, you don't have to assess that. How are you sure he's going to have a hot meal tonight? We're going home, we know we'll have something to eat, but how do you know where his next meal is coming from?'

'But Anthony,' I repeated, 'if you give that beggar money he might use it to go and drink or do something worse. Could you not see the empty beer can beside him?'

'That's not for us to decide,' he said firmly. 'Let's give something at least.' His mind was set. There was no give. The line had been drawn.

As we walked, I reflected that my son was always teaching me. But the real impact of the lesson came later, when we got home and found there was no milk in the fridge. I asked him to pop out and get some, and he said, 'I don't have any money, Mummy.'

'For goodness' sake,' I told him, 'do I have to give a grown man money for milk? You go and buy it yourself.'

He said, 'I put my last pound in that beggar's bowl. Because, Mummy, when we walk home, I know where I'm going. I know I have a meal waiting for me. He doesn't know where he's going and it's cold outside.'

There was a terrible vulnerability to Anthony too. I knew that if he had witnessed the aftermath of one of yesterday's four bombings, he would have been horribly upset, even traumatised.

One occasion came clearly into my mind, when he had returned from work with a rather sad and distant look in his eyes. It turned out that he had heard of the death of his friends' friend – a young man, about his own age. 'He'd been getting his life sorted out,' Anthony said.

'Did you know him well?' I asked.

'Not so much. But he's dead. I just don't understand why he had to die now. He was just slightly younger than me. What is his mother going to do?'

He went into his room, changed, and went straight to bed, and I didn't see him again till the next day. We didn't speak of it again, because I decided to let him be. But I worried about his reaction and his keen sensibilities. He could be hurt so easily.

By this time it was getting light. The cockerel was crowing again, and what a different day was dawning. The certainty and serenity of the morning before had gone.

I put on the television again to see if there was any breaking news, but the same things were churning round and round. It was too early to call Amrit, but I called him anyway. Amrit answered like someone in a dream, yet when I asked if he was awake he admitted he had not slept at all. 'Auntie, I am just trying to ring round the hospitals.'

'You are? How far have you got? Which ones have you done?' I asked.

'Please don't worry,' Amrit said. 'We're getting there. We'll find Anthony. Whatever it takes, we'll find Anthony. Just you stay calm.'

I thanked him. I didn't know it at the time, but Amrit had pictures of Anthony, with Nike, to show to nurses or the police or anyone who might be able to take him to his friend. Other close friends were ringing hospitals too, and they had already put up a website appealing for information. All this was kept from me.

At 6 a.m. my sister came back to the house. There were tears and brave faces as our last hopes dissolved that Anthony might have been in touch with someone, just one of his friends or family, during the night.

My eldest brother, and head of our family, Anthony's much idolised uncle Tom, called from Abuja, Nigeria's capital. He had been sitting in his study all night, waiting by the phone. His own children were in London, and of course he had called all of them and they were OK. But out of kindness, Tom didn't tell me that.

When I asked about them, he claimed he hadn't been able

to reach them yet, but he was confident they were all right. That simple act of charity gave me a little strength, because it was beyond imagination that an entire generation of our family could have been caught up in the tragedy. So I vented a little frustration on the thoughtlessness of youth, and asked everyone, 'Where are they, why can't they call?'

By 7.30 a.m. the inactivity of waiting had become too much. I knew I had to fly to London, even if it meant scouring the streets for Anthony myself. 'Look,' I told Alan, 'this is ridiculous. I'm stupid, aren't I, sitting here?' He was preparing to go to his clinic, and I protested, 'You can't go to work. We haven't heard from Anthony. We have to go to London.'

Alan refused to be panicked. 'Why should I go to London?' he asked quietly. 'Everything is going to be OK. Do you really think that out of everybody in London, something should have happened to our Anthony?'

I grew angry and shouted, 'What is the matter with you? It's not a question of everybody in London – we haven't heard from our son! It isn't that I can't go alone, but you have to go too. I am afraid. You know I don't get frightened easily, but what if he is injured? Alan, you have to come. I have a phobia of hospitals, you know I do. You are the only one that can help Anthony now. You have to go to London. Because if we haven't heard from him, it means that he is in hospital. So he needs us. I don't mind going now, I can go now, I am ready to go now, but I think you should go too.'

Alan weathered the storm of my words. He was strong, because he knew that without his support I would crumple. In the days that followed he never wavered, and I am so grateful for that.

'It is not that I mind going to London,' he said. 'I just don't think there's any need.'

Looking back, I realise that if he had eagerly agreed to leave his patients and fly to London, I would have interpreted that as further proof that my worst fears were coming true.

Difficult though it was for him to act so coolly, his reaction was exactly what I needed most.

I didn't see it that way at the time, however. 'How can you say there isn't any need? His friends are looking for him. We are his parents. We ought to be there. If London was next door, I would have driven there already. If he wasn't 3,000 miles away, I needn't have gone through a sleepless night – I could be out there on the street, asking everybody to tell me where my son is. But I can't just click my fingers and arrive in London. If I had known it would come to this, I would have taken the night flight yesterday with British Airways, but I didn't know. None of us could imagine it. We must take the Virgin Atlantic flight this morning.'

Alan was exasperated. 'Ah! You must be dreaming,' he exclaimed. 'How can we? It's almost eight o'clock and the Virgin flight leaves at ten.'

Defiantly I said, 'I can do it, I can take it, if you are not willing to go.'

It was almost ready to boil up into a family row, but Rosa intervened: 'Stop it! Stop it! This is no time to quarrel. You can't afford this.'

She was right. Yelling was not going to help Anthony. Alan went off to work, promising that he was prepared to fly to London the following day if it should prove necessary.

My husband was right: if I thought I could catch that Virgin flight, I was dreaming. I pleaded down the phone with the bookings office at the airport, but there was nothing they could do to help – I had no ticket and, even if I took no more than my handbag, the flight had already checked in, the passengers were boarding, and the airliner would be taxiing down the runway by the time I had driven across town. My head felt as though it would burst, but I knew I would have to wait for the evening flight with British Airways.

The rest of that day passed in a blur. My hopes surged briefly when Amrit called to say Anthony had been seen in the Euston area in the minutes following the Tube bombings. It

seemed to be positive proof that he could not be lying trapped, perhaps badly injured, in one of the Underground tunnels.

'This woman got in touch, she'd seen Anthony's picture,' Amrit told me. I could hear the excitement in his voice. 'She's certain it was Anthony who helped her with directions when the Tube was evacuated.'

'Where was this?' I wanted to know.

'That's what I'm trying to find out. This lady is a stranger to London – that's why she needed directions. She's not quite sure where they were, but she's definite about the identity. It was Anthony. She said, "Your friend helped me get on a bus. He was fine. You've nothing to worry about, he must be OK. In the middle of all that confusion, he helped me. He seemed like a kind person." '

'That was Anthony,' I said. 'How like him, to stop and help a stranger at a time like that.'

'There's something else we're trying to do,' Amrit said. 'We know he called his office, so I'm hoping his phone company can trace the signal and tell us exactly where that call came from.'

'Is that possible? Can they do that? In that case, why can't they trace his mobile right now and tell us where he is?'

It seemed that every answer only multiplied our questions.

The resources officer from Anthony's office called to ask if I planned to come to England. Anthony had not come in to work, of course, and they were concerned. I told them I would call ahead to let them know when I'd be arriving at Heathrow, but the truth was I was too anxious to be that organised. All thought of calling ahead had evaporated by the time I caught the flight.

An officer from London's Metropolitan Police called too, hours later, wanting to know if I was flying out. He noted the time my flight would land, but to all my questions he was calmly non-committal. I reproach the police for many other things, but I do not blame them for saying nothing during that first call.

At some point, around noon on 8 July, I went to church. I was full of indecision, unsure from one second to the next whether I had the strength to go. A car was on the drive and there was a key on the hook, but I could not trust myself at the wheel. Nor could I make the decision to call for a taxi. Rosa had set off to the airport to help book the flight, when on the spur of the moment I leapt from my chair and marched to the car in my slippers and boubou, the gown I wore around the house.

The next thing I remember, I was standing in the church compound. Just before I went in, I saw the parish priest, and told him again that he had to offer the Mass especially for the victims of the London bombings, the injured and those still missing. As calmly as I could, I reminded him that I still had not heard from Anthony.

He seemed quite confident that all would be well. Inside the church, I discovered there was no one to take the reading. I was trembling with worry, and I had to walk to the lectern. When I read the names of people who needed our prayers, I added my family's. My voice was steady but my legs were not.

The priest was full of praise and words of comfort afterwards. He knew of course that I was waiting for that call from Anthony, and he said the strength I showed in taking the reading was proof that there would be a light at the end of the tunnel. Perhaps the thought was in his mind that, if Anthony were already dead, I would need all my strength in the months and years to come. But he made his words sound upbeat and positive, and I clung to them.

My sister Teresa, who also lives in Abuja, had hoped to join me on the flight to England, but she discovered at the last moment that her visa had expired. One of Anthony's closest friends, Remi, joined me instead. He was a pillar of strength.

Remi came to the house in Lagos with his mum after Amrit or another friend, Ope, called him to break the news that Anthony couldn't be found. They had known each other since they were about sixteen – they went to different schools in England, but they got to know each other through friends. When I told him we still hadn't heard from Anthony, he was emphatic: 'I'm coming with you, Auntie. I'll come with you on the flight; you can't go alone.'

All through the flight he was constantly coming to my seat to ask, 'Are you OK?' and I was saying, 'Yes, I'm OK, OK.' The truth was far from that.

I told him how grateful I was that he was with me, and he said, 'Anthony always looks out for us, and this is the time to look out for him.' All through that long flight, the longest I think anyone can have ever made from Nigeria, he kept coming to look at me, every so often, and saying, 'Auntie, you are not sleeping.'

I said, 'What about yourself, you are not sleeping. And anyway, I am praying.'

All around us people were asleep, but for me there was little chance of that. I was exhausted, yet my nerves were screaming and my head was buzzing. I focused on the thought that I was going to see my Anthony. Nothing more. Nothing unusual. I was simply flying to London, to the city where my son was born, to see him.

The year he was born, the winter was almost interminable. Anthony arrived on 29 January 1979, but the freezing weather went on deep into the springtime. We had a white Easter. The British press labelled it the 'Winter of Discontent', a play on Shakespeare's words that had more to do with politics than snow forecasts. But for me, it was the warmest time of my life.

When my contractions began, I was scared, but also too thrilled to realise how difficult birth could be. I was just twenty-four years old, and Alan was twenty-six. Our adult lives had just begun, and everything was strange and novel.

It is at these times that I truly appreciate the beauty of a loving family, the privileges of an extended family and the blessings of a united and caring family. My parents, my sisters and brothers were all there for us, either in spirit or in person.

What followed proved to be a seriously protracted labour. It went on for about thirty hours before the decision was taken to give me an emergency caesarian section.

That news threw my family into disbelief and near-panic. Alan had to call on his newly developed skills as a professional doctor to calm fears, and perhaps play down the dangers of such an operation after so long a labour.

All I can remember now is being wheeled into the theatre, my vision foggy as I counted like a nursery-school child who was still struggling to wrap her brain round the idea of numbers.

As I came round, my little angel, my special gift of gold from God, was placed in my arms by his adoring young dad, with doting aunties and uncles pressed around. Gradually, groggily, it dawned on me what had happened. As I hugged the flannelled bundle, Alan told me: 'Marie, you've got a lovely baby boy.'

I nervously pushed away the folds to allow me a clear view of the most gorgeous, pretty and charming little baby I had ever seen. Because he was born by caesarian, and his head had not fully engaged during the labour, he came out with clearly defined fine features, the most gorgeous pair of twinkling eyes and lashes of lovely, dark silky hair.

This was a divine moment, and for the family a time of celebration. Anthony was the first grandson for both his sets of grandparents. He seemed destined for us, destined for the joy that he brought to families that had been eagerly awaiting grandchildren.

On my side of the family, I am the last of six children and the last of four girls. We grew up and married, but over the years the family had suffered our full share of disappointments and bitter tears, unfulfilled and shattered hopes and dreams, through a series of miscarriages. My eldest sister, who had waited ten years to become a mother, had to endure the awful pain of a stillbirth: her little boy was delivered dead, by caesarian. All of which culminated in her becoming a victim of unjustified marital indignation.

Over the years I had pondered why, and I had prayed fervently for healthy children to be born to my brothers or sisters long before I got married. I never prayed that for myself, so my family's delight was complete when, three months after Anthony arrived, my eldest brother's wife also had a baby boy. From the moment he was born, Thomas Jr (TJ) was more of a brother than a cousin to Anthony, a constant companion.

I can still savour the wafting whiffs of mingled baby and baby oil aroma as I brought Anthony close to my heart for a cuddle. I can visualise his button mouth, all too ready for another meal, as the upturned dark pupils of his eyes twinkled and sparkled like bright light on liquid crystal.

He looked up right into my eyes with such love as if we had known each other for ever, and as he fed he seized my index finger in his tiny palm as if he was never going to let me go.

My hospital room was a cross between an antiques storeroom, a florist's, a card stand and a chocolate shop. All of the nurses wanted a cuddle and Anthony obliged without a tear. They had a field day and the general opinion seemed to be that this must be a very special baby boy. Once he was fed and changed, he would gently drift off to sleep as the radio played. There's one song that I can never hear without being instantly transported back to those tired, happy days: 'ChiquiChita', by Abba.

As for flowers, the only one I took home with me from the hospital was the potted purple hyacinth. It stayed on my windowsill for years, blooming every season.

As I bustled around the house with my baby, I would murmur a little chant to him:

Anthony, my Anthony, my love, my gold
Anthony, my Anthony, the bringer of joy

Anthony, my Anthony, my bundle of hope
Anthony, my Anthony, the pretty boy that could pass
   for a girl.
Anthony, my Anthony, my handsome, nay pretty prince
Anthony, my baby, Marie's gold from God with a bright
sparkle, a warm chuckle and an infectious gurgle.

The words flowed so easily, from the heart. Anthony loved to hear my voice: he could certainly tell, long before he was able to talk, that he was being showered in praise and love.

Travelling or going shopping with him three months on was a delightful ordeal, for in every shop we entered he exerted a pull, an attraction, as people came bustling around his pushchair. The same thing was exclaimed over and over: 'Oh isn't *she* gorgeous!' Because he was so fair-skinned in comparison to me, I was often asked, 'Where is her mum? She must be over the moon with a baby like this.'

And yes, Mum was.

As I explained that this 'little girl' was a boy, Anthony always beamed away, one of those cheeky, toothless smiles that could melt a heart of ice. Looking back, I realise that from the very first weeks of his life, Anthony had always poured out love and warmth.

Chief John and Victoria Ikimi, my late parents, adored him. Anthony called them Papa and Mama. Papa was a tough man, a strong character, very prim and proper. That's where the boys in my family got their determination and strong dress sense.

He was a very correct person. A tough disciplinarian, very strict with himself and with all of us. He had earned a reputation for his ability to turn stubborn kids around when their behaviour was proving too hard to handle in their own homes. All he believed in was to give us a good education, no matter how he did it and no matter what it cost, because he felt with a good education you can always make your way in life and hold your own anywhere.

And the next thing my parents gave us was our faith. That brought us together. My mother was a stronger churchgoer than my father, though of course he always went to church.

So that is the legacy we drew on, and Anthony used to go to my parents' home at weekends and for short holidays as a small child. They spoilt him silly, though obviously he wasn't *that* spoilt because he came out the way he did, as the man he was.

He was one of those lucky children who knew all four of his grandparents. They showered him with a lot of love, my father in particular, very happy and proud that he had his first grandson. And my mother of course was thrilled, not having had grandchildren for quite a while, and suddenly there was Anthony and all his cousins coming along, and they were all quite happy.

They brought us up as a very close-knit family, telling us what it was to be there for one another. That's why we have this bond of love that has always seen us through good times and bad times: what touches one, touches the other. We're there for one another. It's just a closeness we had from birth, all through our upbringing.

My father was that breed of strong character who says, 'Look, you're a family, and I am the head of the family.' He was a very tough man, but very warm at the same time – he would cane the older ones if necessary, he would do what needed to be done to instil discipline, but at the same time he also knew how to reward you if you met your targets.

My mother was always the one who was the tempering factor. All the boys in my family know how to cook because my mother would call them when my father was not in and let them cool off and learn how to prepare food. But as soon as my father came in, they would scamper off again.

But it paid off: my brothers can hold their own: they can look after themselves. And we girls can do the same thing; we can cope, and have found that the value of education is greater than anything money can buy. That is why I would always go the extra mile, deprive myself of comforts and pleasures, to give my children the best education.

Being the youngest, and quite frail and small when I was growing up, I was lucky. The rest of the family would use me to get things from my father, because they knew he had a soft spot for me and would nearly always grant me my requests.

The others used me a lot to get things they needed, if they were too scared themselves to ask him, or if they thought he would say no because they hadn't done what they were supposed to. Then they'd say, 'OK, so who do we send?' And everybody would look at me and say, 'Come, come, come!'

And then innocently I would go and carry out whatever task they had lined up for me. That was why when my father died I realised that he really wanted to reach out to me, because we were so very close. We drank tea together. At breakfast, whenever I was around, he would call me and we would share toast and marmalade. He loved toast and marmalade and his tea. I was the only one who was always privileged enough to share it with him in the morning.

That's why, years later, when he died and I wasn't in the country, I knew he was trying to reach me to say, 'Where are you?'

When Anthony was a toddler, our little family went back to Nigeria for a time. Alan's late father, Atanda Fatayi-Williams, was then the chief justice of Nigeria, and his official residence was next door to the house of the then vice-president, Dr Alex Ifeanyichukwu Ekwueme.

Anthony often went to Grandma's, because she always wanted him to go there to play. She couldn't wait to have him for the day and make a fuss of him. Anthony was an open child, curious about everything, and when he heard sirens, he would run to the gate to watch this cavalcade of cars going to the next-door house, as the vice-president swept past. And Anthony would always wave.

We didn't know about the waving, of course, until one day

the vice-president phoned my mother-in-law, Irene, and said, 'I always see a little young man at your gates when I'm driving to my house. Who is this?'

'Oh,' Irene said, 'that's my grandson.'

'You must let him come over,' the vice-president decreed. 'I'd like to return his lovely wave.'

So a day or two later, by personal appointment, young Anthony was taken to see the grandee next door. And the first Alan and I knew of it was when Dr Ekwueme sent us a photograph of the two of them in his house. I still have it, signed by the vice-president! Anthony must have been about four years old. Even at that age, he knew how to get to the right people!

As the lights of London shone through the windows of the plane, I felt certain that the 'right people' would be eager to help me find my son. How wrong I was.

5

At Heathrow I went through the unending queue at Customs. There was no one waiting to question me, no one with a news bulletin, which was fine – because as far as I was concerned I was just going to see my Anthony.

It was only when I emerged into the terminal building that I discovered a reception party. I had turned on my phone as I stepped off the plane. All I had was hand luggage. The phone shrilled as Remi and I made our way through the groups of people: several of my cousins and friends were waiting for me. I told them I'd be out in a few moments.

I was pleased to see a group of Anthony's friends had come too, as well as Alan's first cousin, Dupe, all the way from Leicester. I think Amrit was there as well, but after two sleepless nights I was so exhausted that my memories now are blurred. I know some family friends were in the party too, in particular Dr Peter Ewah. They were all there to give emotional and practical support, but part of me wished I could be arriving much less obtrusively, so that I could maintain the private fiction that this was an ordinary trip to England.

As we were heading towards the exits towards the car park, a man approached me in the information hall and asked, 'Are you Mrs Williams? Anthony's mum?'

I said to myself, 'Maybe there's some good news here.'

He introduced himself as a policeman and wanted to know whether I had arrived on the flight as planned. Wondering how he thought I could be there by any other means, I said, 'Was it you I spoke with over the phone?'

'No, no, that was my boss. I'm just here to be sure that you've arrived. Do you need anything? Nothing particular, just anything at all?'

'Yes,' I said, 'I'm hoping that you'll tell me what I need to hear. Is there any news from Anthony yet?'

Did he know? It's impossible to tell, but it's obvious to me now that the tragic news could have been delivered straight-away. Instead, his bureaucratic bosses had dispatched this man not to end my agony of uncertainty, but to ascertain that Mrs Fatayi-Williams had arrived as intended. He assured me that other officers would be making contact during the day, and he left.

My friends and family took me to Anthony's flat in Hendon. It was so full of people, and so empty without him.

'So now,' I said, 'what do we do? Amrit, give me an update. What's been happening? Has anybody heard from Anthony? His phone is still ringing but not taking messages, and this is not at all right. What do we do?'

Ope Ogunbanjo stepped forward. He is one of those who has been a tower of strength to my family over the past few months, and his clear memories of the days following the bombings have been a real help in writing this book, so let me introduce him: a Nigerian by birth, he had been in England for about seven years and, over the previous two or three years, had become a close friend of Anthony. He and I got on well, but it was Anthony's sister Aisha that he was really closest to.

He had just finished a degree and a diploma, studying man-ufacturing, engineering and management at the University of Nottingham. 'Three unforgettable years' he called that: like Anthony, he was a young man who loved to work hard but also relax with friends.

He began to explain how his and Anthony's friends had been scouring the hospitals. Ope was shaken, and to see this usually calm man so upset brought home to me how fraught the past two days had been for all of Anthony's friends.

'When did you first realise that Anthony was missing?' I asked him.

'One of my cousins, the guy that introduced me to Tony, called to check if I was all right. He wanted to know if I had called Tony, but this was the first I'd heard of it. I couldn't reach his mobile so I called Tony's workplace and the lady there said that she had talked to him and everything was cool. They said he was fine. He must be somewhere.'

I nodded. This much I already knew.

Ope continued to fill me in on the details: 'I thought, "Everything's cool," but I kept coming over to this place, several times through the day, to keep on checking, because I thought maybe Tony had walked back and that would take a long time. Since I wasn't going to work that day I thought we could just chill. What I couldn't understand at first was that Tony would have called me, just to check I was OK, because of the explosion. He's like that – always the first to make sure you're all right.'

'That is Anthony,' I agreed. 'The only explanation is that, for some reason, he has not been able to call us. Because he would if he could.'

'I thought probably his phone battery had died,' said Ope. 'The night before, I was with him at just after midnight. You know he had a seminar the day before, and it went really well. He went into town with Amrit, and I was going to meet them in central London, but I decided not to go. I don't have Anthony's energy! So he asked me to come over here and get his car, because I have a key to the flat. I got Tony's car to pick him up from the station. I dropped him off and I went back to my house at between 12.15 and 12.30. 'And I remember that his phone battery was dead because he had forgotten to charge it. So I was thinking, he didn't charge his phone and I know he won't remember my number off the top of his head.'

I shuddered, because Anthony would forget almost anything else, but not to charge his phone. He practically lived on it.

Ope reached across and took my hand. 'You called from Nigeria, and Amrit, Nike and I decided we would have to search every hospital. But we can't find him so far. He isn't on any of the lists of the injured or anything like that. So now I think we have to go through the same process again. There are some hospitals where we haven't been able to get access.'

Everyone agreed. It was the logical thing to do. In all the confusion, it was entirely possible that Anthony had been admitted to a hospital under the wrong name, or that his name had been missed off a list. All we could do was to keep trying. But the task would not be easy.

'There is plenty to stay hopeful about,' insisted Ope.

'Tell me about the hopeful things,' I said eagerly.

'Anthony is a streetwise guy – if he is evacuated from the train because there's been an explosion, he won't get on a bus or anything like that.'

We all agreed. What we didn't know then was that people were being told there had been a power surge, to keep panic to a minimum. If the authorities don't tell people what's really going on, they can't make fully informed decisions.

As we prepared for a second round of hospital checks, Amrit told us what to expect. 'The hospitals are being very, very helpful,' he assured me. 'Obviously it has been a bit of a bad time, they had a lot of work to do, a lot of people to attend to. But they are doing their best, and they really helped. There are a lot of people like us, going to reception and asking if they have a list of the people who have been admitted.'

'I want to go round the hospitals with you,' I said.

Anthony's friends were horrified. 'You can't do that! No, no, you are tired and, believe me, it is not easy work. And anyway, you said you have a phobia of hospitals. You will only make yourself feel worse. Let us do it.'

'But are you getting access to all the places you need to go? Are the hospitals taking you seriously? You're young, and in a situation like this you need to use all the friends and influence you can get. Now I'm here, Dr Peter is here, we can call on some people, medical people, the doctors I know. They might be able to go with you. They'll know their way round, and they'll know who to ask, even if they might not recognise Anthony – that won't matter because you guys will be with them. You have to go to all the hospitals, even the ones outside London, because the news reports are suggesting that so many people have been injured that they're having to use bed-space outside the city.

'We need to marshal a plan of action, because I know how hospitals work: Anthony's father is a medical man, remember. They won't let just anyone through to see patients: Peter agrees with me on this. It isn't enough to say you're his friends. You won't be allowed in to see the survivors unless you can prove you are family. So we need to think how you can get through this barrier. Let's be realistic – some people have more access than others. Some people can just walk in. We need to get them to help us.'

Already in my head I was enlisting people, such as Peter's wife, who is also a consultant, and others of the same calibre: Ayo, Victor, Sheyi, Dizzy, all of them friends or friends' husbands.

I took a deep breath. It was time to confront one of my worst fears. 'Maybe Anthony has been taken to one of the outlying hospitals, but he can't make contact because he doesn't know who he is. The trauma could have caused a memory blackout. Or he might have had a bang on the head, and been unconscious. He could still be unconscious. But if he is injured, we will find him. So let's see what we can organise, let's see who can help.'

That got everyone fired up.

'There's one more thing,' Peter said. 'We need to keep track of all the hospitals we've contacted, but don't forget:

more people are being admitted all the time. Within the past twenty-four hours there will have been new admissions on every ward, and they'll still be trying to identify many of those people.'

That was a start, but it wasn't nearly enough. I was going to leave no stone unturned in my search, and I knew where I would start: at my country's embassy. And, almost as if he had read my mind, Remi came up with the same suggestion.

I reached for the phone. 'I'm going to call the High Commission and find out if there's any message or anything. Maybe they've heard something, or maybe they know something, or maybe someone can help find out who we can go to, which authority can allow us access to all of these hospitals. They have to understand: we have someone who is lost.'

There was, and is, someone I knew at the High Commission – I won't print names, for obvious reasons. I called his personal number and he greeted me warmly: 'How are you, are you in town?' He was quite surprised that I was in London, though this was the Saturday morning, forty-eight hours after the bombing.

'Of course I'm in town,' I said. 'Don't you know what has happened? My son is missing after this attack, and you are asking if I am in town?'

He said, 'Ah! Fatayi? Is that your son? Oh my God! I think someone in the High Commission had a call from the police, maybe last night, about a Fatayi.'

'From the police?' My heart leapt into my mouth and suddenly I could hardly speak.

'I didn't take the call,' he said, 'and the person who did could not get hold of the duty officer. They were not quite sure what to do. When they managed to reach me, I instructed them to take the message, and get the name and number of the police officer, for future reference.'

'So what did the police have to say? What was the message?'

'They asked if we knew anything about a Fatayi-Williams, and said we needed to know that the mother of this Fatayi-Williams was coming in and she would like her son released as early as 6 a.m.'

I almost screamed down the line, 'Would like her son *released*? As early as 6 a.m.? Are they holding him? Is he being questioned? Where is he?'

He said, 'Ah now. That's what I didn't understand. But I'm telling you what was in the message that was passed to me, only by way of information.'

This made little sense, but of course my hopes immediately rose. All sorts of scenarios began to play simultaneously in my head, racing through my mind. Maybe Anthony has been arrested, I told myself. What if, in the aftermath of the bombing, the police suspected the terrorists were still alive and trying to make their escape. Of course the police would be under instructions to detain people all around that area. But why would they stop Anthony and hold him? Maybe because of his double-barrelled name: they'll take one look at his ID and see that Fatayi might be a Muslim name. And of course it is – Anthony's father is a Muslim. So perhaps some officer has thought, 'Ah! Prime suspect!'

I thought about this a little more. It was far-fetched, but it made sense, especially in the light of that cryptic message: 'the mother would like her son released as early as 6 a.m.' After all, Anthony was mixed race – his paternal grandmother was a white Englishwoman from Sussex, born Irene Violet Lofts. His looks showed his lineage: he had a fair complexion, and of course he was a young man.

I weighed the possibilities silently: perhaps they really are holding him. Or perhaps he is one of those who is injured and unidentified, a victim who does not know who he is. Perhaps he has had a mental block, because this whole thing has affected him so badly. If he has been caught up in carnage, he might not be able to cope with the trauma. He can't stand all that sort of thing. It's easy to imagine that he's in a police station somewhere, sitting with his interrogators, looking at them, and they are talking to him and he can't give satisfactory answers. It's very possible they know his name, because he always goes to the office with his work ID on him. And at some point the detectives will have taken note of the band on his wrist, the green-and-white one he always wears, which bears the slogan, 'Nigeria making progress'. They won't need Sherlock Holmes to tell them Anthony must have something to do with Nigeria. So what's their next step? They call the Nigerian High Commission to find out more. That fits: wasn't I just told that their first question to them was, 'Do you know anything about a man named Fatayi-Williams?'

All this passed through my mind in a matter of seconds. I clenched the phone and told the official, 'I am coming straight to your place. You have got to take me to see these police people. Take me to them now, let me identify Anthony and let me tell them that he is not a terrorist. And let them release him to me.'

My hopes were right up. Before I set out to collect him, I tried to reach the High Commissioner himself, Dr Christopher Kolade. I got through on a private number to a very close personal contact of his, someone very highly placed.

I introduced myself and asked to speak with the High Commissioner. He wasn't there, I was told, he was still at Gleneagles in Scotland, where the G8 summit was taking place. The person on the phone went on, 'His Excellency is very busy with the head of state, President Olusegun Obasanjo. He is dealing with some very important issues. But when he comes back, I will tell him that you have called and that the boy they are looking for is your son and he's Nigerian. In fact, only last night I saw that name, Fatayi, on the news, and I said, "That sounds like a Nigerian name," but I wasn't sure.'

'Very busy . . . some very important issues'. It was the third day since my son had disappeared, and someone my family knew, in a top position at the High Commission, was saying these things to me. I had to swallow my confusion and my bitter disappointment. To get angry and to rant and rail would make a bad situation worse.

'It is a Nigerian name,' I confirmed, keeping my tone respectful. 'It is my son's name.'

'If you can find your way to the High Commission on Northumberland Avenue, off Trafalgar Square, I will instruct an officer to meet you there at some point and see what we can do.'

On the way there, we stopped to pick up the official I'd spoken with earlier and together we drove to the High Commission. When I explained to this man that I was expecting to be met by somebody, he suggested I should stay in the car while he went in to find the official.

At length, he emerged, alone. 'I'm ready to go,' I said, wondering where the other official was. 'Take me to the police, bring whatever documents you have too, and let's get Anthony released.'

The official began to prevaricate: 'Let's not rush into this. I've spoken to my colleagues, and it was suggested that the first thing to do is to call the police back.'

I said, 'Half an hour ago you wanted to take me to get Anthony released. Why are you blowing hot and cold? What has changed your mind? And I was told, by somebody very close to the High Commissioner, that a senior official would be here to meet me. Where is he? I understood that his one and only priority was now to help me find my son. Why hasn't he come out to talk to me, or invited me in to meet him? Is he so busy that he can't even greet me?'

Later, I was told that this official had been handed another assignment, one that was 'more important'.

I was becoming rather impatient with my acquaintance, and I insisted he had to do something fast. He mustered all his diplomatic skills and said, 'We have to do it a certain way. We have to talk to the police later. Maybe you should go home first, because my colleagues have spoken to the police from here, inside the High Commission, and I understand there are things to discuss before we call in person. That is something that can be done later.'

All my hopes were crashing around me. The sense of frustration was overwhelming.

'What's happening here?' I said. 'Why did you call the police? Why didn't you call me in to hear it? Who was it who called?'

The official backtracked: 'No, you misunderstand me. It wasn't anyone at the High Commission who called the police – they phoned us. They rang to ask who it was they had spoken to last night, because apparently they didn't make a note of the name. And my colleague asked to speak to the officer who phoned originally, and that person was not there, so the police suggested we should wait a few hours to call back.'

This was all becoming impossibly confused, and my head was reeling. As I stood there, trying to make sense of it all, more of Anthony's friends had arrived, as well as my brother's children.

A call came through on my mobile phone. The caller asked if I was Mrs Fatayi-Williams.

'Who is this? Do you have news of my son?' I asked.

'No, madam. This is the Metropolitan Police. Are you at home?'

I was dumbstruck. The policeman repeated his name, and then all my questions poured out of me in a flood – where were they holding Anthony? Why had they told the High Commission that I wanted my son released at 6 a.m.? When was he going to be released?

'I'm afraid I have no information for you at this time, madam. I'm calling to find out when it would be convenient for you to answer a few questions. Are you at home?'

'No I am not, because – *oh!*' This was too much. But if I lost my composure, that wouldn't help Anthony. And helping Anthony was the only thing that mattered. I drew a deep breath.

'OK, it's 12.20. I can be home by 1 p.m. If you want to interview me any time after that, I'm happy to answer all of your questions as fully as I am able. In the meantime, is there a number I can ring to start getting some answers?'

There was no number. I was told simply to wait for further information.

For a minute or two I lingered at the High Commission, desperate to know more, reluctant to leave when I'd been so certain, thirty minutes earlier, that they could take me to Anthony. It was brutally clear now that this wasn't going to happen.

It was only later that I realised that, for example, South Africa had not lost anyone in this tragedy, yet at a memorial spot on Tavistock Square where people were laying flowers, there was already a South African flag flying in sympathy and solidarity. They had a presence. Nigeria did not, though Anthony was not the only Nigerian to die in the atrocities. Three Nigerians out of fifty-two dead is a sizeable proportion.

The impression I got later was that Anthony was not regarded as a Nigerian: they said he was a British citizen because he carried a British passport, he worked in London, and his grandmother was British. But his grandfather was a former chief justice of Nigeria. And everyone there knew that. But even if he was a 'nobody' in their eyes, even if he wasn't my son, any life is important. The people at the High Commission didn't have to know me or any Nigerian victim personally.

I called them for assistance because my son had disappeared in London, barely a mile from the High Commission. And all they could say to me was that H. E., His Excellency, was very busy on important matters. H. E. was coming back to London with the president. To them, that was important – and to them, Anthony was just one small boy, not important. But what had happened to him might have happened to anybody.

When I listened to my High Commission's evasions and utterances, I felt sorry for my country. I thought, 'Yes, actually, we do have the colonialist mentality.'

At times the officials ceased to know why they were there. And I know that most other embassies would not do that. The British or American embassy would never behave like that. The first question those embassies ask after a disaster is, 'Are there any British people involved? Any Americans involved?' But when I called on the Nigerian High Commission and said, 'Look, it's very likely that my son was involved,' they told me there were more important matters.

At 2 p.m. I had the first visit of many from the police and heard the mantra that would be repeated endlessly over the coming days: 'No, nothing yet.' Do you have any information for us? 'No, nothing yet.' Have you been told if my son is being held? 'No, nothing yet.' Is there any word on when Anthony will be released? 'No, nothing yet.'

They explained they were going to assign someone who would be liaising with us on a continuous basis, a family liaison officer, but I had to understand that police resources were extremely stretched. There was a lot to be done and they couldn't give me any information – except, 'No, nothing yet.'

But, they promised, as soon as they had information, they would let me know. The family liaison officer would keep me up to date and informed, so I was not to worry – I should just keep in touch with them, they would keep in touch with me, and things would progress from there. Officers would come to talk with me and ask me questions.

'Fine,' I said, 'I am willing to answer anything you ask me. I am eager to help. Ask away.' But that was not the purpose of this visit: the questions would come later. I thought it was little wonder that the Met's resources were overstretched if officers were despatched to tell people they would be getting a visit from the police later on.

Eventually detectives came and the questions started. We sat down and for more than two hours they conducted a detailed interview: my name, my background, my family, everything. Then the questions about Anthony: who was he, how old was he, what did he do, where did he work, what was his background? Anything and everything about Anthony and about me. I was sure that there was light at the end of the tunnel because it was very in-depth. They clearly wanted real answers, not vague replies, but full and accurate information, and I was more than happy to supply it.

At one point I told them bluntly: 'You want to clear up that I am not a terrorist, don't you? I am not a terrorist and I do not have terrorist descendants! Anthony is not a terrorist, I can assure you of that, so if there is anything I can say to assist your investigation, just keep asking.'

They did. And I kept answering, because I was clinging to that strange message: 'His mother wants him released as early as 6 a.m.' Of course in the weeks to come I realised that this was probably a reference to Anthony's body, that there might originally have been an intention to hand over his remains to his family at this time. Perhaps when the High Commission did not provide them with the information they wanted, the police changed their minds. But at the time, that interpretation did not occur to me. My mind was utterly focused on hope and staying positive, and my belief that I had to convince the police that neither my son nor I were terrorists.

No matter how many questions I answered, the detectives gave nothing back. They wouldn't confirm or deny anything to me. It was a matter of, 'Once we get any information we'll let you know.' That was all. Nothing more. When I asked, 'Is he injured, is he hurt, is he in hospital?' back came that reply: 'Once we get any information we'll let you know.'

Whether the family liaison officers were aware from the first that Anthony was dead, I am not sure. But the detectives who questioned me must have known something. They must have. All of them must have known. But I think they had to act in unison because they were gathering information. By the end of the week I had realised they were sucking out as much information as they could from anybody and everybody. Anyone who called the helpline, asking for information about Anthony, was traced and questioned.

They were keen on knowing who else was coming to London from Nigeria – was my husband coming, when would he be coming, which flight, would anyone else be with him, why had he not come earlier? I explained that my husband had professional duties, that he was a doctor and other people's lives depended on him. The police said I should try to get him to fly over, because they would have to talk to him as well. I asked, 'Why?' and they were vague: they would have to know about him further. 'Why? What if he isn't coming?'

For a long time all they would say was that they needed to speak with him as well. Eventually they said they might have to 'take some samples and stuff'. That set alarm bells clanging, and I demanded to know what they meant, what kind of samples were needed. 'It's just a routine thing,' they insisted. 'You know, DNA.'

'DNA! What, is there anything wrong?'

'Oh, no, no, no, it's just a normal procedure.'

They could have told me then. I have never received any explanation from the police as to why I was explicitly told that the DNA samples were required as a matter of routine and normal procedure, when they later admitted they were used to confirm the identification of my son's body.

At the end of this long inquisition, they took all my telephone numbers and other contact details, and revealed that two family liaison officers had been assigned to us. They arrived later that day and introduced themselves: Sharon and Gill. Sometimes both would arrive together, sometimes just the one, but both were polite, sympathetic and professional: 'Anything you want to discuss with us, we'll be the ones you'll talk to. Don't hesitate to ask us any questions. We'll keep you fully informed. Here are our pager numbers, we'll be coming back tomorrow, and as soon as Alan is here you must tell us – the minute he arrives. In fact, tell us before he arrives so we can go and meet him.'

I believed them and agreed to it all. I was so determined to show them that Anthony could not possibly be a terrorist.

Then came the warnings against talking to reporters. 'We're your liaison with the outside world. You have to trust us, because it can create all sorts of difficulties if you talk to other people. Keep yourselves to yourselves, and don't talk to the press. If they ask questions, don't answer them. You can never tell who's out there, how they will treat the information you tell them. It's not nice, but that's the way the world is.'

How the world really was, I was only just beginning to find out.

6

When the family liaison officers left, I had a piece of paper in my hand, the emergency services' helpline number which I could call for assistance and information. It was a service provided for all the families. And after so many hours of 'No, nothing yet' and 'Once we get any information we'll let you know', I was ready for information. Maybe there'd be someone on the end of the phone who hadn't heard the order: tell *nothing* to Mrs Fatayi-Williams!

What I got, instead, was someone who had never heard the name Fatayi-Williams at all. Despite the fact that this helpline had been set up to assist families of people who were still unaccounted for, they had nothing on file about Anthony.

'I've told our life stories to your officers,' I insisted. 'They even know what size shoes Anthony wears. Don't tell me you have no record even of his name. There have been so many people calling to find him.'

My inner voice piped up: 'Keep calm, Marie. You have to work with these people. They are not deliberately trying to make your life even harder.'

The helpline operator was polite and seemed genuinely to be trying to be helpful. 'It's shocking that we haven't got your family's details on the database,' she agreed. 'The computers have been struggling to cope with all the information over the past day or two, and of course it's possible that the detectives who questioned you haven't had a chance yet to input everything – they're pretty overloaded too, as you can imagine.

Perhaps you wouldn't mind running through the details again. What is your son's name?'

'Anthony,' I sighed. 'His surname is a double-barrelled name, Fatayi, spelt this way: Foxtrot-Alpha-Tango-Alpha-Yankee-India, hyphen and a Williams.' And so the questions began again – age, nationality, date of birth, occupation. The operator assured me: 'I am just asking these things so that, from now on, anyone who calls can access the information. Now, does Anthony have any peculiar marks, does he travel on this line on the Underground, where does he work?'

The following day, the police came to take the first batch of DNA samples. Alan had just arrived from Lagos, and no sooner had he arrived than he was put through a marathon interview session. The police, as he put it, 'wanted to know my life history as well as that of all my ancestors, descendants and associates'.

Alan answered their endless questions patiently, as I had, providing all the same answers. Perhaps the detectives wanted to be sure that our stories tallied at all points. 'Anything is good enough for me as long as, at the end of it all, they bring my son alive to me,' he said. 'I will prove to anyone that I am not a terrorist and neither is my son.' Each time the police showed up he obliged with answers, and we both agreed that we were always doing the answering and never seemed to be receiving any answers to our one and only question.

I was hopeful that the DNA tests could lead to some kind of instant breakthrough, but Alan was more worldly-wise. The swabs had been taken with meticulous care, he conceded, and the chance of mistakes seemed minimal, but he knew the pace of government and police bureaucracy: it could be at least two weeks before the results were known.

Two weeks! They might as well have asked us to wait for ever.

During the DNA testing, the police asked whether I could give them Anthony's computer. I knew what they were driving at: if Anthony had been a terrorist, there would be clues on his hard drive: e-mails and browser histories would reveal a trail. But the implications were becoming harder to bear. How dare these police officers insinuate that my son could have ever played a part in the atrocities? I was having to exercise more self-control than I had ever imagined I possessed.

My husband's professional calm helped to give me inspiration. He'd been dealing with pressure all his working life. My older brother, Tom Ikimi, also flew to join us as soon as he could; he is the former foreign minister of Nigeria, and his career has many times rested on his ability to master his emotions. The support of these two strong men during the whole period helped me to bear up.

'The computer,' I said. 'Of course I would be happy to let you take it away, to comb through it, in case there is any clue hidden in some obscure file that might point to Anthony's whereabouts. But it is a laptop, not a home computer.'

'Why would that make a difference, madam?' asked a detective.

'Because I guess he had it with him. He must have done, because you can see it is not here. It is his work computer. And if he was carrying it when he was injured, or when perhaps he was arrested, or when whatever has happened took place, then it is likely that the police have already picked it up.'

Later, they asked: 'Did he used to wear glasses?'

The casual use of the past tense sent a momentary chill through me. For one terrible second I thought, do they know Anthony is dead? No, that is unimaginable. No one could be so inhuman as to ask these questions and not tell me what they knew, when it is evident how much my son's life means to me and all of us.

'Yes, he wears glasses,' I answered, 'but I don't know whether he was wearing his glasses that morning because I wasn't here. He doesn't wear them all the time; he has them for reading. Where is all this leading to? Where is Anthony?'

'Not to worry, Mrs Williams. Once we get any information, we'll let you know.'

By now we had been able to contact various friends who
were doctors, ready for a fresh trawl through the hospitals.
Knowing that these professionals would be able to use their
credentials to gain access to the wards, I had arranged for
photos of Anthony to be copied, and I armed my friends
with these. They managed to get two teams together,
intending to search for Anthony wherever there was the
remotest chance he might be.

At some hospitals they were allowed to go in, at others
they were not. Most of these places were still struggling to
maintain a basic level of functioning. They were in danger of
being swamped by the hundreds of casualties and the
thousands of anxious relatives. I am full of admiration for
the doctors and nurses who worked for days without sleep,
but I can't help asking: what if the casualties had been far
worse? What if there had been not 52 innocent victims, but
520? Or thousands, as there were in New York? What would
have happened to the injured when the system hit meltdown?
And what is the British government doing now to reassure its
citizens, and ensure that in the future it is prepared even for
the very worst scenarios?

As our medical friends reported back that evening, it was
clear they had been unable to find Anthony. And yet hope
still burned. Quite a number of the injured were in wards
where no one was permitted to go, in intensive care. It was a
thought too horrible to contemplate, and I cannot say that I
hoped Anthony was in intensive care – but at the same time,
I knew that people could recover from even the worst
injuries. The strength of Anthony's friends showed me
clearly that, even if my son faced a battle of months and years
to pull through, he would have love and support every inch
of the way.

There were other bright spots among the embers of our
hopes. We had not yet visited all the hospitals outside

London. We still had no explanation for that odd message to the Nigerian mission: 'his mother wants him released as early as 6 a.m.'

A rumour gleaned from television news reports added weight to the suggestion that some of the witnesses of the bus bombing in Tavistock Square could have been held. A cordon had been thrown around the area very quickly, and footage was shown of one man who had been left miracu-lously unscathed – but shortly afterwards, he could not be found. Could he have been rounded up? If the police knew where he was, they weren't saying. Looking back, I realise my mind had strayed into the zone of conspiracy theories and spy films, but at the time any hope was better than no hope.

I told Alan, 'I have a sneaky feeling that our boy, because of the name that he bears, or maybe his looks, is being questioned in some police cell. Why else would they want to inspect his computer? They must want to make their checks, to be sure that he is my son and that what he's telling them and I'm telling them is the truth. Eventually they will reconcile our stories, because this information we're giving them is just too detailed to be dismissed. On the other hand, if someone is dead, you don't need all that information. They wouldn't have to be asking me the story of my life.'

Remi told me later that Anthony's friends had the same theory, far-fetched but a vestige of hope, even though on the Sunday morning, he admitted, he woke up with a gut feeling that Tony was dead. Remi said, 'Amrit tried to work it out. He broke it down to us. Everything was eliminated. But we hit on some crazy theory that one suicide bomber hadn't killed himself but he was injured, and the police were keeping all the survivors who were on that bus and were unidentified, and they were holding them for security reasons. That was our wild scenario. We had convinced ourselves it was our last chance. Any hope that you can cling to.'

I don't want to sound as if I blame the police for all of the pain during those few days. I will never accept that it was right for them to withhold the news of my son's death, but at the same time I can accept the security services have their own problems. They have to get through a lot of bureaucratic barriers.

The family liaison officers, for example, were fantastic, but there was a limit to what they could do. We told them what we needed and they tried to deliver; they said, 'OK, we'll take this information back and we'll try and see what we can do, and we'll get back to you.' But that was all they could offer. They worked on one level, and they couldn't go any further up the ladder. It wasn't as if we were dealing with the chief commissioner. There were procedures they had to go through. I found that when I asked for specific information, it could take three or four days for the family liaison officers to get back to me – not because there was incompetence or because they did not have sympathy for me. The two female family liaison officers were wonderful women. But I believe that the bureaucratic set-up was such that they could not break the glass ceiling.

By now it was Monday 11 July. We were drawing blanks. The Nigerian High Commission was not helping. We were not hearing anything new from anyone. I'd been in Britain for forty-eight hours and nothing was happening. I had talked so much that the saliva in my mouth had dried up.

What could we do? Where were we going to turn next? I didn't know anybody in MI5 that I could turn to, I didn't know anyone at Westminster, I had no friends among the highest echelons in Britain. I am just me, a mother. How was I going to make people realise that I was looking for my son? How could I make the authorities help me? There could be no more waiting. We needed to find Anthony because the ordeal was becoming too much to bear for any longer.

And that was when the idea of a press conference, a televised appeal for help, started to develop. What I wanted to do was to actually go out there, into the streets, and cry out, 'Anthony!' To call to him, so that if he heard my voice, something would click in his brain and he might wake up and say, 'Yeah, OK, my mother is here.'

Of course, he would not hear my voice if I simply wandered the streets with a megaphone. That's exactly what my instinct was, however – to go into the streets and shout myself hoarse.

But maybe, I said to myself, if I could get myself on television, I could make an appeal. My son might be lying on a ward somewhere, bewildered, not knowing who he is. When he hears my voice, his mind will click into focus and he'll tell the doctors, 'Oh, that's my mother.' And the doctors will draw a picture from there. I would do anything to find this boy, I would take any help, please help me . . .

I came out of my reverie. I looked around. My friends and family were with me, but in the outside world nobody was helping. No one was telling us anything. At that moment I made the decision: I had to share this thought with someone. Who better but Amrit, who had been such a tremendous support and who had already made some inroads with the press.

To my surprise, before I could speak, he blurted out the same thoughts.

From then on, the utmost teamwork was required. The success of the press conference was due to a combination of all of us. Amrit has a clear, incisive mind, and he realised immediately that it was not simply a question of 'going on the telly'. We had to target this appeal.

'One of our options,' he suggested carefully, 'is to talk to the press.'

I shied a little. I am instinctively respectful of authority, and the police had told me clearly that I was not to speak to reporters. I told Amrit my reservations.

'That may be so,' Amrit agreed, 'but if the police are not helping us, Auntie, what do they expect us to do?'

All the young people chimed in, to convince me. 'People become lost every week,' Ope pointed out, ever the realist.

'What the relatives always do is go to the media to appeal. And then they show their picture and they appeal to the missing person. We've been doing it on a tiny scale, approaching people on the street to show them Anthony's photograph, talking to nurses and receptionists in hospitals. And the response has been incredibly helpful. People want to help. But if I stop a man on the street, he's just one guy. He might want to help but, if he doesn't know anything, he can't. If you talk to the television cameras, millions will see the appeal. It's like stopping ten million people on the street, in one moment.'

'I have already been on television,' mused Amrit. 'We have to do something with real impact.'

The day before, Amrit had been visiting the hospitals, and at the Royal Free in Hampstead he had approached a knot of reporters and cameramen. Sky's news team were there, interviewing relatives of the victims, and he had showed them Anthony's photograph. The clip had lasted no more than a few seconds, but it had been repeated several times, perhaps because of its emotional impact: Amrit had not slept for days, like all of us, and he was clearly distraught.

That news item was a start, but I could see that Amrit had more ambitious plans. He sat with me, quietly, away from the others, and set about explaining how we could capture the attention of the world's media.

'Why talk to the press?' I said, doubtfully. 'Isn't it usual for the police to organise a conference? It would be better to work with the authorities.'

'If the police wanted us to do that,' he pointed out, 'they would already have suggested it. Auntie, let's work through this. We know Anthony was in that general area of Tavistock Square. I went to the phone company, and they managed to pinpoint the position of his last calls.

'Even if he was in Tavistock Square itself when the bomb exploded, we think he probably wasn't on the bus itself. There is nothing he would be doing on a Number 30 because that doesn't go to his office. But he could have been in the vicinity when the bus exploded. Maybe he got hit by flying debris. Or, another possibility, Anthony's the sort of person who can't abide suffering and pain, so maybe he did all he could do as a first-aider and then he lost it and he's just walking, roaming, thinking. Maybe he'll be huddled up somewhere, close to a television or a radio. It's only through the media that he has a chance to hear your voice.'

'What if the police decide to stop us?'

'I don't think they will, Auntie. What would be their reason? We are only helping them out.'

I was convinced. 'I have to tell the press, "This is Anthony, this is his picture." So – which picture? We need a very clear picture of him. Not just a good likeness, but one that captures his whole personality, so that viewers will see and immediately recognise him or feel real sympathy, and understand why we are so desperate.'

I had to force myself to be strong and not to dissolve into tears as I sorted through the few pictures of Anthony that we had. There was one I loved especially, taken a year earlier at the silver wedding anniversary celebrations for Alan and me.

Anthony was holding me close to him. It was the same in every photograph: he was either cuddling me in a protective way or giving me a kiss, just loving me for who I am. When he pulled me close for a photo, he would always say, 'Mummy, you're just the best.' Look at any picture of me with Anthony, ever since he was a small boy, and we are always tête-à-tête, head-to-head.

'We'll use this one,' I said. 'Amrit, can you organise all this? Do you know where to start?'

'Auntie,' he said truthfully, 'I don't know how I'll manage, but all I can do is try. I'll get as many people as possible to this thing, but I cannot tell you what to say. You'll just have to reach out to Anthony. Call out for him. Just talk to him. Tell him you want to see him, tell him to come out wherever he is and let us see him. What on earth else can we do?'

Later that day, as people ran in and out of the flat, deep in conversation or chattering into mobiles, I caught hold of Remi and asked him how it was progressing.

'Amrit is the brains,' he said. 'He's incredible. He's got all of us youngsters running round, trying to get the television and the newspapers and the radio involved. We're letting all of them know so that everyone can be there. It is quite a daunting task, I can tell you. And without Amrit leading everyone in the right direction, delegating everything, I can't imagine how we'd do it.'

There was no way for me to help in the organisation. I would only get in the way. I just sat on my bed distraught and thinking, what am I going to say, how do I say it? I wrote down a few lines. Part of my speech just came to me, and I jotted it down. A couple of the young ladies keeping watch with me offered to type whatever I could manage to write. But I knew I was going to have to ad-lib the greater part.

Maybe Mr Blair would see it and be moved, and say to the police, 'Release her son. You don't need to hold him any more. Without doubt he's not a terrorist.'

But then I suddenly thought, what if Anthony is dead? And instantly, I managed to banish that notion from my mind. He can't be dead. He has to be alive. He is my only son.

I clung on to what my elder brother Tom had said to me in Lagos: 'Anthony dead? Oh please, forget about that. There is nothing wrong with Anthony. Out of everybody in London, why should Anthony be affected?' I held on to that all night.

At some point in the dark and sleepless night, a new and terrible thought stole across me. What if the terrorists have taken him as a hostage? Amrit and Remi think that one of the terrorists might have survived. I found myself taking this thought a stage further – what if the killers did not die, but they could not escape? So maybe they rounded up survivors at gunpoint, and are now holding Anthony as a pawn?

This horrible fantasy grew larger and larger in my mind,

until I had to say to myself, 'Suppose it is true. Anthony is a hostage. He cannot get away. How do I get them to listen to me? I'll beg them: "Look at me! Please! He is my only son. He's all I have. He's a young man going to work to earn a living. He doesn't hate you nor have anything against you. Just release my son to me. Please. I beg you from the bottom of my heart. Hatred will not get us anywhere. He doesn't hate you, I don't hate you. I'll pray for you. Just release my son to me, please. He's all I have. I need him. I want him." '

I broke out in a hot and cold sweat. My fears and my grief were twisting the situation into hideous shapes that I could never have imagined. I could not let this idea alone: the terrorists have him. I have to get through to them. I have to appeal to them. To show them the futility of this action. I will say, 'People have died. Those who have been killed, look at them. They are like me. If you have my Anthony, look at them. They didn't do anything. Give me my Anthony, and you will make me very happy to have my child, but I will also feel very sorry for those other people who have lost their children. What about them? If you are holding other people's children, release them as well. Please let my appeal for Anthony free every other hostage.'

This was my last chance: a simple, human message that would touch their hearts.

But how should I word my message? I could directly address the head of the terrorists, through the cameras – but the media seemed to know nothing of hostages. They might easily assume I was unhinged by grief, and ignore my appeal altogether. I might even be blundering, for if Anthony was a hostage the negotiations would certainly be delicate. Perhaps I was not allowed to know. To reveal what I had guessed could be a terrible mistake.

I decided my message to them had to be as broad as possible: 'I am not going to stand on hard ground, I am not a decision-maker, I'm not the government – just help me. Give me my Anthony.'

The morning came at last and, with the light, reason returned. There were several ways that my son might be found safe. All of them were slender chances, but I had to hold on to them all. All I could do was deliver the most heartfelt, coherent message that my heart could supply.

That was how my journey to Tavistock Square came about.

7

The scene that greeted me was not in the least what I was expecting. We went by car, with Amrit driving, and it's a good thing he knew the way because to this day I couldn't point to the place on a map and say, 'That's Tavistock Square.' For the life of me, I couldn't place it and I would not want to.

It was only later I learned that, very close to the site where the cameras were being set up, was the wreckage of the bus.

Tavistock Square: the name had been a blank to me. I had never had cause to go there. Maybe I had passed through it, I might have ridden through in a taxi or a friend's car, more than once. But that name had never registered in my mind before, and I wish I could still say that.

All the same, I had a general idea of where we were. The British Museum was not far away, and I had passed through Marylebone many times, not so far away. But as I stepped out of the car, the skyline and the buildings looked no different to any of a thousand spots in London. This place seemed to have no special resonance.

Other cars followed us, filled with Anthony's friends. They were so wonderful. Everyone came with us, his cousins, and his pals. Amrit is a Sikh, and not for the first time I was struck that so many of Anthony's friends were of different religions. That was natural, for Anthony was the first child of a marriage between two faiths, Alan a Muslim and I a Christian. Remi too had a Muslim father and a Christian mother, a combination that is not uncommon in Nigeria. I remember that Alan's father was quite reserved towards me because of my faith, until his son and his wife both pointed out that Irene was Christian herself! He had to concede that point.

I stepped out of the car with Alan. I am not especially tall, and all I could see was this forest of microphones and cameras. That was a shock. I had thought I was just going to speak to one or two people. I imagined what you see on television, where the presenter sits in a little room, and I was trembling.

I thought of Anthony and said, 'Get a grip on yourself, Marie. Just get a grip on yourself.'

My husband took my arm. 'Oh Alan, what are we going to do?' I whispered. 'I have to speak to these people and there are so many microphones. My heart is pounding.'

A favourite childhood auntie of mine, fondly called Mama Leye, was firmly beside me. She had come to London to see her new granddaughter, yet she abandoned them to stay with me and play the role of my eldest sister, Grace, her very close friend, who was not yet around.

I was clutching my piece of paper, with a few words jotted on it. As soon as we had walked a few steps from the car, the cameras started to click and clatter.

A huge banner photograph of Anthony had been erected behind the microphones where I was to stand. I was taken aback. This was a photograph I'd never seen before and Anthony looked so alive. His warm smile and his eyes were welcoming me, as if to say, 'Yes, Mummy, I knew it, I knew you'd come to look for me.' The boys had turned it into a backdrop.

Then I noticed the slogan on top of the photograph: 'How Many More?' And I thought, 'Why? How many more what? Innocent victims? Was Anthony one of them, already dead? You mean I'll have nothing to keep of him but just a picture? Oh no, no, no! He *has* to come back to me.' My emotions were running riot.

And then I saw the T-shirts – the boys had managed to make a handful of T-shirts, about six, with that photograph on the front. It was as if they were saying, 'Auntie, look, we are all doing everything we can. We're leaving no stone unturned.'

What in God's name have I let myself in for, I thought. And then, steadying my nerves, I decided: OK, we are here for Anthony. He has to be well, and whether it's the police or the terrorists or the hospitals that have him, they have to release him. That's why I am here.

I asked the newsmen, 'Where do I stand?'

They said, 'On that little thing.' There was a small bench or box. I stepped up, just to be on the same level as the microphones, and I looked at a sea of heads. Every one seemed to bob under a microphone. So many microphones, big, small, fluffy, red-meshed. And I couldn't recognise any face at all.

But when I looked at the back of the crowd I spotted one of my nephews, Christo, and that gave me reassurance: OK, someone that I know is in the crowd. That could be Anthony. I can imagine him walking up to me. OK, fine.

Then I lifted up the silver wedding anniversary photograph, and I said, 'This is my son, Anthony. It is five days now and I haven't heard from him. I don't know where he is.'

The words just came to me, how he was the head of my family, all the things he said to me: 'Mummy, I'll do great things for you, you'll see. I'll always be here for you, holding you tight.' I'm not referring to the text of my speech at this moment, and I don't know it by heart – far from it – but the immense love and longing I felt for my boy flowed in every word I spoke.

The first few lines had been prepared, as well as bullet points, but within a couple of minutes I was just giving vent to my feelings. Whatever was in my heart, I kept saying it, because I could feel Anthony there. His presence was all around.

I felt so sure that Anthony was going to appear after this –

he had to come out from wherever he was. So I just lit up and I said the words in my heart. I don't know whether I cried but now when I look at the footage I see my expression and I can see I was so distraught.

That speech came to be because it just came to be – something was pushing me, something was directing me, something was eating me and I knew it was the spirit of God. I knew I wasn't the only one who felt this way. There were many other people, hurting out there.

As the speech gathered power and emotion, I more or less broke down. Mama Leye squeezed my arm reassuringly, while Alan held me to steady my trembling frame. I remember Remi, the friend of Anthony's who came with me from Lagos and who gave me such strength on that flight; he was the one who was holding Anthony's picture, and when in the middle I couldn't cope, he was the one who put his hand on my shoulder and whispered, 'Auntie, Auntie, you're doing fine. Just hold it in and take a deep breath, don't cave in now, Auntie, Anthony needs you.'

As soon as he said that and I heard 'Anthony needs you', I picked up again. And Amrit said, 'Yes, Auntie, Anthony needs you.' That's how I managed to make it to the end.

As I stepped back from the microphones, I told the boys, 'I can't answer any questions.'

They said, 'No, you don't have to,' and we went straight to the car. As we drove away I suddenly felt cold, as if all the heat had drained out of the day. It was the middle of July and the weather wasn't cold – it was hot, but I was so cold.

After a mile or two, Amrit pulled the car over and we stopped. That was clever of him, because we had driven off in a direction that none of the reporters could have guessed, and then we'd stopped. That made sure the media could not hound me – for half an hour, we were the only people in London who knew where we were. We had departed so quickly that the crews had no time to stow away their cameras.

We sat down in a small café, and we ordered some coffee and some tea. Nike poured some tea for me and I tried to drink it, but I was shaking. There was a little shop up the street, and Nike quietly slipped away for a few minutes. When she came back, she had bought a shawl for me, a warm, black one. I wrapped it round my shoulders as she remarked that I was shaking.

'Yes, I am feeling very cold, very cold.' I couldn't drink the tea, I couldn't do anything, I was just trembling. So I wrapped myself more closely in the shawl, and my whole world had suddenly shrunk to the space of that café. My heart was numb, as if the cold in my body had spread throughout it.

I had poured out my plea, and Anthony had not come walking out of the crowd. My brain had always known I could not will him into existence with the sheer force of a mother's love, but that was what I had tried to do. Now there was nothing else, nothing I could do but wait, and no energy left inside to drive me forwards. I simply sat with my hands wrapped around the hot mug of tea, unable even to sip from it.

At length the boys said, 'We'd better go home.' Soon after we got back to the flat, other friends and family started to arrive, asking where we had got to. And the phones started to ring.

The phone calls did not come directly to me. The press were calling Anthony's friends, who had been giving out their mobile numbers. The flat was packed with young people, and within an hour it seemed as if all of them were talking away on their phones. Every reporter in London wanted to know more about the hunt for Anthony. I should have been relieved – it looked like my appeal had generated some interest. How much interest, of course, I had no idea.

So the press had a field day with cousins and friends and people who were at school with Anthony. They didn't chase me, but I'm sure they could have if they'd wanted to. My guess is that they saw my distress, and they saw that it wasn't anything to celebrate, it wasn't anything to joyride about. It was a sad thing, and the men and women of the media had the decency to respect that.

That scene in Tavistock Square was a very traumatic moment for me and for everyone around us. It was not play-acting, not a fake. I was what I appeared to be: a mother who had lost her son and was looking for him.

Because I was so drained, and because all the focus I could muster was directed at waiting for news of Anthony, waiting for information, waiting for the family liaison officers to come and tell us that he had been found, I took little notice of the hubbub of activity around me. I barely glanced at myself on the television. But Remi came to me, and offered me reassurance that I had done everything I could. Our press conference had delivered far more impact than anyone could have dared to dream.

'Auntie, it was unbelievably effective,' he said. 'I could never have imagined doing that. Two days ago, we were thinking, "What's the best thing we can do?" And now we have done it. You were inspirational, exactly what we all expected and knew you were capable of.'

'You all helped,' I said. 'Thank you.'

'It was just a case of being by your side and getting you through it. For ten or fifteen minutes you had to be as strong as we know you can be, just for those particular minutes in front of the cameras. And yes, you were brilliant.'

How I wished the comfort and praise of Anthony's friends and my family, and all the reports and reviews I was later to read in the newspapers, could have brought my Anthony back.

Later, while I was going through some papers, looking for anything that might give us a clue in our search, I came upon some notes Anthony had made for the nutritionist at his Holmes Place gym. As I read it I could not help tearfully smiling to myself:

Eating Pattern:
I endeavour to eat five fruits a day as a minimum: I always have at least one banana, one apple, two oranges, and then perhaps grapes or a plum or another banana. I use the fruits to curb the desire to eat continuously!
Breakfast:
2 parts
A/ Cereal, with (banana), Crunchy Nut cornflakes, Frosties, Coco Puffs. Sometimes Alpen, but not recently. Fruit juice. One or two fruits (7.30 a.m.)
B/ A bagel; usually ham and scrambled egg, tuna mix (i.e. peppers mixed) or a sandwich; usually not so healthy, e.g. chicken and bacon, with mayo. Two or three fruits (10–10.30)
Lunch:
Now almost always a baked potato with chilli con carne (v. boring but tasty as hell) (1.15–2.00)
Three or four fruits – usually a banana (4.00–4.45)
GYM!!
Dinner:
Never usually before 9.00! TERRIBLE! Dinner could be anything. I have bought quite a bit of muscle fuel from Joe, so I hope to perhaps use this to supplement my eating, e.g. especially in the evenings, so as not to eat too late. Monday to Friday, I drink approximately two litres of water a day. I do not take any vitamins or supplements, but I am open to suggestions.

I took this piece of paper and showed it to some of his young friends. They all smiled and agreed, 'That's Anthony, all right. He is the healthiest guy we know!'

'He is a very healthy eater,' I agreed, scanning the list. 'He likes his food. That's why all of his friends have been saying to me, "Anthony will be all right because even if he is injured, he is so strong and healthy. If that's all that is needed to come out of this thing, he will come out of it. Because he is just too fit and he cares so much about what goes into his stomach and how he trains and in getting the right nutrition, drinking the right things." '

'You know he started this five fruits thing at his office?' someone chipped in. 'He always goes to this same vendor, this greengrocer, and he always buys his fruit from him. Then he goes round to all his friends in the office and tells them, "OK, here's your fruit, here's your apple, here's your banana" – he takes his bag around and asks his colleagues, which of these fruits do you want?'

'And he does his keep-fit so passionately,' another added. 'You know how he likes to look good. He is always very determined. When he sets his mind to something and says, "I'm going to do this," he sticks at it. I think it started off with him thinking, "I'm a little tubby," which to me he never was. But he wanted to look better and be healthier. And then he wanted all his friends to join in.'

I smiled wryly.

'He is like that with all of us,' said Amaka. 'He tells us, "Rather than having toast with a lot of butter, why don't you have a bagel with cream cheese?" Of course he spends a lot of time, if not every evening, at the gym, and he is trying to push us girls in the nicest way, in a very supportive way, to get active too.'

It was so good to talk about him like this. Everything about Anthony was so positive; it had been a terrible drain to be fearing for him and fighting off the negative thoughts. I was in my stride now. As I ran my finger down the list Anthony had written out for the nutritionist, I thought: he is forever cautioning me, 'Mummy – Mummy! Cholesterol! It's not good for you, you're putting on too much weight, Mummy. You've got to watch what you eat, you know.' And he is always wanting me to go to the gym with him. He actually did register me, but I never went once and my membership lapsed. He said, 'I don't know what else to do to get you to go to the gym, you've *got* to go!' I smiled and said, 'You're doing the gym for me, *you* keep going!'

My group of lovely young ladies and I laughed and cried. Strange, but Anthony was offering me support even then because these were all his friends, each one special, each one with a special compartment in my son's large heart.

When I think about him now, I know he didn't get his healthy eating pattern from me, because I'm a picky eater – I don't really eat very well. I lost a lot of weight after Anthony's death, but about Christmas I went on a binge, eating and eating, and I have gained more than half my weight again. I am one-and-a-half times the size I was, because I have just let things go. I don't each much, but I'm eating the wrong things – a lot of sugary things and puddings – instead of real food.

But now I can imagine Anthony saying, '*Mummyyyy . . .* you *know* you shouldn't be doing that.' So now I'm getting to the stage where I say to myself, 'OK, I can re-psyche myself, to try and do the things that Anthony had more or less been ordering me to do: following the correct way of eating and exercising; not eating too much fat because of the cholesterol; thinking about my blood pressure.'

'Oh Anthony, *please*,' I used to say to him when he nagged me about the importance of exercise and eating well, but he was insistent: 'No no, that's no good, you have to eat well. Don't cook that stuff.' He used to buy olive oil, the very best, and then he would make something delicious and serve it up with a flourish: 'Pasta's very good for you, better than rice. Eat what I have made! That plateful has got the right mix of vitamins; it's filled with veg!'

And I'd say, 'Anthony, you're not trying to kill us, are you? Loads of salads, oh no!'

He loved to do the right things and wanted to be the best in everything he did. His credo was, 'Live correctly, live life to the full.' He had such dreams of what he wanted to do, and he was so conscious of being the head of the family – he had his sisters, and he often told them, 'I've got to stay healthy. I've got to be there for you guys.'

* * *

The following day, we were visited again by detectives. It wasn't enough that they had DNA samples; now they wanted dental records. The police had combed through Anthony's medical records, and they wanted to know who his dentist was.

'Have we not given you that answer, and many more answers besides?' I sighed. I was exhausted, and it felt as if there was not the most minute fact about my son that had not been seized upon and labelled and locked in a jar by the police. 'Dentists,' I said; 'well, he has never really had a dental problem, so he never really goes to dentists much. This is a young man with a healthy diet, who takes care of his body.'

Alan reminded me: 'Uncle Sunny . . .' Alan's face was ashen. Much later he told me that this was the moment he realised the police almost certainly believed that Anthony was dead and that they had his body in a morgue. Dental records are required for post-mortem identification. In my shattered state, that connection did not really occur to me: I was simply struggling to maintain hope and a positive attitude, because only then would I be able to do my utmost to find Anthony.

Uncle Sunny was a friend of Anthony's grandfather. More properly he was Prince Sunny Akpabio, MBE, and had been the family dentist in London for as long as Alan could remember. The friendship between Sunny and Atanda probably dated back to the 1940s, when Alan's father had become one of the first Nigerians to study law abroad. He went to Trinity Hall, Cambridge, becoming a fellow, and earning one particularly rare privilege: he was permitted to walk on the lawns. Of that, he remained justifiably proud to the end of his life.

He met Irene while he was in England; she volunteered for the RAF during the war, and in my favourite photograph of her she is wearing her uniform. Irene adored Anthony, and we were heartbroken when she died in the mid-1990s.

When Atanda Fatayi-Williams returned to Nigeria, he joined the judiciary, rising through the ranks to become a crown counsel, in the days of the colonial system before the judiciary was handed over to the Nigerian government. He became the fourth Nigerian chief justice after independence, but he always maintained his close friendships in England, and Uncle Sunny had always been part of Alan's extended family.

'Anthony probably had a check-up with Uncle Sunny while he was at school in England, at Sevenoaks Secondary in Kent,' I said. 'The practice is on Finchley Road. I could probably fetch his records for you.'

The detectives were quietly emphatic: they would do the fetching. We gave them Uncle Sunny's address, and when they were gone we decided to call him.

Uncle Sunny was horrified. 'Do you mean it was Anthony they have been talking about? I'll check my records and I'll send them everything – I haven't seen him recently but I have his childhood records. I think he came once and I think I did some work, he had an X-ray or something. I'll get the records right away.'

Alan also called Anthony's dentist in Lagos and his records were promptly e-mailed that same day, with the X-rays following by courier. Meanwhile the police had returned, saying they couldn't reach Uncle Sunny. It turned out they were calling an old number, from his former practice. We had to put them right, but while the police were talking to us he called again, and they were able to interview him immediately.

The following day Uncle Sunny came round, clutching a wad of aged brown envelopes under his left arm. 'I was able to find some of Anthony's records and dental X-rays,' he announced with authority. 'I hope they will be of help.' The family liaison officers came over straightaway, and forms were filled out, handwritten records inspected, and X-rays deposited in exhibit bags that were duly tagged and taken away.

I tell this story to stress that everybody around Anthony was striving to be as helpful as possible. No one could have done more to assist the police. When I criticise the chaos of the investigation, I do so in the knowledge that his friends and family did all we could.

The entire investigation seemed to be an awful mess. Nobody in authority seemed to be thinking of us as people with emotions. It was just a matter of getting from us as much information as they could – and not giving us any information in return. Looking back, I say to myself, 'God forbid that this had been an atrocity on the scale of the 9/11 assaults on New York and Washington, when thousands died and many thousands more were injured. How would the British emergency services have coped?'

The system would have collapsed. With fifty-four people dead, including the bombers, they couldn't cope – the computers were crashing every minute. Each time I managed to get through to someone on the phone, it was like starting from day one again, as if everything was being entered into a huge handwritten log that made data retrieval impossible.

They issued us with new log-in numbers each time we phoned. Yet each time I called I was still the same person, calling about the same Anthony, who apparently couldn't be found on the system.

I'm more than happy to concede that, during the initial stages of the investigation, it would not have been possible to keep all the channels open and running smoothly. After four blasts like that, right in the centre of London, and with the utter disruption to communications and transport, no one could expect the system to function at full efficiency.

But the chaos wouldn't go away. It stayed at what seemed like maximum confusion for a week. With the ultra-fast, ultra-reliable computers we have these days, system overload shouldn't be triggered by fifty-four deaths.

Even if fifty anxious relatives have phoned in the past ten minutes, and fifty reference numbers have been assigned, is that such an impossible task to co-ordinate within a week? Surely it should be easy for the person manning a helpline to enter my name, or my son's name, into a search engine and instantly gain access to my records? Surely I could have been identified by just one reference number, instead of having a different one assigned each time I called?

Some time around the sixth day – and it is hard for me to be more precise, because of the emotional stress I was under – I rang the helpline to see what was happening. It was one of the few positive, active things I could do: it turned waiting into action. But it also turned anticipation into frustration.

The voice on the other end of the line said, 'I don't recognise the reference numbers you're quoting. Are you sure you have the right ones?'

'Sure?! Yes I'm sure! The boys who have been chasing around to find my son have four different numbers. I gave you two of them just now and you say you can't find his name. So this is his name: Anthony Fatayi-Williams.'

'Fatayi-Williams? Have I got that right? I don't seem to see any records, could you spell it please?'

'Not again! Not on your life!' I said.

There was a silence. If I didn't want to play their games, that didn't seem to bother them. But if I couldn't make them find out where Anthony was, that bothered me a lot.

'OK, let's do something,' I said. 'Please, I'm fed up. Let's start from scratch. Let's take it as if this is day one. This is his name. Anthony is his first name. Fatayi: Fred-Alpha-Tango-Alpha-Yankee-Indigo Williams. It's a double-barrelled name. That's his name. Date of birth, 29 January 1979. So now let's put it in and let's have a single reference number. Please. Can you not give me a reference number? And synchronise every other entry?'

The voice said, 'Yes, yes, that's what we should do. This is your number.' She reeled off a string of figures.

I read them back. 'Good,' I said. 'Now we know that anyone who calls about Anthony Fatayi-Williams can be placed in the right context. And when my son is able to make contact, he will see his file is all in one place, and he will know we have been trying to reach out to him, even though he was unaware.'

Later that very day, a policeman called and identified himself as Police Inspector Somebody. For a moment my hopes soared. He dashed them with one question, so callous and cruel that I still cannot believe it: 'Have you heard from your son?'

I caught my breath. 'Have I heard from my son? I'm waiting to hear from you, to say you have heard from my son. How can you ask me that?'

'OK,' he said, 'not to worry.'

'How am I supposed to have heard from my son?' I demanded. 'And if you're a policeman, aren't you supposed to go through my family liaison officer?'

Let me spell this out: this policeman phoned me to ask if I had heard from my son, when Anthony was lying in a police mortuary. It beggars belief: 'Have you heard from your son?'

'I just thought maybe you might have heard from him,' he suggested. 'I was just wondering if you'd had a phone call. But anyway, I'll need to ask you a few questions again, just for us to get things straightened out.'

The very same answers that I had spent so long repeating in interview after interview, the very same questions I had worked through over and over, these were the things he quizzed me about now: did Anthony have any peculiar marks, did he have any identifying documents, what clothes did he wear, did he travel on this Underground line, where does he work, what does he do? And on, and on.

I was in shock, shedding tears of anger: 'I have only just finished answering these questions for the umpteenth time, and here is the reference number with all that data.'

'Well,' said the police inspector (if that's what he was), 'you've got to go through them all again with me, madam.'

And for Anthony's sake, for the love of my son, I did that. I answered every question again.

But when that police officer had rung off, I got to thinking: no one could be so callous as to grill me that way, on the off chance that my story might change. It must be so obvious now that Anthony was not a terrorist. So perhaps something else triggered that call. Perhaps they know more than they are saying. They wouldn't need to know where he worked, if they thought Anthony was dead. So they must know he is alive!'

I reached for the phone. I called the helpline. I gave them Anthony's name, and the reference number that had so laboriously been acquired.

And the voice said: 'I'm sorry. That reference number is not showing up. Could you spell that name, please?'

The following day when Sharon, one of my family liaison officers, came, I said to her, 'You told me not to speak to anyone! Not to discuss anything! But I have had someone on the phone, asking me whether I have heard from my son! And he says he is a police inspector. And then he asked me the very same questions that you have all asked, over and over.'

Sharon calmed me down: 'That's very bad, that shouldn't have happened. They know the practice. No one should call you directly any more, once you have been assigned a family liaison officer. They should always go through me.'

I said, 'But when I tried to tell him that you, the family liaison officers, had all this information already, he said to me, "I am not the family liaison officer, I'm me." Why does he have to put me through this? All I am trying to do is look for my son.'

I was not alone in suffering this ordeal. I've heard the same story from family after family at group meetings.

At one meeting, some were even more outspoken. They said they had cried so much, yet all the police had wanted to do was suck out information and suck out more, and not give any information back. Each time the police called it was to ask more and more questions. And the relatives were waiting for news, but they couldn't even get a consistent reference number. Some did not even have family liaison officers assigned to them. When family friends called on their behalf, the calls were traced, 'for security reasons' – as if everyone who died in the bombing was automatically a suspected terrorist, and all their family and friends were possible leads in the war against terror. Where is the sanity in this system?

Months have passed, and everybody has been given an accolade for a job well done.

At some point the next day, someone pressed a letter into my hand that had been passed on by Anthony's office. It was a tribute to Anthony, one of the first of many, and it came from three colleagues who had met him at the seminar, the day before the bombing.

I cried so much when I read it. It seemed impossible that my Anthony had been so much to the forefront on Wednesday, impressing everyone with his charm and sharp mind, and that a day later he could not be found.

The letter read:

We were all shocked to see that Anthony Fatayi-Williams is amongst the list of missing persons following last week's horrendous explosions in the London transport systems. We did not know Anthony very well, but his impact at our Nigerian oil and gas seminar was tremendous last Wednesday afternoon, the afternoon before these fateful explosions.

Four of our PLLG team met him and were all tremendously impressed by his articulateness and intelligence, his courtesy and manners. We were planning on working with him further. Anthony has real expert knowledge about Nigeria. We had earlier read one of his previous presentations and one of our other colleagues commented that it was one of the best in the industry.

[We hope that] something may still happen at this

very difficult time and we will all be watching the media for further announcements.

It was signed by three of the group's senior managers.

Two days after the journey to Tavistock Square, a Mass was held at our flat. As Alan put it, the flat had been 'transformed into a mini-chapel to suit the purpose'. The Ethiopian Catholic priest, the Reverend Father Bogel, had kindly offered to give us Communion. This was on the seventh day since Anthony had disappeared, and it was the third Mass we'd had at home: one was said when I got there, and another the next day.

The police had been there in the morning, of course, but now the day was wearing on into evening. Both my brothers were there, and my sister Teresa, my tower of strength, had arrived. Many friends were there too.

Naturally Alan prayed with us, even though he is a Muslim. My husband is a man of God, and God will hear our prayers however we say them, whatever our religion.

Many people have expressed surprise that Anthony was the son of a Muslim and a Christian, but to us there is nothing remarkable in the union. Islam, like Christianity, is a faith founded on peace, and perhaps Anthony was a doubly peace-loving man because he came from twin traditions.

I prayed, 'whatever the news might be, let us hear something of Anthony. If he's OK, but he's injured in hospital, we will bring him home to us. If he is unconscious or he doesn't know who or where he is, let your Spirit touch him and let him come out of whatever dark place he is in. May he be safe. Deliver him from evil.'

I was breathing hard, but my emotions were under control as I came to the most difficult part of my prayer: 'If it is that you have called him to yourself, then Lord, your will be done, but let us know. And show us where he is. Let us at least know one way or the other if he's ill, if he's been hurt, if he's been maimed, if he's gone, at least let us find him. Let us find him.'

My brother Tom prayed the same prayer: 'Lord, relieve this pain and suffering by letting us know what has happened to Anthony, that wherever he may be, no matter what the circumstances are, he may be returned to us.'

About two hours after that Mass I spotted that the family liaison officers had arrived and were talking outside the room to my husband and my brothers. I was used to that. They'd done it many times before, twice a day, talk, talk, talk.

I did not realise that, this time, it was different.

8

My friends were sitting with me, comforting me, but when I saw the family liaison officers with my husband outside, I thought I ought to go out and greet them.

They were sitting in the corner, as they often did. These visits had become a regular feature.

'How are you? Hi Sharon, hi Gill, any news yet?' I asked.

And they said, as always, 'No, nothing yet, Marie.'

I said 'OK' and returned to my friends. After a long while, I noticed that Sharon and Gill were leaving, so we went out to be with Alan and the other men. I saw that quite a number of people were there. Usually they would leave and come back in the morning, but this evening they didn't seem to be going. So I said, 'Alan, what's happening?'

And he said, 'Oh no, no, no, nothing.'

That didn't satisfy me. 'What more news have they for us?' I demanded. 'What have they said now?'

Everybody said, 'Oh no, nothing. The police just said they'd be coming back tomorrow.'

It was not until about midnight that all the others had gone, and it was just me and my family. Then Alan and Tom sat me down, and said they needed to talk with me.

I said, 'You've been talking with me all day. What is so special that you have to talk with me now?'

And then I saw Alan's face. All through that evening, after the family liaison officers had left, he had not been himself. I had wondered about this, but I thought that if they knew something, they'd tell me, wouldn't they?'

Alan came and sat down with me and he said, 'We really need to talk.'

'About what?'

'The news is not very good.'

'What is not very good?'

Alan said, 'We prayed that Anthony should be found, alive or dead. And we have waited this long, and at least, thank God, he has been found. But not in the way that we would have wanted him to be found. Tomorrow I will go and see him.'

'What do you mean, you will go and see him? You mean he is not coming to see us?' I was still clinging to a faint glimmer of hope.

Alan said, 'Anthony can't come to see us.' I let out a cry. At that point I knew.

The family liaison officers had told only the two of them, Alan and Tom – my husband and my elder brother. They then told the other doctors who were around and who agreed a time with the family liaison officers when they could go with Alan to see Anthony. So everything had been organised. The only thing they were wondering about was whether to include me.

They could have put off telling me until the next morning, but they wanted to see how I felt, how I reacted. That would decide whether I should be a part of the group that went to identify Anthony. The family liaison officers needed to know who was going, because no one could go in their own car: the morgue, which we eventually learned was in Shoreditch, east London, was a secure site.

So that was it. My most deep-seated fears, which I had banished to the innermost recesses of my heart, now flooded over me, and that night was like the devilish, evil night of the first day. I was waiting for the dawn, as if it was going to be 8 July again. And I cried.

Anthony was lost. I was lost. I wanted to scream but I couldn't. And then I thought, how do we tell the girls? What do we tell them? Anthony had put them on the flight to Lagos for a holiday, just one week earlier. I thought of the discussion I had in Lagos with Lauretta, the girl Anthony called Lolsy-bubs, and how she had said, 'Don't worry, Mummy. Anthony's all right. Nothing can happen to Anthony. You know that. Nothing can happen to Anthony.'

My brother, with his political sixth sense, realised that we had to break the news to Lauretta and Aisha, and my niece Rita, as well as my sisters Grace and Rosa who were with them, before they heard it via the media. My eldest sister, Grace, is well into her sixties and had cared for Anthony in his first couple of years at the International Secondary School in Ibadan, before he left for the British School of Paris. He fondly called her 'Auntie Kabliye' – whatever that meant, only he knew.

Alan agreed with my brother, and I was able to grasp, even through the layers of pain and shock, that we needed to act. I said, 'Before the news gets out in Lagos, we had better do something.'

The others were grim-faced, and with mounting horror I realised that the news was already out in Lagos. Our mission, which had done nothing for my family so far, had apparently trumpeted Anthony's death to two television stations.

We were already barely on speaking terms with the High Commission, after they had made it plain that they considered the search for Anthony to be of relatively little importance. Relations grew worse when it started to look as if they were trying to take the credit for what Anthony's friends helped me to do with that speech in Tavistock Square.

And then, before I even knew my own son was dead, someone went and broke the news in Lagos. A couple of television stations were already carrying reports, and nobody had told my daughters or the rest of my family in Nigeria.

If the embassy did this, then I believe they must have done

so to show themselves to be on top of things. Yes, they had found Anthony Fatayi-Williams; yes, he was now confirmed dead. Their thoughtlessness meant my husband and my brother had to make certain that our young and very vulnerable daughters did not find out from the television or from a reporter's phone call that their brother was dead.

The first broadcasts, I was later told, went out at about 8 p.m., four hours before I was told. Thankfully, the girls did not see them, but there were many people in Nigeria watching those particular television stations. They started phoning my husband, so within minutes of hearing the news themselves, Alan and my brother were having to make sure that no one answered the phone at the flat except them in case it was the girls.

And the phones, I later learned, had glowed red hot. So many friends were calling to ask, 'Is it true? You mean, after all this time?' Others were journalists, calling for confirmation: they'd seen the breaking news on television and wanted to run it on their front pages.

My husband's attitude was curt and compressed: 'I don't know where you guys got your information from, but you must have got it quickly because we were told only a few hours ago and we have not called anybody in Nigeria. Even my wife does not know.'

Many journalists had chief Tom Ikimi's number, of course. When he took the first call, his reaction was to say, 'What?' But of course he was soon forced to confirm to them that it was true.

Who at the High Commission was responsible, we never learned. It still upsets and bewilders me: if they were so aware of my family's plight and the impact it was having in Nigeria, why did the embassy staff have to distance themselves from us?

With the television stations reporting the news, we had to be both delicate and decisive. I rang my parish priest in Lagos, waking him up well past midnight. We knew we needed somebody from outside the family to help.

For my eldest sister, this would be a disastrous blow. I tried to think who should break the news – I needed someone with a special touch, firm but with feelings. My mind flashed to one long-standing friend, a well-educated and widely travelled diplomat's wife. Yes, I had to call Amina, the wife of the retired Ambasador Hamzat Ahmadu, now the Wali of Sokoto Caliphate.

I woke Amina up. The moment I said, 'Ufan', which means 'friend', as we fondly call each other, her voice suddenly sounded as if she was already wide awake. In fact, she had been in a deep sleep.

Amina said, 'Oh, ufan, ufan, you are in our prayers. There is nothing God cannot do.'

I said, 'True, ufan. That is why I need you now, more than ever, to be strong for me.' I broke down and could not carry on any more. I guess Alan or Teresa told her what she had to do: break the news to my family. It had to be done quickly, because by the morning it would probably be on the BBC, as well as in the newspapers, and that would be unspeakable for the girls.

And so it was that at about 2.30 a.m. Amina made her way to my home, to be joined later on by the priest. They told the news to Grace and Rosa. A couple of other family members were also in my house, and they too were told.

I cannot blame the media. The news was confirmed to them from a credible source. It was their duty to report what they were told. But at that stage, the High Commission had not even phoned to offer us their condolences.

They had done their bit, they had passed the news on, they were 'on top of it', they had shown they were 'one step ahead'.

When someone somehow realised the goof that had been made, I think they eventually called the television station and told them to stop broadcasting the announcement. So the station went on the rebound and said that Anthony's death was actually not yet confirmed; they had understood it had

97

been officially announced, but it hadn't. Of course, by that time, the harm had been done. By the morning, the journalists who had phoned us had splashed the news in six-inch headlines.

Some of my friends feel I should make an official complaint. My feeling is: what good will come of it? The officials know how I feel because I put it across candidly. Of course His Excellency the High Commissioner did try days later to come and pay his condolences, but he had to speak to my husband – I was not around to meet him.

He came to the flat while I was out. By the time I came home, he'd gone, but he left a letter conveying his condolences as the representative of the head of state. But that was condolence for our loss, not an apology for any actions. No one has ever mentioned that.

In the morning, about 8 a.m. in Lagos, the girls were brought down. Another priest, Rev. Fr. O'Leary, who was more familiar to the girls, Amina and some mothers and friends from the church broke the news. The girls' reaction was disbelief: it couldn't be true, it could not happen. Not Anthony.

The shock hit them dreadfully hard. Alan and I decided they should stay in Nigeria for that week. It would have been too much for them to fly to Britain. They had only just arrived back, and it was better to let them stay there until it was time for the funeral.

Several months on, Amina told me: 'Ufan, that was one of the toughest assignments I have ever had to carry out. Not even all my years in diplomatic life were preparation enough.'

My sisters feel they owe her and all the other friends and mothers a debt of gratitude for their show of love and strength.

I could not bring myself to go to the morgue. My anguish was too great, too consuming. Gently, my husband showed me that I could not delude myself by pretending that Anthony was not dead, or that his body had been wrongly identified: the dental records had removed any shadow of a doubt. But to have to gaze upon my son's remains that day – that would have been too much.

Alan was accompanied by friends and family: Peter, a urologist; Ayo, Segun and Ndubuisi, all consultants; Seyi, a paediatrician; Nigel, a solicitor, and Yomi, his young cousin.

'Anthony was at peace,' Alan told me when they returned. 'There was the trace of a smile upon his face.'

I steeled myself. 'Tell me what happened.'

Alan gathered his thoughts. 'We rendezvoused at a hotel. That was a security measure to keep I-don't-know-who off our trail. We were driven into an underground car park, and from there ushered to a room on the fifth floor. Coffee and biscuits were served. An officer had been delegated to give us a "pep talk" before the ordeal.

'I thought I was brave, but had never in my wildest dreams imagined that I would ever be called upon to identify the remains of my own son. But there were eight of us, and I could not have asked for better company. I shall remain eternally grateful for their support.

'A security van took us on the final leg of the journey, to a huge temporary mortuary of white canopies in a garden park. The police were everywhere.

'Anthony was lying on his back in a secluded area with his head and face exposed, and he had a hint of a smile on his face. He indeed looked as if he was asleep. I now appreciate the phrase "Gone to rest". There were no burns, no cuts, only a slight bruising visible on the left side of his face. It was a tremendous relief. At least I can tell my family that he had not suffered and that death had come sharply, quickly and perhaps painlessly. It is a small comfort.

'I wanted to touch him, to hold him – to say, "Anthony, Daddy's here, we'll be going home soon." A Salvation Army officer offered me a glass of water. I felt stunned. I sat down. I didn't want to leave without him. After a while Peter said, "Alan, it's time to go now."'

'That is the last time I will ever see my son.'

There are no words to describe how bereft my husband seemed.

It is now clear that the police had Anthony's body all along. They had known who he was, because of the personal effects they returned to me later: his distinctive green-and-white wristband with the inscription, 'Nigeria Making Progress'. He always wore it, and now I am wearing it.

That wristband meant a lot to him, because he was of the generation that harbours dreams about going back to Nigeria and helping to make it great. He was really looking forward to going back and pouring his energy into society, to fight poverty and build a future for the less privileged.

The police also returned his St Benedict's cross medallion, on a long white-gold chain, which he always wore round his neck. I took the pendant, Lauretta took the chain. Then they brought back his Oyster tube pass as well as his work I.D. badge. They brought the pens that had been in his pocket and his business cards. Eventually they returned his briefcase. It even had a receipt in it, showing some banking transaction that had been carried out on his father's behalf. They knew all the time who he was; he must have been among the first people they had found.

They had all the personal effects. What possible reason could they have had for not telling us? Yes, they had to be sure that I was not a terrorist, that much was obvious from the kind of things they were asking me. But, equally, my answers would have made it instantly plain that we were innocent victims.

The friends and cousins who phoned on Anthony's behalf were traced and questioned too. The police were looking for whoever committed the atrocity – the families, and the dead, and everything else, were secondary.

Every other family suffered the same thing. When I went to a group meeting in September 2005, all the families there had the same complaint, some more than others. They were incensed. For some families it was simply too much – to suffer such loss and anguish, and then to be a suspect because of your name or the colour of your skin.

When I knew for sure that Anthony was dead, I thought I would just collapse and die. My heart would not be able to take it, my thoughts would not be able to take it, my pain would explode through my veins.

The outpouring of love, the support from the other grieving families, the consolation and the comfort from friends, from parishioners, from people in the church, both in London and Nigeria: I can't start to quantify it. Some unseen hand was just helping me, something to hold on to, and it came alive in me more than ever before.

In the hours after I was told that Anthony was no more, I experienced a ghastly sense of anti-climax: it was over, yet it was not over, and it never could be. It was as though a horrible nightmare had ended, but I was not going to wake up in the morning and say, 'Oh! Thank God it was all a dream.'

How can it be that I will not hear this boy talk to me again? How can it be that when I call his cellphone number, which is still listed in my handset, he will not pick it up and say, 'Mummy, I'll call you back, love you lots'? How can it be that I won't hear him grumbling early in the morning when he's preparing for work, and he peeps outside and sees it is raining, knowing that he can't drive his car to the office?

How can it be that I won't feel his strong, comforting arms around me, or catch that special wink, or break into French with him when we did not want his father, or some other listener, to be in on our conversation?

How will the girls cope? How does one begin to explain to Aisha about her dear brother, Mr T, as she called him, who cares so much about her? Is this it? Is this the end? Is this what I have slaved for? All my personal sacrifices? Is this what he has slaved for in his short life that was just blossoming?

No. It cannot be. If this is so, it cannot be right. There must be some mistake somewhere. His life, my life, our lives, must be worth more than this. Is it right for some stranger to get up in the morning and decide he is going to end the lives of people he doesn't know and who have never hurt him? To take life that he can never give back, even if he could wish to?

If there is a cause that the bombers were fighting for, how has killing my Anthony and fifty-one other innocent people helped that cause? And if the cause had developed out of anger towards the Iraq war, then the injustice becomes even more painful for a simple reason: Anthony was a young man who did not support the war. Like most people, he felt that, when a cat is preying on doves, you must catch the killer cat without slaughtering doves in the process.

When I was studying for my masters degree in international relations, I got excellent marks for an essay on just and unjust wars. I included an analysis of the Iraq war which had just begun, and which I believe was not justified for several reasons: I cited the existence (or non-existence) of weapons of mass destruction; the go-ahead that was essential from the security council if we were not to find ourselves swimming in uncharted waters; and, above all, the fall-out of any war, which is the death of innocents.

The perpetrators of the war, for the sake of their peace of mind, coined a new phraseology – 'the coalition of the willing', 'precision bombing'. Worst of all was the dismissal of those dead innocents as 'collateral damage'. In these two words is summed up all the futility of war. In these two words is contained all man's inhumanity to man.

How much collateral damage was necessary to put a stop to the excesses of one man, Saddam Hussein? How many doves would have to be slaughtered before the cat was caught? And after the cat was in a bag, how many more doves would die?

My Anthony was a dove. He was collateral damage in a war he cared little for. He died alongside fifty-one others in London, and alongside many thousands around the world, part of an ever-growing tally of victims of political and religious extremists. How can this be justified, by any side or whatever party, in this terrible, costly, painful and murderous game of war and terror?

As I tried to find a scrap of sense amid the insanity, suddenly my mind travelled to another plane. I asked myself, where was Anthony's guardian angel? Where were the guardian angels of all who lost their lives that fateful day? Our guardians, they say, never slumber, never sleep.

If only we could put back the hands of time, if only Anthony could wake and pour out his heart to me or tell me some sweet nothings, perhaps give me one last, tight hug, before falling back and 'going to sleep'.

O that I could lie down and that sleep would come. And O that I could wake to see Anthony standing in front of me, saying, 'Taa-raaahh! I fooled you guys! Just wanted to see how much you loved me! Cane me all you want – I am back and I am not going anywhere!'

Sitting in my favourite spot in the sitting-room, waiting for him to return from work – that was another exercise in futility. In fact, I thought I saw him once, coming in with his computer bag slung across one shoulder and his gym bag across the other, throwing a quick 'Evening, Mummy, any food? I am starving', as he used to do. Then I woke up with a start and a smile, ready to reproach him, before telling him what food we had kept warm for him – only to realise I had drifted off, just for a split second.

Why? Why? Why? I was lost for words, lost for answers, empty with loss. I couldn't move from the chair, and sat each night, waiting for my daughters to come back. I knew they felt all the loss too. For now, until the date and place of the funeral had been decided, I was unable to do anything but sit and stare. I was a mechanism for breathing and hurting, a robot of grief.

I couldn't stop thinking about death. How does death happen? There was a human brain behind the bombers' evil plot, but how did death select or reject its victims? Each individual experience must be different, even when death seized a group of victims together.

When I was a child at primary school, I loved to learn poems from the *Oxford English Reader*. I still remember many of them now. Poems express many things that simple prose cannot. After Anthony died, I wrote two poems, one about death and one about loss, in an effort to express feelings for which there scarcely seemed any words.

Later I was to pour all of my grief and my energy and my heart into preparing, to the very last detail, the funeral brochure for Anthony. The songs, the readings, the prayers, everything had to be just right. He had to feel our collective and individual love for him right through to the end.

There is someone whom I will never forget: Mother Benedicta, the mother abbess of the monastery in Lagos. Its name is the Ave Mother of the Church Monastery, in Lekki, Lagos, and it is still under construction.

If my Anthony was a gift of gold and an angel, Mother Benedicta was the second angel to be sent to me from heaven. She called me every day in London, as soon as she heard that Anthony was no more. And for fifteen minutes or more she would be on the phone to me, not saying much, just a few little words and then, 'Maria, talk to me, say anything. Don't worry, God is with you, God loves you much, Maria. Don't worry, His Mother is looking after you. I pray much for you and Anthony.'

And she would ask me to say just one Hail Mary with her. I would think to myself: just one? Shouldn't we say ten, or fifty?

Almost as if she read my thoughts, she would say, 'Just one.' And we would say that one prayer together and she would follow this with a gentle blessing, a soothing balm. The relief in me was indescribable.

She would phone me and talk to me – that was all she did, but I have never experienced such kindness. I drew so much strength and support from just that, the time we would have on the line, knowing that she was at the other end. She just had that gift, to give me calm. I don't know how, or where, or why. Many priests phoned me, God bless them, trying to comfort me, but when she called me, it was like a silent understanding, like a balm poured on my heart.

I cried, and I am not able to cry usually when others are on the phone. But I would go into my own room when she phoned, and take the call and let my tears flow. Maybe she knew I was crying and maybe she didn't, but she would call my name once and I found myself saying simply, 'Yes, Mother.'

'It's OK, Tony is with Jesus. Hold on to your faith, Maria.' That's all she said, and then, 'I will call you again tomorrow.'

The monastery was the first of its kind in the Lagos archdiocese. It is not one where you can go to see the monks or the nuns. When I go there now, I don't see her face as she is in total enclosure – I just hear her, talking to me from behind a screen. That's where I go for peace, where I draw my inspiration. I go and talk to her.

The monastery had a Mass for Anthony six months on – in fact, there has been a Mass on every 7th of the month since he died. Because I asked her, Mother Benedicta started this tradition, for all the victims of the 7/7 atrocities. It is wonderful of them. That's the kind of support I am getting. I go there and I talk to the priest who is the spiritual director, I read, and I share my thoughts and my revelations with them. They help me to pray and tell me, 'It's OK to ask why. Just let yourself go.'

And I have come through. You can't ever put a price on that kind of support.

In my heart, Anthony is not among the dead. He is living, he is happy, he has no injuries, he is hale and hearty, and yet – the pain at times is so bad. Sometimes my mystery voice asks, 'If you believe he is with God, why aren't you happy?'

I answer: 'How can I be? It's my humanity. I had such

worldly plans, that he would support me and be there for his two sisters and carry on the family name. That was my patchwork world. It is a different patchwork now.'

When the reality dawned on me that Anthony had died, and I understood the way it happened, I saw the senselessness of this whole unimaginable, unacceptable situation. It was as if the impossible had been made possible.

And I believe that, for me, this was the ultimate test of whatever I've held dear. Faith ought not to be something simple and shallow, where we can praise God when everything's good and rosy, but when things go wrong we say, 'You're an evil God, you're not worthy of our praises,' or even, 'There's no God, he doesn't exist.'

I believe that my path of life has been mapped out by God in such a way that I have to go through what I am going through. For what, I don't know, but for me it's like a pre-ordained thing. My life has been rough and very tough at times, but I have come through happily. And then, my son is taken away from me!

I have a strong belief in my life, because I have no other. I pray, but I am only human and I often have to ask, 'Why? Why me, why Anthony?' And I asked for quite a while, 'Lord, what did I *not* do, what have I done wrong? Am I such a sinner, is there some bad thing that I have done somewhere that I deserve a great punishment?

And then my mystery voice comes to me, and says, 'Stop this, don't do this to yourself. I'm telling you, if you believe and you have faith and trust in God, then you must accept: yes it is true, Anthony was taken. God allowed it to happen. If you believe Anthony is with God and you believe in God, then hurt, I know you must, but remember also that he is with God. So don't grieve like one who has no hope.'

I always imagined that Anthony would grow up and achieve many ambitions, that he would marry and have children. That is every mother's wish. So many of my friends have had this joy.

And then good, kind and loving people around the whole world, those who didn't know me and those who did, opened up and I was supported by their prayers for me and their love and their strength. Each time I wanted to fall into the depths of pain and I felt this sword piercing my heart, strength came. Something was removing the sword and rubbing my heart, as if to close the wounds.

Where it was coming from I don't know, but my heart responded to it because I ought to have died. I never contemplated suicide. No, not at all. But if anyone had told me, immediately after Anthony was killed, that I would be sitting here six months later, writing these words, I would have said, 'Forget it. By killing him, they kill me.'

9

Anthony had often attended the parish church of the Sacred Heart in Mill Hill, and when it was confirmed that he was one of the bomb-blast victims, the parish poured a great deal of thought and love into offering support to our family. As well as individual prayers and visits, Father Jack Harris, CM and Father Phillip Walshe, CM, the parish priest, wanted to have a memorial service. They came up with what Diana Klein, a catechetical adviser in the Westminster diocese, called 'candles and compassion': an evening of prayer structured around the ordinary evening Mass, accompanied by poems, songs by the choir and a guitarist.

The Tablet magazine described the celebration as follows: 'The church was filled to capacity and spilling over with family and friends, Anthony's colleagues from the city and with parishioners . . . The adoration that followed took the form of a simple candle procession to the front of the church as 52 people were requested to come forward and light a candle, each to represent each person to have died in the blasts . . . Anyone who had suffered the loss of a loved one within the past year was free to come forward and light a candle. It was a most moving and spirit-filled celebration . . . what started as a simple procession with the rendition of "My God loves me" saw an overflow of candles from the stands to the sanctuary floor.'

Diana said later: 'There were hundreds of lights. It was as if the liturgy had taken on a life of its own. This simple and moving procession touched all of us who were there, those of our faith, those of other faiths and those of no faith.'

The celebration came to a close with the recitation by myself of the poem 'Footprints in the Sand', while another parishioner recited a poem by William Crocket, 'A People Place'. Later, when the memorial service at St Paul's turned out to be a state occasion with barely a thought for the people who had suffered physical and emotional agonies after the bombings, my mind often returned to the parish church in Mill Hill. That community showed how a memorial service could really move the heart and touch the spirit.

A week later, on Thursday 21 July, a service of songs was held in the garden in Hendon in memory of Anthony. That night, another mental journey started. A close family friend, Dr Benedette Ewah, who was helping us by liaising with the funeral director, had asked for items for Anthony – his suit and so on. One of the three things I insisted she did for me was to anoint him with the olive oil that I had bought and blessed at the church of the Holy Sepulchre in Jerusalem, where I had been on pilgrimage about a decade before. I had kept that special vial of pure holy oil on my private altar for all these years.

I also asked Benedette to give him the amber and silver rosary brought for him by my friend Maria from Poland and blessed by Monsignor Langham, as well as the red rose and crucifix sent to him by Mother Benedicta.

The following evening, his body was received in the Sacred Heart church in Mill Hill. The minute I spotted the white hearse at the porch of the church, containing Anthony's casket, my heart almost flew out of my mouth. So it was really true. My Anthony, my love, was gone.

I pinched myself to be sure I was still alive. By this time I had been helped out of the car by Tom and Alan. I clung to them for dear life. As Anthony was brought out of the hearse, I turned my eyes up to the bright summer evening sky, expecting to see I don't know who – but suddenly a refrain of a Latin hymn came to my lips and I just kept repeating in lamentation, 'O Jesu Dulcis, O Jesu Pie, O Jesu Jesu Fili Mariae': 'Oh sweet Jesus, oh kind Jesus, oh Jesus, Jesus son of Mary'.

The burning tears streamed down my face, etching deeply into my cheeks. It was as if I were pleading with the Lord to raise Anthony up as he did with Lazarus. By now we were in the church. The celebration of Mass was followed by a few hours of quiet prayer by the family. Then Anthony was peacefully left there all night under the watchful presence of the angels.

Anthony's funeral Mass was held at Westminster Cathedral on Saturday 23 July 2005. We decided that he would be buried in England. He was my first-born, and a sense of Nigerian tradition demanded that we should take him home. But where was home? He was born in Britain, the grandson of an English woman; he was partly educated in Britain; he worked in London and he died there. He had also been to school in France, and spent much of his childhood in Nigeria, travelling widely. So he was a citizen of the world and it felt right to bury him in London, where most of his friends were and where he had spent much of his brief adult life.

At the Catholic resource centre in Lagos, thanks to very dear friends, a simultaneous Mass was being held, while a memorial Mass was held a week later at the Church of the Assumption, with all Anthony's friends and family present.

The service at Westminster was conducted by the cathedral's auxiliary bishop, Alan Hopes, who was assisted by the cathedral's administrator, Monsignor Langham, Father Jack Harris and a family priest from Rome, Father Mike Banjo; Cardinal Cormac Murphy-O'Connor, the leader of the Roman Catholics in England and Wales, was there to speak as well.

There were well over one thousand mourners, people of all faiths, and under their gaze I found the strength from somewhere to stand and speak from my heart. I told them,

'Anthony had promised that when I was feeble, old and grey, his healthy arms would have been my strength and he would have soothed my pain away. Alas, that was not to be, but God knows best.'

And then I was moved to sing. With my eyes lingering on his casket, the saddest sight in the world, and with his photographs around me, I sang, in French, just for the two of us, to the tune of 'Auld Lang Syne': 'Ce n'est qu'un au-revoir, mon fils Antoine, ce n'est qu'un au-revoir; oui nous nous reverrons Antoine, ce n'est qu'un au-revoir.' ['This is not goodbye, we will meet again.']

Then, almost inaudibly, I added, 'Au paradis, au paradis' – 'until we meet again in paradise'.

In his address, Bishop Alan Hopes echoed my words from the speech in Tavistock Square, to urge the congregation not to 'yield to the abyss of revenge'.

Cardinal Murphy-O'Connor directed his words to me from the pulpit: 'You have spoken of Anthony as a sacrificial victim, whose sacrifice must not be in vain. You have spoken movingly of the need to reject violence, of the obligation to resist hatred, and by your words you have set before us all a beacon of light to guide our response to terrorism.'

The journalist Molara Woods movingly captured the mood in an article titled 'Bouquet for Mother Courage' recently published in the *Guardian* in Nigeria: 'In the time of the testing of faiths, Marie was holding tight to hers. Really here was an occasion on which one could not deny the soothing role of religion in people's lives. Watching Cardinal Murphy-O'Connor praying and spreading incense around Anthony's coffin, watching the time-honoured rituals commemorating a life come to an abrupt end, it seemed possible to extract some meaning from the violent death of a promising young man in a mindless act of terrorism. There seemed to be a balm over the congregation and we felt elevated, wanting to be strong in spite of the sadness.'

Alan and I had talked long and deeply, trying to decide

how we could establish a lasting memorial to our son that would mean he had not died in vain. Now my husband announced the setting-up of the Anthony Fatayi-Williams Foundation for Peace and Conflict Resolution. 'Anthony was a peace-loving person, and his values we will strive to immortalise,' he said.

Nigerian tradition demands that parents are not physically present when the casket is lowered into the ground, but his sisters, cousins, young friends and other members of the family, as well as my friends, went from the cathedral to the Cemetery. As his body was interred, just before four o'clock in the afternoon, four doves were released. When I went to see the grave after Mass on Sunday, I could hardly believe there was anything underneath the huge bed of flowers that had been brought, accompanied by messages of love and prayers.

Looking back again on the messages from his family, it is heart-rending to read the ones from the young people. Lauretta wrote, 'I love you forever and I promise not to be a coconut head. Love you, your "Lolsy-bubs".'

Her older sister Aisha said, 'Tony-T, I love you lots with my heart and soul. You will always be my darling brother and I promise to be the best. Your "Zaiz-gabs".'

His cousins poured out their grief too, in simple tributes: 'The pain in my heart and in the hearts of so many others is testament to your truly caring and benevolent nature,' wrote Benjamin.

'You were the embodiment of compassion, hope and unconditional love. Your memory will live on in my heart forever,' said Judita.

'My love for you is forever founded in your legacy: Compassion, Respect, Family,' wrote Christopher.

'I love you, I will miss you and I will never forget you,' said Margarita, who was always 'Reets' to Anthony.

His cousin TJ wrote, 'You will be with me forever, and my love for you transcends the boundaries of our mortality.' He is Tom Ikimi Junior, and while I have been writing this book, TJ has been working on a documentary.

TJ and Anthony were born three months apart, Anthony being the eldest, but TJ is the first son of his dad, my eldest brother. They were very close, and Anthony's death shook him deeply. He delivered a deeply touching tribute during the service, describing the two of them as a pair of empty glasses that were gradually filled by life. Amrit, on behalf of 'the boys' did a moving tribute, while Nike read a poem by an anonymous writer titled 'Miss me but let me go' – you could hear a pin drop for the silence.

A handful of our Nigerian friends, also worshippers at the cathedral, came together with other kind-hearted individuals to sing a traditional Nigerian offertory hymn. Outside the cathedral, Julie gave a moving eulogy to reporters: 'Anthony was a wonderful child. His father is a Muslim, his mother is a Catholic. If the bombers thought they were going to spread hatred, to turn us against each other, they reckoned without Anthony. They reckoned without Marie.'

I managed to say a little to the press too, when they asked how I was feeling: 'Of course I am sad. I lost my only son. I am distraught. I am distraught, but I am trying not to be angry. I could be very angry, but if I was angry, what would that do? Anger begets hatred, begets more violence, so let's forgive. I cannot bring Anthony back. But I can make sure that he did not die in vain. If I can manage to stop even one potential suicide bomber to have a change of heart and not to kill people, then I would have achieved something.'

At the Mass, prayers were offered for all the fifty-one other victims of the atrocities. I felt deep in my spirit that I knew each one of them, because each of them must have meant to their families as much as my Anthony meant to me.

However, it was that spirit of forgiveness that had enabled me to offer a prayer for the bombers during the service. *The Sunday Times* called it 'a display of unity between Muslims and Christians', since Anthony's Muslim friends were there as well as mine, Alan's uncles, his older brother Tunde and his family, and his younger brother's wife.

Cardinal Cormac Murphy-O'Connor also wrote about the service for the national newspapers: 'To seek vengeance, or to lapse into resentment, would soon render Anthony's death insignificant. He would be a victim, and no more. But like another Mary at the foot of the Cross, Mrs Fatayi-Williams has struggled through the shock and desolation and found, in her son's death, a meaning for our terrorised city. Hers is the truly radical response.

'It is by listening to people such as Mrs Fatayi-Williams, and by resisting the dynamism of fear, that we will overcome the temptations of terrorism – indeed, terrorism itself.'

10

Cardinal Murphy-O'Connor had written a kind and touching letter of condolence to us before the funeral:

> Archbishop's House, Westminster,
> 20 July 2005

My dear Mr and Mrs Fatayi-Williams,
I am writing to express my deepest sympathy with you both on the tragic death of your son, Anthony. I understand so well your grief and pain at your terrible loss. It seems everyone who knew Anthony spoke highly of him as an extremely kind, generous and good young man. May the God who loves us all console you at this time. I know you will be strengthened by the support and the prayers of your friends and particularly by those in your parish.

For my part I want you to know that I will pray for the repose of the soul of Anthony and also that I will remember you both and your family in my prayers at this sad time. May the good Lord comfort and bless you always.

With deepest sympathy and my prayers, Yours devotedly in Christ
Cormac Cardinal Murphy-O'Connor
Archbishop of Westminster

One of the most moving letters came from the Prince of Wales and his new wife, the only members of 'the Establishment' to show deep concern:

Highgrove House
25 July 2005

Dear Mr and Mrs Williams
Although whatever words we use seem so profoundly inadequate in these heart-rending circumstances, both my wife and I wanted you to know how deeply we feel for you and your family as you endure the most indescribable horror and anguish that has been inflicted upon you.

To lose a loved one at any time is utterly soul-destroying, but to be confronted by such a callous disregard for humanity, and for life itself, is almost unendurable and our hearts go out to you.

I can well recall the intense despair, and many other emotions I initially experienced, when my beloved great-uncle, Lord Mountbatten, was murdered – together with my godson and my godmother – by the IRA in 1979. In some small way I can perhaps begin to understand something of the emptiness and confusion that invades one's whole being when our entire world is shattered in such a cruel, ugly and devastating way.

I realise that whatever I say cannot possibly provide any genuine comfort, but please just know that you are so much in our thoughts and prayers at this most agonising of times.

Yours, with the greatest possible sympathy
Charles and Camilla

My interview on BBC Radio 2 prompted a letter from producer Hilary Robinson, which I read over and over:

BBC Radio 2
25 July 2005

Dear Marie

It was such a pleasure to meet you on Sunday morning [the day after Anthony's funeral] and we are so grateful you found the courage and strength to join us on the programme. So many people have been touched and inspired by your words that I have no doubt your peace initiative will have considerable effect.

Most of the day I thought about you, your family and Anthony, and was disturbed by the senseless waste of it all – yet equally I thought of how your actions will mean that Anthony's death will not have been in vain and I have no doubt other lives will be saved as a consequence of your fortitude.

We felt most privileged that you found the strength to come in on Sunday. It must be Anthony's spirit as well which is empowering you – and that, in him, is enriching the lives of all of us that have the pleasure to meet you. He must have been so special.

With love and best wishes
Hilary Robinson
Producer, *Good Morning Sunday*, BBC Radio 2

Nigeria's ambassador to China, J. O. Coker, a good friend and well-travelled career diplomat, poured out his heart:

Embassy of the Federal Republic of Nigeria,
Beijing
18 July 2005

Dear Sister Marie

Our hearts were filled with sorrow, our eyes filled with tears and our parental instincts were filled with painful emotions when we learned that Anthony, Anthony our

119

brother, Anthony our son, Anthony our compatriot, was one of the victims of that dastardly terrorist attack on the City of London on 07 July 2005.

We have cried, we have wailed and we have exhibited enormous sorrow, not because we are the biological parents of Anthony, but because we are all his parents today, we know the magnitude of the loss and we know what it is and the parental labour involved in raising up a 26-year-old man and for him to be cut down in the prime of youth. A large amount of youthful ambition, energy and parental hope have gone down in destruction. We are all, by virtue of our profession, the 'parents' of Anthony, as indeed we are the parents of all Nigerians outside our national frontiers.

Please accept, our dear Sister Marie, my deepest condolences and those of my wife, entire family and staff. We pray that the almighty God continue to grant you the strength and fortitude to bear the loss, the strength and fortitude that you have already manifested in your character when you rendered that internationally inspiring eulogy at the site of the attacked bus in London.

We pray that our creator will wipe tears from your eyes and assist you in filling the void created by Anthony's passing on. We are aware that the void of a successful 26-year-old man cannot be filled in a family, yet we pray to God that help from above will assist you and your family in coping with the loss and in continuing the fruitful work and legacy which Anthony has left behind.

Yours sincerely
Jonathan Oluwole Coker
Ambassador of Nigeria to China

The House of Representatives in Abuja, through a motion by the deputy speaker Austin Okpara, held a moving one-minute silence for Anthony and all other Nigerian victims of the bomb-blast.

And his friends, bosses and colleagues at Amec paid a wide-ranging tribute:

Tribute to Anthony Fatayi-Williams, Amec Offshore Industries

In November 2001 Anthony joined us in Amec as a graduate in our management systems group. Anthony immediately impressed us with his style, mature manner and communications skills. Additionally his sense of humour, his support to his colleagues, his positive 'can do' attitude and most of all the enthusiasm he exuded when he passed us in the corridor or visited our desks lifted us all as time went by.

This was a man with a five-year plan and a determination to succeed and make a difference. And so he became involved in international projects and joint ventures ranging from the Caspian to South Korea to Nigeria before finally holding an executive role in our West Africa region.

So you can see that from our perspective he was a vital and potent force in our organisation and one who will be dearly missed.

More importantly we should also reflect on Anthony as a friend. And so I have captured just a few of the thoughts expressed in a Book of Condolences we have raised in Anthony's memory.

These quotes are from a diverse range of young and old, men and women across all creeds and ranks in our business from around the world.

I quote:

'His enthusiasm and ambition was obvious from day one, his thirst for knowledge and experience was unending, sometimes leaving his colleagues and superiors struggling to keep up!'

I quote:

'We shared many happy times. We laughed together and now we are crying for him – it is so unfair. He inspired me and others to live life to the full and I promise I will continue to, just as Anthony would have done.'

I quote:

'I know you are in heaven chilling out, enjoying yourself in peace, and laughing at us for worrying so much about you when of course you are more than all right.'

I quote:

'Ray of sunshine would be an understatement to describe you; always smiling, joking, full of ideas and living life to the fullest. You served as a source of inspiration to me as a fellow Nigerian during the short time that I knew you.'

I quote:

'There are friends who walk through your life and out the other side, then there are friends like Tony who come into your life and shine a light. The way he conveyed his love and respect for his family and friends was immeasurable, always declaring his unconditional support for their well-being and hoping they would be proud of him in everything he did. A proud Nigerian, he was always committed to make his mark on this world for the good of those around him, and man, didn't he dress well! No lies and nothing false, just a man who showed people true respect, dignity and kindness!'

But one quote perhaps points the way forward in how we deal with such a great loss:

'Anthony will be sadly missed but remembered always with a nudge, a wink and a smile.'

'Anthony – we will always remember you!'

But no tribute tore at my heart more than the words of his sister, sixteen-year-old Lauretta. Sometimes she was Lolsy-Bubs, sometimes she was Lo-Lo to him.

Lo-Lo and her big brother had started to bond very well. She was a young teenager who would talk to him and tell him all the things going on in her head, and he'd listen and advise her. She acted as his fashion consultant, because he realised she had a good sense of what clothes went well together. And he'd say, 'Do you like what I'm wearing here? Is it cool, yeah? I'll get you whatever you want, just tell me the truth.' And he was always cool.

They really started bonding when Lauretta was fourteen and Anthony was twenty-four. When *he* was fourteen, she was just four, so they didn't have that much in common then, especially as he was away at boarding school for much of the time.

Aisha was his special girl and for Aisha, Anthony was everything, her world. He said to her, 'I know you will always tell me the truth. You are in my heart, I have you here. Do you like my girlfriend? Are you sure? You like her? Thank you, I knew you'd approve.'

Anthony liked to dance, but he danced in his own way! That's one of the reasons that the bonding between him and Lauretta had been so strong during the last couple of years, because Lauretta had grown up to a level where they could relate. Now she was a young teenager, she would teach him how to dance, she said.

He'd say, 'What is the latest step?' and she'd say, 'This is it.' I remember them standing in the sitting-room one evening, and he said to her, 'Yeah, I'm going out tonight, what's the latest step?'

Lauretta had said she wouldn't tell him unless she

was sure he was going to buy her credit for her phone! But Anthony had said, '*Please*, I have to show them some real style tonight.'

And Lauretta had said, 'You have two left feet, Anthony! You dance like Daddy!'

Anthony said, 'No, no, no, I *can't* be as bad as Daddy. I need to know the right dance steps.' And Lauretta had done the moves, while Anthony had been saying, 'Slow down, slow down, it's too fast!'

And I had been laughing and smiling, as his little sister told him, 'Nooo, Anthony, it's like *this*.'

I remember those moments now.

That's why Lauretta feels as if life was a dream. Sometimes she asks, 'Was Anthony really there?' To her, he was the most important thing in the world. She loved him so. Even her friends were in awe: 'Ooh Lauretta, your brother is handsome, a cool guy.'

He would go to pick her up from school and he was always ready to help anybody who wanted a lift home. I remember a day when we took Lauretta back to her boarding school, and a number of young girls had their suitcases and the porters weren't yet there to help take the bags up. We knew we had to help Lauretta get settled into her room before we left. So Anthony carried her bags up three flights, and then he said to her friends, 'Which are your bags? Which are your rooms?' And he insisted on taking their bags upstairs for them.

And all the girls were saying, 'Lauretta, your brother is so kind, so helpful.'

He just did that kind of thing for her. If he was taking her out, and anybody else wanted to come, they could. But even when they were in Lagos, if there was something that Lauretta wanted to go to, Anthony had to give his approval. He had to look at it and say, 'Yeah, OK, you can go there. But you can't go to that.'

He would make sure he was there to collect her. He

was always there, holding the end of the line for her. She said to me, 'He was my everything, my emotional support, my confidant. We could talk, and we were always sending e-mails and chatting, and if I wasn't doing certain things he would say, "Better concentrate. If you work hard and excel and you're not a coconut head, I will give you this and I will give you that. I myself, when you graduate, you'll see, *I* will buy you a car. By then I will be very successful." Anthony had big dreams. Mummy.'

This is what she wrote:

Love Personified – Tony

A Brother's love is a bond, a knot that can never be untied. A tie which is based on understanding.

You understand me, Tony, probably because we are so alike. Our likeness ranges from similarities in the way we look, to the way we think and our outlook on life.

Our meaningful conversations were my source of enlightenment. Our discussions varied from the exchange of playful banter, to intellectual conversations on our lives in the past, present and what we desired them to be like in the future.

You were extremely protective, which was natural. Sometimes I would complain, but secretly I enjoyed it, and you knew I did.

I would constantly bug you and then you would complain, but I knew you enjoyed it and you too were aware of this.

Un-boundless love is unique, and this is the unique love Tony and I share. We grew closer over the last few years, because we began to realise we had more in common than we thought.

You know when someone has that boundless love for you when:

- They constantly talk about you and are proud to show you off to others.
- They continuously talk to you.
- They always remind you of what is important.
- You can see in their eyes the plans they want you to be a part of in the future without them having to tell you.

You always told me, 'I will always be here for you; all you have to do is call me.' And aside from how reliable you are and from the powerful meaning and dedication of those words, your baritone voice reassured and soothed me each time we spoke.

You would also tell me, 'Life is not always going to be easy, you know, and one day Mummy won't be here to do everything for you and neither will I. You have to start working hard from now on if you want the good things in life later on.'

I knew you would not always be there every single time I needed you, probably because you would be far away working in a position where you couldn't do much. Or something could have simply gone wrong, but not death.

In my eyes, you were invincible, the strongest member of my family. The thought of you dying, under no circumstances crossed my mind – ever. I can't emphasise enough how your passing away was not conceivable in my thoughts.

Now, under the actions of the wicked people in this world, the inconceivable and the unthinkable has happened.

I question God numerous times every day. I stop what I'm doing, my thoughts are interrupted, and then I utter only the word, 'Why?'

I want to know why he had to go this way . . . why now. I want to know why his life was abruptly ended without him being able to finish actualising all his projects and dreams . . . I want to know why my role model, the person I looked up to, is gone . . . I want to know why now the thought that he is in a better place doesn't console me . . . I want to know why we will never be able to do everything he said we would do together . . . I want to know why I will never be able to see him smiling as he approaches me at Victoria station, each time he comes to pick me up, when I come down to London for a break . . . I want to know why I will never be able to smell his musky scent, a mix of cologne and cigarettes . . . I want to know why I am afraid to let go of any of his personal belongings . . . I simply want to know why . . . The least God could do after taking him away is answer my questions, right? I could ask a million and one questions, every single day for the rest of my life, and I may never get any answers, but I know that each day that passes brings me closer to the day when we will meet again. Maybe on that day all my questions will be answered.

You helped me through my A-level choices; you promised that when I turned seventeen, you would be the first one to teach me how to drive. You loved the good things in life, and you promised to give me all the good things in life. I was supposed to mature and go through school, through university and through life with you by my side guiding me and advising me. I was supposed to do all that you did for me for any children you had, but this dream won't be fulfilled and these are my growing pains.

The thought that you won't be here to experience life with me hurts, but although you are not physically here, I can still feel your presence. I never really understood the term 'life after death' but now I do. People say life goes on, but I don't want to move on. I feel that if I move on I will forget you, and you won't be happy that

I am moving on so soon, but I am beginning to realise moving on is not forgetting – it is remembering and cherishing. I hold on to everything you said to me, every time we spent together and every memory of you, as if my life depended on it.

I do still expect you to walk through the door after work. I still expect you to knock on the window at 2 a.m., begging me to open the door because you forgot your keys. I still expect you to pick up the phone when I call you. I still expect you to call me and say, 'So you can't call me, hey?' I still expect you to reply to my e-mails. I still expect you to wake me up at seven in the morning when you are getting ready for work, because you need to talk about something that has been bugging you and most of the time it's about a girl. I still expect you to walk through the door of the room and call me a coconut head because I haven't tidied it. I still expect you and Mummy to argue over how you were late picking her up because you were at Bill Gates the barber, cutting your hair, almost every Sunday. I'm still in disbelief, and I'm really just waiting for everything to go back to normal.

Although things will never go back to normal, you, Tony, my brother – your memory will remain etched in my mind for the rest of my life.

I now know the meaning of the common saying, 'You never know what you have until it's gone.' You were and still are the personification of love. I never knew what love was and what it really meant until now. I don't know why I couldn't tell that you were the embodiment of love, but you and your love are special. You were not meant to be tied down for too long. A love like yours is rare and I may never find it again but you are free now. You don't have to battle the hardships life brings anymore.

I will try my best to fill your very expensive shoes

and buy even more expensive ones, and it's not going to be easy, but you are guiding me so I'm confident.

The warmth of your smile, the confidence of your words and the reassurance in your eyes will never die.

11

During the next few months, we tried to stick together as much as possible as a family. After the service in Nigeria on the 30th, we kept the girls with us at home for the rest of the holiday. I brought them back to England to start school again at the beginning of September.

I never went to the official counselling service. I heard other families say that the kind of psychological help and treatment that was on offer was not the kind that they needed, as it was rather ad hoc and incoherent. The personal touch was not there. Obviously I can't really comment on what I didn't see for myself, but judging on what other people said, it seemed that nobody was very impressed by what had been set in place as a support system for the families.

My only support system was my immediate family, close friends and my faith. I couldn't draw on anything else. Alan was a great source of strength. He is strong in his personality and strong in his will. He is the kind of man who might not show his grief outwardly, but I know that deep down he is hurting. He is keeping it in because he knows that if he crumbles, what happens to the rest of the family that he has to support?

He shares in my deep pain, he shares in my sorrow, he shares in my greatest moments of weakness, as he sees all the suffering coming out of me. In front of everybody else I forced myself to put on a brave face. But I relied, and still do rely, on Alan enormously, even though at times I do give vent to my pain – we have had our moments, when I would seize him and demand answers to my questions.

I would ask him, 'Are you feeling anything at all?'

And he would reply, 'Of course, Marie, what do you want me to do? We have to face the reality: Anthony's gone. It's very sad that he's gone, I didn't expect my son to go like this, and so soon, but that is the reality.'

'Are you sure you are really hurting?' I demanded hotly one evening. 'How are you processing all of this? Maybe it's because you're a doctor. The medical profession has prepared you for this?'

Alan answered with infinite patience: 'Marie, you can say that, but, believe me, no preparation can make you ready for the loss of your own son.'

And with that one statement, I realised how deeply he was hurting and yet not allowing it to crush him. You need that: you have to be there for each other. Because if you don't close ranks in a family, especially at a time like this, what do you have left?

It is also the love that people have shared with me that has kept me going. My family and friends have been paramount, but I have also gained great comfort and strength from letters and e-mails from people who learned about Anthony via the television.

One letter from a complete stranger was addressed simply to, 'Anthony's Mum, the London bombing victim'. That reached me. Another was sent to me via the cathedral: 'Mrs Fatayi-Williams, after the funeral, Westminster Cathedral'. It got there and reached me.

People sent their prayers, and said how much they respected what I stood for and what Anthony's death meant to them. They made reference to the peace foundation, saying how necessary it was, and told me how much they admired my determination to make good come out of evil: yes, they say, it is high time that something is done.

Others were just connecting, to say, 'We have a son as well, and we can't imagine what it would be like to lose him. You are coping by the grace of God, and we are praying for you and send our support.'

Others have lost their own children, and they say, 'We can imagine what you are going through. But who else can imagine it? Just hold on, be strong, we're praying for you. We lit a candle here, and all the people in the parish church are being supportive and praying for you.'

I am so glad when I open a letter from someone I have never met, and they tell me a candle has been lit at Walsingham, at Lourdes or at one of many other places. An American family told me they had gone all the way to the national shrine to light a candle for Anthony. I thought of all his friends in the States.

Even the foundation website gets so much e-mail. People want to know how they can help; they want to know what they can do for the foundation. Every message emphasises that we must stop this killing and this terrorism. They say, 'Let there be peace in the world. The message you gave has touched everyone. We need to make this evil stop.'

I never knew how people felt until they wrote to tell me. Here is just one of very many letters: it was written three weeks after Anthony died, by a lady called Jo Anderson in Norwich:

Dear Marie and Alan,
As a complete stranger I hope you will not find it intrusive if I write with a small donation (£5) to the Peace Foundation you are setting up in memory of your son, Anthony. In appearances on television and radio, I have been moved by your courage, dignity, goodness and love. Your public call to 'end this vicious cycle of killing' was the only truly wise message delivered in the present tragic times. To have said that from the heart of personal grief won the admiration of many, I'm sure, and may your call be heard everywhere. As Dr Martin

Luther King once said, 'Violence only begets violence on a night already devoid of stars.' Your words too are a light shining in the darkness which will not go out.

It is impossible to read such a letter, from a woman I have never met, and not to be deeply moved.

Newspapers in Nigeria, including the *National Interest*, *This Day* and the *Guardian*, marked Anthony's death with a photograph the full length and half the width of their front pages. It showed him with his ever-present smile, wearing a perfectly knotted tie and business jacket. One headline said simply, 'Fatayi-Williams, Ikimi families lose first grandson'. The caption read, 'Anthony Adebayo Omoregie Fatayi-Williams, 1979–2005'.

Another paper, the Saturday *Sun*, ran a page of e-mails from around the world. By reprinting a few of them here, I hope to convey a sense of how intensely my son's murder affected so many:

'I was at first speechless. And in tears. As a mother I grieve with her. My heart breaks for her. I will continue to pray for her precious son and everyone affected by the bombings . . .'

'As a mother who has lost her son, I feel her pain. She has expressed only what anguish can express in the face of this evil that is gripping the world. I pray that God and his goodness prevail, and that Marie and all mothers who have lost their children find some measure of comfort . . .'

'As a veteran of World War Two, what this wonderful woman says breaks my heart and makes me weep. I am desolated by her words because she speaks the truth about us. We should hang our heads in shame for the mockery we have made of Christ's teachings. I feel such shame and such love for this woman and her great loss. May she find peace in her heart again some day . . .'

'Shall we continue living this way? Terrorism is not the

answer to our problems. We can't deliver peace by killing our fellow human beings . . .'

'I have two sons and cannot imagine the pain you must be suffering . . .'

'I want to send my deepest sympathy to Marie. Her words so eloquently expressed her feelings. Why, why, why are we trying to solve the problem of violence by creating more violence? This woman has expressed the utter devastation of heart and soul that the death of your child causes . . .'

'In utter disbelief and sorrow, I keep following the news broadcasts and the wire services, still not truly able to comprehend what is happening around us. Distances mean nothing in situations like this. The only way to overcome the consequences is to help each other . . .'

'I hope you can at least feel a little comfort from the love and prayers of all of us who know of your terrible sadness. Please keep speaking out your message that hatred only breeds more hatred . . .'

In a way, Anthony had become everybody's son. And that was natural: Anthony was the first grandson of both my family and Alan's, so he always was 'everybody's child'. He had many aunties and uncles, or many mums and many dads. And they were all his favourites. He shared his love with everybody.

When he was with each of his aunties he called them 'Mummy', and when he came back to me he called me 'Mummy'. Two of my sisters don't have children, so right from a tender age – and I don't know what instinct made him do this – he called them 'Mummy' when he was with them. He did this even at our home, if I wasn't there. But when I came back, he called me 'Mummy' and my sisters were 'Aunties'. I had no idea he did this, until my sisters, laughing, told me.

Friends of mine used to say, 'Marie, this boy is so polite and well-behaved. How have you done it? He goes to church, he looks after his sisters, how did you achieve this?'

I would say, 'I don't know, it's just by God's grace.'

Even when he was nine years old, people would say, 'Marie, do you know your son is very respectful? Can you imagine a young boy of nine coming and standing with his two hands behind his back and greeting you? He shows a lot of deference to people. Good manners.'

I remember his tenth birthday. At his party he wore a tuxedo, looking like a little man in all the photographs. He was always the leader, he was not a follower. He stood for a photograph with all the boys, who refused to be photographed with the girls. And then he gathered the girls round him, and they all had their picture taken, but he had to be at the centre!

Quite a few of the children who were his friends at that age, especially from Corona school in Ikoyi, have phoned me to say how shocked they were to hear Anthony had been killed, and a lot of his secondary schoolfriends too. He inspired loyalty, and lasting friendships. He went to the British School of Paris from the age of twelve and he did his GCSEs there. They followed the British curriculum. He spoke French very well – in fact, he was really bi-lingual, as I am. That foxed his dad, because we could have secret conversations and Alan would never quite know what we were talking about! That was why when I sang to him in French at the funeral, it was just for the two of us – a final intimate moment shared.

The school didn't have boarders, so Anthony lodged with a French family. They were terribly upset when he died. So many people from those days have come to see me, or made contact by letter, phone or e-mail. There was one who made contact from Mexico, just from a hotel, with no contact number or anything. They said, 'Do you remember us? Our son went to school with Anthony. We send our best wishes to you and we are so sad – we can't believe it, not Anthony, not him. What can we say? We are praying for you.' Other old school mates came to the funeral from Paris and Holland, where they now live. Anthony was back in France for the World Cup in 1998. He loved the game – Anthony was definitely a bit of a football supporter. He went to cheer the Nigerian team. His club in Britain was Arsenal, though he didn't go to every match, because he enjoyed the game most when he could watch it on television. But for the World Cup, he said, 'I don't know when I'll get another chance so I'd better go, because France is only next door.' To a young man with Anthony's energy, that really seemed true – he could hop across the Channel and think nothing of it.

Anthony had graduated with honours from Bradford University after studying economics and politics. He had a very strong character, and he could be difficult if he wanted to be. He'd make a stand. If he thought someone was taking advantage of him, he'd say, 'I just can't accept that any more. It's not going to happen. You might think I'm a fool, but I am not. I will just go this far and no further.'

I could see a lot of me in him, no doubt. That was what he was like – headstrong and headlong! He was strong-willed and very clear on what he wanted to do. Having said that, he was easily hurt and very passionate. So most times he had to put on a strong front.

He didn't want people to think he was being over-pushy or pretending to be something he wasn't, because he hurt very easily and that's what many people didn't know. Acquaintances saw him and they thought, 'This is such a strong guy. He's so together, in control, nothing can ever hurt him.' But the smallest things could. That's why TJ added in his tribute in the church, 'Anthony was one guy who could cry.' TJ told me he doesn't know too many men who can cry, but Anthony was one such person.

That's a lot like me. People don't know that I hurt, but I hurt very badly and very easily. But I always have to go in the other room, cry, clean my face and come out smiling, saying, 'Hi – hi, how's everything? I'm fine.' Nothing is allowed to get out. I know I cannot let myself crack and crumble. I can't just sit and flop, or nothing will change.

Anthony would cry at the little things. If something hurt him deeply, especially when somebody died, he just couldn't take it. And it hurt him to see that there is so much injustice in the world. I used to say to him that no one could change the world, and he would say, 'But Mummy, we can try our little best!'

That's what I am doing now, with the peace foundation in his memory: trying my little best.

When he thought about Nigeria he would say, 'I must go back. That country needs every one of us that it can get. When I have gathered enough experience in Britain, I must go back and put it to use in Nigeria.'

That was his ambition. That was why he never removed his wristband, the green-and-white rubber bracelet that says, 'Nigeria making progress'. He was sure that one day there would be progress and he was going to be part of that.

Anthony wanted to go into politics. That was his ultimate ambition. I knew it, though he would never talk about it. And his immediate aim – what he really wanted to do and what he had discussed with his friends – was to travel to two or three developing countries first. He wanted to work with some of the poorest people, and help them, like a gap year he never took. He wanted to reach out and see something of the world. He was already planning to take time off work, because he always had a passion for the excluded, for people at the fringes of society.

Recognising this very sensitive aspect in his character, I tried to talk things through with him whenever I could. He was always there for me and I was always there for him, whether it was issues with work or distress at stories in the news.

We had long discussions about poverty, suffering and destruction, and the place of religion and God in all of this. Much as he respected my views, he still challenged quite a lot of my assertions. 'You'll find out when your own children arrive,' I would tell him. 'You'll try to give them understanding, but they can only come to it through their own experience.'

He saw love and hate, good and evil, suffering and luxury, riches and poverty, inclusion and exclusion, peace and war, pain and gain, life and death, and the sheer scale of the injustice in the world angered and bewildered him. But he wasn't going to sit back. He was going to fight it and contribute his quota.

The grand plan was to go out and help in poverty-stricken places for a while, perhaps as an aid worker, and then come back to Nigeria and be part of its economic development and eventually go into politics. He was going to do great things for Nigeria. He had his eyes open and he knew he belonged to the generation that would bring change to bear.

In his personal, everyday life, his philosophy was completely positive: do whatever you can with all your heart and with love. Eat right, play right, train right, work right. And he had time for everybody. He had a shoulder for everyone, for anybody who wanted it.

Friends used to say to me, long before he died, 'Oh, do you know we saw Anthony, and he stopped and asked us if we were all right and would we like a lift? He stopped just because he recognised us.' He was polite to everyone, and he always had hugs for the children – he loved kids a lot and they loved him in return.

His friends told me of one occasion when he bumped into a schoolfriend he hadn't seen for ages. They'd lost touch, but they got chatting and exchanged phone numbers. A week later he called her and she said it was her sister's birthday but, because they were short of money, they weren't planning to celebrate. 'We're a bit broke, and we're just sort of sitting around,' she said.

So Anthony went round to the house and told the sister, 'You know what? This is your birthday! You can't just sit at home. I'm taking you and all your friends to McDonald's. My treat.'

They were about his age, so it's not as if he were taking his little sisters and their friends out. His attitude was, you've got to celebrate. That's what life is about.

It's not as if he was handing out money, or as though he had much to give away. That in itself did not bother him. Anthony could live without money and say, 'There will be a better day.' And he was looking forward to that better day. What little he did have though, if someone needed it then he would spread it.

His cousin Benjy, who is nineteen, said that Anthony would always phone him and ask if everything was OK. He'd tell him, 'Remember I am there for you if you should need anything.' Not that he had that much, at least not financially, but he told Benjy, 'If you need anything, don't hesitate to call me.'

Benjy is at University College London. He has written a little book, a short story called *Pessions*, containing a lot of imagination, depth and philosophy, which he has dedicated to Anthony. When Anthony died he retreated into himself and wrote the story, and now a firm in India has published it. All this Benjy organised himself, without the help of anyone.

Christopher, Anthony's other cousin, a graduate of Kings and a traditional artist by vocation, took it upon himself to design the logo for the AFW Foundation.

Anthony was conscious of his position as the first son, the first grandson, the brother – he took it seriously and he felt there was a lot of responsibility on his shoulders, with more to come. And there was so much love riding on him, he felt he had to make his life work out right.

While I was studying, I came across a book that said first-born children are natural leaders, and that this had been proven psychologically and scientifically. I told him about it and he was excited by the idea: 'Show me, let me read it! Yeah, I can see myself in that, that's true.' And that little bit of science seemed to give him a lot of food for thought. Suddenly, he didn't fret so much about his instinct to lead and to nurture. He realised he was just fulfilling his natural role.

If there was a family rift, he'd try to be the reconciler. At times he'd come and look at me and say, 'Smile, come on, give us a smile, give us that smile.' You knew he just didn't like to see you moody or unhappy. And when he did something wrong and was chided for it, he might be macho and go off, but five or ten minutes later he was back, saying, 'OK, Mummy, I apologise for that. I hope I didn't hurt you – you know I didn't mean it.'

Even though there were times when Alan and I could have gone the extra mile for him and done a lot more, we sometimes held back, because we felt he had to grow and achieve these things for himself. That way, he would appreciate them all the more. So if for a while he didn't have a car, it was not because one of his uncles couldn't have afforded to add some money to his salary to help him buy a car, but because when you work for it yourself then it means more.

He wasn't too pleased about that at first but we told him, 'Anthony, you are the head of the family with two girls growing up after you. You must learn to make your own successes, because all your life you will have to be looking out for other people. Maybe in the past you have had a problem with people who say, "Hey, you should get this, you should own that, every guy has this-and-this," but you are not "every guy". You are you, you are Anthony, you are different. People will respect you for who you are, not what you own. If they don't respect you, too bad. What you've got is what you've got.'

12

As the weeks passed, I felt increasing frustration about the government's apparent inaction. There was no kind of official contact about anything. The atrocity had been a mighty wake-up call – so why did the official world still seem to be asleep?

The government seemed to be wishing the whole affair away, in a calculated refusal to face the obvious. Did they believe that by never referring to 7/7, never discussing it, never staging a public inquiry, they could persuade the public to forget about it? Perhaps.

Did they imagine bereaved families could forget their loved ones and the way they had died? Will the badly injured be wished away? How were we to ensure that never again would innocents be butchered by terrorists on city streets?

At a discussion with other families who had lost loved ones in the bombings, I quickly got the feeling that I was not alone in my frustration. Everybody was bemused that nothing was happening. It was as if the officials whose chief duty was to protect the people could not brush the bombings aside fast enough.

At the first meeting for families that I attended, the most common complaint was about the endless questions of the police and their relentless focus on drawing information out of us. We were also aware that the Home Affairs committee at the House of Commons was to sit on 13 September, to hear evidence on what was termed 'Issues Arising from the London Bombings'. Witnesses would include the Metropolitan Police Commissioner Sir Ian Blair, mayor of London Ken Livingstone, various government ministers, and the secretary-general of the Muslim Council of Britain, Sir Iqbal Sacranie.

None of the families had received any official correspondence about this, either inviting us to participate or asking if we had any contributions to make. Now there were only a couple of days until the hearing, and people who tried to attend were told they could not even be assured of seats in the gallery.

Looking back, we should have heard the alarm bells then. This was how things would be, until the government finally admitted there would be no public inquiry. Back in the early autumn of 2005, however, we were all still hopeful and trusting.

We made up our minds that we were going to start writing to ministers, our MPs and councillors, to find out what was going on and why we were being cut out of the loop. Too many things had happened where the authorities had turned a deaf ear and a blind eye to us as grieving families.

What effect those letters had, I cannot truly say: I attended only the first meeting, though I have kept in touch by phone with some of the other families.

To the bereaved relatives at that first meeting, I suggested that we should organise something to mark 7 October 2005. I came up with the slogan 'three months on, too soon to forget', because we felt people were already forgetting about the atrocities. The idea was not simply that they should remember the people who had died, but also that they should never forget that, 'Terrorism exists. This thing could happen again. People in the government should be more forthcoming towards us than just sending us paperwork advising us to claim £11,000.'

That was a seriously vexed issue for many families: the government's Criminal Injuries Compensation Authority had announced at the beginning of August that relatives of the people killed in the bombings would receive £11,000 as 'compensation', with children to be paid £2,000 a year until they were eighteen for 'loss of parental services'. The Authority's chief executive, Howard Webber, called this 'efficient, fair and compassionate'. Most of the relatives felt it was a calculated insult.

I don't even want to go into the issue of compensation; I don't want to discuss it here, because it is ridiculous to imagine that money could be set in a balance against Anthony's life. To me, though, the very offer of £11,000 was proof that his murder was just another death as far as the civil servants were concerned, and the bombing was just another criminal act. The fact that it was terrorism was irrelevant to them: this was a crime, and the victims were no more notable than any other victims of anti-social behaviour. If the government was aware that the families of the people who died in the 9/11 attacks were each awarded £2.1 million, they did not refer to it. Nor was Lockerbie referred to either.

'Three months on, too soon to forget.' That was how I came to do the first flier that was given out at Tube stations. Anthony's friends came out to help once more, and I also got volunteers from round the borough. We didn't have time or funds to hire a professional distribution firm, so his friends stepped in to hand the leaflets out at King's Cross, Liverpool Street, and at the memorial site in the Embankment Gardens. I would have liked to cover all the bomb sites, including Tavistock Square, but we did what we could.

Something was egging me on. I knew that I was inspired, and it was not only Anthony's spirit: I was fired up by the whole of the world and the state it was in. I was driven by the mere fact that out there were people who thought they had the right to take life, and that we should just sit there and accept it and hope that life would go on.

I set out to plan my first campaign, and I realised I needed to design a pamphlet and a bookmark. This wasn't my idea alone: I sat down with my daughters, and I said, 'I am planning to set up this foundation, but how am I going to let people know about it? How am I going to get them talking about peace? We need to get word out. Let's give out fliers in the station, just so that people know.'

These were the first small steps by the AFW Foundation. My niece Judita helped me to design the bookmark, with a photograph of the bus prominent on it. It is a picture that needs no explanation. The wording on the bookmark was this: 'Three months on, too soon to forget. Dialogue, prayer and mutual understanding till differences no longer make a difference. Start by taking a Peace Pause today and every day. Think Peace, not War, not Terror.'

What I really wanted to do was to reach out to as many people as possible and tell them, 'Let us stop a minute for peace.' I was moved by the two-minute silence that all of Britain had held in the wake of the bombings, when millions of office workers streamed out of their buildings to stand in the streets in silent tribute to the victims. The power of that collective emotion could be harnessed, if only I knew how.

Television might have helped, but I didn't have the strength. I might have the courage, but I was just too weak, too tired, to face it. My real hope was that a journalist would pick up on the fliers and approach me, and ask to talk in more detail. And even if just one person saw that flier and was inspired to pause for peace, and to think about what it meant, then that might inspire other people. It might be a way to spread the idea.

I started with the Tube stations, not because I wanted to frighten anyone going to catch a train, but because I wanted to remind everybody that the threat of terror had not gone away. With another close friend, I came up with the wording: 'Victims of terror are alert . . . you need to be too.' We aimed to send a crisp message, setting out what we stood for and what we were intending to preach: that good will come out of this evil.

Anthony was blessed with his friends. He attracted good people to him, and they didn't fade away. Their willingness to help with the pamphlets was just one example among many. In the months since the bombing, I have sat many times with them, reminiscing and often learning more about my son. Even at his posthumous 27th birthday on the 29th January, when his cousin T. J. organised a 'meet and greet', his friends reminded me that they were all now my 'adopted' sons and daughters. God bless them for their love.

I have made a note of some of the most touching and revealing comments, and in my mind all those conversations melt into one, like an afternoon chat that makes the evening pass in a blink and lasts late into the night. Benjy and TJ are there, Ope and Ibrahim, his childhood buddy Saudiq, who is now married to Peggy and lives in Paris, and Adeniyi, and Aisha, Ego, Amaka, Will, Remi, Nike, Amrit, and a crowd of other young men and women.

And to set things off, I might tease them a little and say that I don't like rap music because some of the lyrics are not very . . . let's say, 'elevated'. Anthony loved to rap, and I urged him to write lyrics with a more uplifting message.

'When Tony wrote his lyrics, he put his true feelings in them,' insists one of the guys. 'It doesn't matter what words you use; what counts is the things that you say.'

'He was just being real, realistic about the way he feels,' agrees one of the girls.

The quiet Ope chimes in: 'One thing Anthony did with his friends was to talk about wars and world issues. And in his lyrics or his poems, because really they were actually poems, he was speaking out about them. He liked to challenge other people's prejudices and pre-conceived ideas.

'A lot of people might want to sugar-coat things. Tony never dreamed of sugar-coating anything, he didn't believe in that. Because in the end we don't all live in a lovely, beautiful paradise. And I think the more you sugar-coat something, the more you poison the mind. I am not saying kids should be

exposed to certain things, no. But if you are an adult, you deserve the truth. That was what he was trying to put down, and I am very, very proud of him. It might not always have come out in that "elevated" way, but we all have to have our differences. It creates a platform for debate. That's what Tony loved. He liked the fact that not everyone saw everything the same way.'

'You and Anthony were always talking about music,' I say.

Ope nods: 'Anthony and I started up a record company together. Tony had been writing music for a very long time, but he hadn't been to the studio in a while, and last year I encouraged him to start going again. Sometime in May we wrote a song and produced it together. I gave that CD to Lauretta because she wanted to have it as a keepsake. We didn't complete the song – his part was finished but there was still some work to do on the chorus.

'The song was called 12th Disciple. Tony wrote the lyric. From the name, you can sort of figure out what he's talking about. Jesus had 12 disciples, but the twelfth was Judas, the person who betrayed him. Tony and I had been through experiences in the same way – we knew people who were supposedly our friends, but who had done things behind our backs that we didn't appreciate. I think that the whole idea was to write a song that said no matter how much someone does you wrong, don't hate him. If you loved someone once, you can't hate him because of something he has done, even though you might not be able to be his close friend again.

'And the song was also a warning: be careful about the people that you hang around with. Beware the people who can haul you down, how money and material things can pollute the minds of people you are close to and your friendships.'

'I've seen his lyrics, and heard them, and they are like poems,' I agree. 'I didn't know how much he wrote, though, till you told me.'

Everyone starts talking and laughing, remembering Tony the performer. 'He was so gregarious,' says someone.

'Not shy at all,' whoops another.

'I wish I could find those lyrics now,' I say.

'He wrote a lot of stuff on his phone, dictating into it,' Adeniyi points out. 'That's why we can't find a lot of it now. The police say his phone wasn't among the things they recovered. Anthony said lyrics just come to you any time, anywhere. There were times when I called him from Lagos to say hello, late at night, and he would recruit me as a solo audience for his latest inspirational lyric.'

'That was one side of him,' agrees Remi. 'He was a very versatile guy who liked doing a lot of different things. He liked reading. He loved his music, loved his gym, loved his friends, loved his family. He was always trying hard to better himself and be a better man, and with every year that went past he was getting better and better. He was like a fine wine, getting better with age. The last two or three years he was just an amazing friend. He was determined to be the best he could. He loved to go out, have a few drinks and go clubbing, being with his boys. He loved it when everybody was happy, having a good time. He loved travelling. Miami was a big favourite.'

'Even as a kid, he went out to Florida with my brother and his family,' I say.

'He was passionate about going back to Nigeria and really working for the country. We all were. Even though we were all in school here, every summer and every holiday we would all go back to Nigeria. We would meet up there from all the different schools and all the different families, and just became very close. We'd been doing that for four or five years. We bonded very closely. Tony was such a generous, loving, loyal person, you can't describe him. The ideal friend. Once he liked you he was loyal to the end, you were immediately family to him and he would do anything for you.

'As we grew older and busier, we separated, and it would always be Tony who called you and said, "Come on, let's go out if we can, let's meet up." He was, almost without even

knowing it, the gel in the whole group. He kept us together, and he didn't realise it, and we didn't realise it ourselves, until later on. I think we'd all agree, his loss has affected the way all his friends relate, because it's made us a lot closer again. When we were younger, Tony used to look up to me. He wanted to be my friend. I kind of took it for granted that he'd be around. Now it's me looking up to him, wishing he was there.'

Some of the girls are trying to hold back tears, and even the boys are struggling to put on brave faces.

'He placed a high importance on family and close friends,' one of the girls says, 'but he also warmed to people who weren't in his circle of friends. He made a lot of friends, at the gym for example, and he'd meet someone once and the next time he saw them he'd be chatting to them like he'd known them for years. He was always so friendly to everyone.'

Someone close to him chips in, 'One day we left the gym and he was chatting to someone for ages. I was complaining and saying, "Can we go?" but he was chatting to this person and getting their number and promising to call, and I was like, "Well, who's that?"

'And he said, "Well, I don't actually know his name! He's on the bus every morning going to work, but I've never really chatted to him." And they'd been talking like they'd known each other for years. He just made a lot of friends.'

'Anthony's contacts and friends wherever he went cut across all ages, creeds and ranks,' I say. 'He could hold a fulfilling conversation with the lift man, as with a driver or a chief executive, and make each one feel equally well respected and special.'

'And he was such a sharp dresser,' adds a girl admiringly; 'very smart. He was an extremely well-spoken person too, and liked to look the part, liked to look good, in a smart way, not trendy. Quite conservative in a nice way, but also with a fashionable side. He made a strong impression on people immediately. I happened to bump into my doctor when I was

with Anthony one day, and they talked for a few minutes. Well, after everything happened, I visited my doctor and I said, "Do you remember Anthony?" Right away, he said, "Oh, you mean the extremely well-spoken chap. He looked very nice, how is he?" And he could not believe that Anthony was dead.'

Everyone wants to talk at once now, sharing their memories.

'He pulled you in as soon as he met you,' says one. 'He could tell if this was a person whose company he would enjoy, and he made everyone feel warm and welcome as soon as he met them. As soon as you met him you were introduced to his family. He would say, "Oh come and hang around with me and my family, come and meet my mum, come and meet my sisters." On his sisters' birthdays, all his friends would ring the girls. He made his family feel like your family, so he always made you feel very "at home" with him.'

Ope nods his head. 'That really affected him, anything to do with family. It was his family that was the main thing. Once he showed you love, he showed you excess love – but if you ever took that for granted, he really hated it.'

'His sisters miss him so much,' I say, sadly. 'He was so good at caring for Aisha, helping with her learning disability. He'd go to her college open days: I always knew, if I wasn't around, he'd go. One of the last e-mails he sent to me was about an assessment for her education, and he sent me this perfect report about what happened, what the teachers were trying to do, what to do next, and what he thought should happen, and then the last line was: "Mummy, when next you're here, we'll sit and discuss this and know where we're going from here."

'Really, his Achilles' heel was his family – do not joke or poke fun at any member of his family, as he was prepared to lay down his life for them and would dare anyone to try him. Such was his bond and love for family. It was a love that left everybody feeling special, as if he had created compartments in his heart for each one, yet with ample space for friends, colleagues and the needy.'

'Even his barber was part of the family,' laughs someone. 'He was there every week!'

'We had rough times over that,' I exclaim. 'I didn't like it when Anthony shaved his head. He told me, "Mummy, I can be clean like this." But one of you guys told me he was getting very particular about his receding hairline. He was very conscious of his hairline so he decided to keep everything one level: "OK, I'm going low-cut." He never scraped it, but because of his complexion, when you looked at it, you thought it was all shaved. He did that the first time and I told him, "You cannot do that, Anthony. It's just not on. You can't be a skinhead. Everybody knows your age, so it isn't as if people will see a receding hairline and think you are old!" He just had to keep a correct look.'

Ibrahim, the more meditative young man, has a serious point to make: 'Anthony was much more than skin-deep. He always wanted to learn and make the most of life. He spoke perfect French. I used to speak French with him and Saudiq, and listen to the stories of their escapades!'

'Anthony was going to teach me French, if I would teach him one of the Nigerian languages, Yoruba,' adds Ope. 'So whenever we were with people who spoke French, he would try to make me speak French, and whenever I went out and spoke Yoruba, he would want to take part and he'd ask me, "What did you mean there?" He loved learning.

'I warned him, "It is a very different language to European languages: the tones are heavier, much heavier. The pronunciation is not as hard as in French, but the grammar might be just as difficult." But speaking it is not as difficult as it seems. And for younger people, there's a lot of slang that you can mix with the hardcore language. He was adamant about learning it. We started early last year when we came back from Nigeria. He was always thinking, his mind was always ticking, he was always hyper in a kind of good way, always on the ball. He noticed things very very fast and you might think he didn't see something, but believe me he saw it.

'And once he set his mind to do something, there was no stopping him. So with learning Yoruba, he would never wait for me to start a lesson – he would do it by himself. We would go to a car wash, and there were a couple of Nigerian guys working there, and when we got there I would be the one to talk to them. I wouldn't be expecting Anthony to say anything, but he'll just say, "Bawo Ni?" which is "How are you?" and he'll just start talking. He was getting on fine with it. It would have taken a bit more time to make him fluent, but he was getting there.'

Nike adds, 'He made friends everywhere. I actually bumped into someone at church, a couple of months after he died, and she said, "I recognise you." I'd been introduced to her once at the gym. She was a lot older than Anthony, but he'd spend some time talking to her, about exercises or whatever, and he'd also speak to her about spirituality. Things hadn't worked out in her life very well, and she'd told him about it. He spoke to her about faith, and spirituality, and that was why she started coming to church. In fact, that was her first time at church. She said she owed a lot of that to him, and she was really grateful for her relationship with him. She learnt a lot from him, she said. I think he did touch a lot of people. The way he passed away affected a lot of people as well, made a lot of people rethink things. For something like this to have happened . . . I believe Anthony was put here to touch people. He did affect everyone.'

One of the boys says, 'I remember in the middle of last year we used to go to evening Mass, and as we came out of the church we got into his car and he put on some hip-hop music. And he said, "I wonder what people will think? They will assume I don't know what I am doing in church!" But what he had was faith, a belief. He didn't see religion as a barrier to having fun, because he loved life.'

'He went to church with me sometimes,' I say. 'Sometimes I think he went more often when I was not around than when I was here. There were days when he would go with us in the morning, and there were days when he would say, "Mummy, I don't have to do exactly as you do. I'll decide which Mass I'll go to."

'And for a while I thought he wasn't going at all, until I realised he was going in the evening. I said, "OK, I should let this boy be. He should follow his own path." All I wanted was that he should pray and go to church. But we can't make or force people to do things. He couldn't make me go to the gym! Gym and church are not comparable in any way, of course, but what I mean is, I left Anthony to make his choice and follow his path. When it comes to religion you have got to give what you have, plant the good seed, water the soil, tend it the best you can, watch it grow and allow it to blossom the best way it is able.'

'Anthony didn't hide his spiritual side at all,' says Ope. 'If he was comfortable with you he would say anything, no matter what. He was not the kind of person who was ashamed of anything, in front of his friends. He was there for you to see all his ups and downs, once he trusted you. He wasn't concerned if he seemed unmanly. He wasn't afraid to cry. He would cry. He could be very blatant and outspoken, transparent in front of us.'

'He was a brave guy, and physically imposing, though!' exclaims another friend. 'What about that nightclub, the time when some guy slapped a girl? Anthony did not take this girl to the party. He only just met her. But he stepped in. We tried to hold him; we didn't think it was any of our business, but Anthony says, "What do you mean, mind my own business? Why should he slap her? We can't all just stand around and watch this thing happen. Do you mean, if he had killed her, we would all just stand here and let him?"

'He went up to this guy and said, "Hey, what did she do to you? Why did you hit her? What's with you?" And then he went to this girl and asked her, "Did this guy hurt you?" The guy lashed out at him, and Anthony actually took a punch. Luckily the girl had called someone on the phone who came and broke it up before it became a brawl. After we left, we told him, "What if he had brought out a knife and stabbed you?"

'Anthony said, "Well, I didn't think of that and I take your point. But I couldn't just stand back." '

Remi has been quiet. He was one of the pall bearers alongside Amrit, Ope, Christo, T. J., Sadiq, Iyke and Adeniyi. Now he says, 'For me, the first month after the funeral was very hard. Just very, very painful. But I knew what Tony was about, because he really did live his life to the full. When it was time to be serious in the office and do his work he was extremely serious, and when it was time to be out at the weekend he partied the hardest. But come Monday morning he was back ready for the office. He was doing long days coupled with his studies, very dedicated, but also he loved to take life a bit easier with his boys and live comfortably.'

'We did talk about his beliefs in life after death, once or twice,' says someone, 'but Tony did not focus a lot on that. He focused on living this life that was here. He was always saying, "Come out, let's just do it, you know. Not out of control, but don't retreat into yourself, be out there more. The future is going to be the present very soon, so why not just live the present?" And I just know a lot more people and I'm into a lot more things because of him.

'Work hard, play hard: that's the perfect description. He had that energy that the rest of us don't have. He could do things. He could party till midnight, and next day he'll go to work fresh. Too much energy, in my opinion!'

13

There will be no public inquiry into the terrorist atrocity that claimed Anthony's life, killed fifty-one other innocent people, wounded 700 more and left London in paralysis and shock. The four bombers were young British men of Asian and Caribbean descent; two of them had been watched by the security services for as long as eighteen months before the attacks. Despite this, government ministers and senior police officers say an official inquiry would be a 'distraction' from their efforts to prevent further acts of terrorism. Instead, a 'public narrative' is to be published some time in 2006, a selective sequence of those events that Downing Street is prepared to acknowledge, without the awkward need to address difficult questions. One of the most important questions – who masterminded the attacks, and where is this criminal now? – has been completely ignored.

To me, this simply is not fair. It's playing politics with people's lives. Put plainly, that is wrong. Fifty-two people have died. That isn't 3,000-plus as it was for the USA on 9/11, but for fifty-two families, it is just as devastating. We cannot bring our loved ones back, and that hurts us dreadfully. Let no others hurt like us. Let London learn. Let's make sure that there is change. Let's know that after these lives that have been lost, there will not be others.

But instead the government wishes to keep everything closed and tries to hurriedly draw a line under 7/7, saying it will get everything sorted out by sending around a copy of a report. I say: 'What do you think that does to me, and what does that say to me about my son who has been killed unnecessarily? That it is fair or it is good, or that this makes everything all right? I don't think so. If you don't have a public or independent investigation, the suspicion must be there is something that you are hiding. If that isn't the case, then have the investigation and we'll all see the results and we'll all draw a line under it.

'We can't go on living in fear. That's what the terrorists want. To allay the fears of society, you must allow us to come forward and ask the necessary questions: "What happened? What did you know? What didn't we know? What could we have done? What could we have done better? What didn't we do? Where were the alert systems – were they down, were they set at high, were they low? How have things changed between then and now? How safe is public transport now? How safe is the Tube? How vigilant are the police and the security forces?" '

Anthony couldn't drive to work because there is nowhere to park in Old Street. So he had to take the train, and when there was no train he had to take the bus. People will keep on taking trains and buses for generations to come. It is not by sticking our heads in the cupboard, with our whole backsides sticking outside, that we will solve the problem. It happened, and it can happen again. It isn't enough to say, 'Londoners are brave, stubborn people and the city coped well. That's it, everybody move on, and we'll pretend 7/7 never really happened.'

The powers-that-be want to sweep everything under the carpet and not talk of it. That's why they don't want to have a proper memorial. There is a small slab in the Embankment Gardens, below a plaque and an Oak tree commemorating the Queen's coronation. At least her plaque is raised up: the 'memorial' to the victims of the bombings is a scuffed, grubby postage stamp of marble, scattered with gravel. Three months after the attacks, I went with a few other bereaved families to have a private moment of remembrance in the Gardens, and what we found were magnificent monuments to dukes and generals and composers, and a half-buried piece of marble. I looked at it incredulously and I thought, 'How sad' – not for those that it was meant to commemorate, whose names were not even on it, but rather for the people who thought that this would suffice.

I am not a cynical person, but I don't know what else to believe: as far as I'm concerned, the government wants to ignore the evidence, sweep everything under the carpet, and say, 'The bombings? They never really happened – let's go on to 2012 and the Olympics. A big memorial somewhere? No.'

That is not the attitude in the USA. There, the threat of terrorism is taken with the utmost gravity. In that country you can meet anyone in the street and discuss 9/11 and get feedback. Any member of the public will be well appraised of the latest developments, and everyone will know the current level of security alert. The American government has done so many things to make its citizens feel safer. At the airport, when the security guards tell you to take off your belt or take out your hairpins, you know they're doing it for a reason.

But in the UK, any mention of 7/7 provokes an uneasy response. That's not right. I was involved in the aftermath of those atrocities: am I supposed not to talk about it? Am I supposed to make myself believe that I never had a son called Anthony who was killed in the bombings? Am I expected to sit back while the security services appoint themselves judge and jury? Am I to accept without question the 'public narrative' that might one day be published? Is this the behaviour of a civilised society?

I am in agreement with Sir Iqbal Sacranie, the head of the Muslim Council of Britain, who has said a public inquiry would be 'in the interest of all Britons . . . There has to be a full public inquiry so that we will be better prepared to prevent such a tragedy happening again.'

After all, the UK had been expecting this kind of assault

for a long time. After the Madrid bombing that killed 192 people in March 2004, there was a widespread expectation that London would be next. And what could have been a more dangerous time for the capital than the day after the Olympic Committee announced London would host the 2012 Games? Meanwhile in Scotland, the world's most powerful leaders were gathering for the G8 conference at Gleneagles?

If ever there was a time when we should have been prepared and alert, it should have been then, at the time of Gleneagles. And yet we left our underbelly open and vulnerable. How did that happen? How can it be prevented in the future? And aren't these questions worth a more far-reaching inquiry?

I cannot conduct my own inquiry but, with the help of friends at national newspapers, I have been able to assemble a database of cuttings that set out the events of 7 July 2005. I have at least been able to find out what the scene was during the last minutes of Anthony's life, even if some questions will always remain a mystery.

All the reports agree that at about 8.50 a.m., three bombs were detonated on the London underground within seconds of each other – one in a Circle Line tunnel just beyond Aldgate station, one on the Piccadilly Line departing from King's Cross, and a third, also on the Circle Line, westbound outside Edgware Road station. The bombers were Islamic extremists seeking vengeance for the death of Muslims in Iraq and Afghanistan, according to a 200-word statement released by al-Qaeda at noon that same day.

The Aldgate bomber was twenty-two-year-old Shahzad Tanweer from Leeds, a cricket fan and the son of a fish-and-chip shop owner. The King's Cross bomber was Jamal, or Germaine, Lindsay, nineteen, a Jamaican-born convert to Islam who lived in Aylesbury, Buckinghamshire, and whose wife was expecting their second baby. The Edgware Road bomber was the leader of the group and the oldest,

Mohammad Sidique Khan, thirty, a former classroom assistant from Dewsbury in Yorkshire and the father of a baby girl.
All were killed instantly. Some commentators have, strangely,
speculated that the killers might have thought they were
priming the devices instead of detonating them. They had
arrived in London that morning with return tickets, and none
of them left a suicide note.

There was a fourth member of the squad. Closed circuit
television footage shows four men arriving at King's Cross
with their rucksacks, looking like hitch-hikers, going off in
separate directions after brief goodbyes. The youngest of
them, a heavy-set boy of eighteen called Hasib Hussain, had
left his parents' home in Leeds the day before, saying he was
visiting the capital to attend a religious lecture. 'I'll be back on
Thursday,' he told his mother, Maniza.

Hasib Hussain did not get on a Tube train. Perhaps he lost
his nerve, or his bearings: security experts think he had been
told to take the northbound Northern Line, so that the four
simultaneous explosions would create a burning cross
centred on King's Cross. The trains were running, but instead
Hussain wandered out of the station, trying to get a phone
signal perhaps to call his fellow bombers. CCTV cameras
picked him up, walking aimlessly through Boot's the
Chemist's and buying a burger in McDonald's. When he left
the station for the last time, he walked towards Euston.

Hussain caught a bus heading north. He was supposedly
the newest recruit to the bomb squad, and had not taken part
in a 'bonding trip' to an adventure centre in Bala, North
Wales, a few days earlier, where the others had gone white-
water rafting. He regularly visited the same mosque in
Dewsbury that Khan used, however, and it seems likely he
was a late replacement for a bomber who dropped out of the
suicide mission. That would explain why he acted with little
of the robotic sense of purpose the others displayed.

The bus became gridlocked in the chaotic traffic caused by
his fellow bombers. Other passengers observed him getting

more and more agitated. At last he appeared to lose patience, scrambled off the bus and, minutes later, boarded another bus – a Number 30 – travelling from Hackney to Marble Arch and back, which had been diverted because the King's Cross area was cordoned off.

This bus was crowded, and its driver, George Psaradakis, allegedly was urging people to get off and walk if they were bound for King's Cross.

Richard Jones, a sixty-one-year-old IT consultant, was one of those who got off. He had been standing at the back, and a young man with a rucksack had repeatedly jostled him. 'It was standing room only,' recalled Mr Jones. 'You can imagine the crush. This chap kept dipping down into his bag and then getting up again. He was becoming more and more frustrated. He did it about a dozen times in two or three minutes, and was looking extremely agitated. He was fiddling away, and he kept getting annoyed with something. He kept bumping into me – it was getting on my nerves. I remember him vividly because he was annoying me.'

Others also noticed him. They described him as muttering to himself and dipping frequently into the rucksack, as if he were grabbing pieces of fruit or bread.

A retired journalist, John Falding, was talking on the phone to one of the passengers on the bus, his girlfriend Anat Rosenberg. Mr Falding had been campaigning against cuts in the fire services, and Anat had called him to say that London's emergency crews seemed to be working at full stretch that morning, with sirens wailing on every street. 'I told her there had been an incident,' Mr Falding said. 'Just then, I heard a scream in the background. It was like nothing I have ever heard before. It was ghastly, not of this world. It didn't sound like a woman's scream. It was horrible, high-pitched, and I think it might have been a man.' That was the last time he ever spoke to Anat.

Richard Jones, walking away from the bus, heard the scream too, before a massive explosion obliterated it a second later. The bus driver's first thought was that a tyre had blown. Then he looked round to see that the roof of the bus had been punched open like a paper bag.

The British Medical Association's headquarters was just a few yards away, and the BMA's head of ethics, Ann Somerville, was in the car nearest to the bus when the bomb detonated. 'There was a loud explosion and the roof peeled off the bus like a banana skin,' she said. 'You could hear cries. There were plumes of smoke and lumps of debris flying everywhere at all angles. It smelt like gunpowder. I was just amazed. I couldn't work out whether to get out of the car and run and help, or move my vehicle out of the way of the emergency services.'

On the pavement 20 yards away, film storyboard artist Joe Dor was on his mobile, warning his employers he would be late in to work. His girlfriend, Vicki Dokas, was with him. 'As I put the phone down,' he said, 'I heard a massive bang and I felt this enormous power hit me in the face. I froze, but my girlfriend shouted out, "Run!" '

In a 999 call, made public months later during the London Assembly's review of the response to the bombings by emergency services, an office worker told the operator: 'There's a bus just exploded in Tavistock Square, just outside my window. There's people lying in the road, there's people trying to get out. I think there's ambulances on the way but there's people dead and everything by the look of it.'

Dr Peter Holden, preparing for a meeting with colleagues inside the BMA building, said that, at the moment of the blast, everything turned pale pink for an instant. Then he saw 'white smoke and debris raining down on the square'. Taking charge, he organised a party of doctors to improvise immediate treatment for the casualties who had managed to crawl from the bus.

The driver, like the majority of the people at the front of the bus, was unhurt, but he could not understand how he had survived. Explosives experts have suggested that the worst of the blast was channelled up the stairwell at the back of the bus, which perhaps explains why the roof was ripped open by a bomb supposedly on the lower deck. One of the passengers who died was twenty-year-old Shahara Islam, the daughter of another bus driver.

George's wife, Androulla, said his first reaction, after he had done as much as he could to help the injured, was to phone her: 'He was saying, "My passengers are dead, all my passengers are dead." It was all he could say. My husband's been saved by a miracle. He carries a picture of Mary, mother of Jesus, around with him at all times and I think that's what saved him. When I spoke to him on the phone at the hospital, he said, "The picture saved my life." '

Tavistock Square had for many years been a focal point for the peace movement, with its statue of Gandhi, its cherry tree commemorating Hiroshima and its memorial to the victims of the Holocaust. In footage being beamed worldwide within minutes, a red double-decker bus, a shattered icon of London, would come to symbolise the attack on the capital.

At 11 a.m., one of Hasib Hussain's sisters phoned their mother in Leeds to let her know there had been bombings in London. Hussain's older brother, Imran, took the call. The evening before, Imran had been playing cricket with Shazad Tanweer. Now, he tried to contact his younger brother by mobile, without success. With rising anxiety, all the Hussains tried to reach the teenager throughout the day, until at 10.20 p.m. Maniza phoned the police to tell them her son was missing.

Because there has been no official inquiry, it is impossible to know what the immediate police response was to that call, but Hussain's father, Mohammed, has little doubt: Maniza's call alerted the police to a Leeds link, even though the family had no idea that their son was a bomber and not an innocent victim. 'I like to think that we may have helped in some way,' one of the family told reporters. 'Before we called, police had no idea that Hasib was there.'

The little that has been made public about the bomber's life reveals that he was deeply misguided, trapped into committing a terrible crime by evil men, but probably not evil himself. His parents insist he had been a gentle boy: 'If a fly came into the house, he would catch it and take it outside,' said Mohammed, who had moved to the Holbeck district of Leeds from Pakistan some thirty years earlier. 'If there was a caterpillar in the garden, he would make sure it was safe. I can only imagine he was brainwashed into doing this. I keep thinking that this must be some kind of mistake. That it must have been someone else who did this.'

Although he was not marked out as a troublemaker at school, he had to be disciplined for shoplifting and spraying graffiti. He was withdrawn by his teachers from his GCSE exams, and left school at sixteen with just a single GNVQ, in business studies.

Without school or football to fill his life, Hussain drifted. His home was said to be devoutly Islamic, but that form of religion didn't seem to satisfy him. Instead, he was drawn to radical, extremist Islam. Because there has been no public inquiry, it is hard to know whether he was recruited to this perversion of his religion in the UK or abroad, but most reports suggest he visited Pakistan at least once, for a family wedding.

A cousin said, 'Hasib went off the rails and his parents were very worried. They wanted to instil some discipline in him. I don't know what happened but two years before he died, Hasib suddenly changed.' He grew a beard and began dressing in traditional Muslim clothes. Before his death, he shaved off his beard. Anti-terrorism analysts have claimed that this is a textbook indication that a radicalised Muslim is about to undertake a terrorist mission, but it might just as easily have been a reflection of Hussain's vacillating mind. He allegedly told friends that he disliked the way an imam at one mosque would preach one set of rules about beards and hair, and another would dictate something quite different.

'Forget it,' he told one friend. 'I will go my own way.'

My impression is that this boy was weak-willed and under-achieving, desperate for meaning in his life but without the natural discipline to make anything of himself. He needed direction: unfortunately, he got it from men whose minds are dripping with poison and hatred.

These are some of the problems that face society today, and that need careful study and unravelling. Education and a sense of self-respect are an integral part of the key to saving such young men as these.

When Hussain died, he probably didn't intend to kill himself. He probably had opted out of the co-ordinated attack an hour earlier, and his behaviour on the Number 30 bus did not seem that of a man steeling himself to commit suicide according to these reports. In those last minutes, agitated and frustrated, constantly dipping into his rucksack, he might have been trying to disarm his bomb. His chilling scream reported by John Falding and Richard Jones was probably Hussain's last instant of horror, the terrorist plunged into terror by his own deed.

Whether suicide or accident, Hussain killed twelve innocent people by his action, and injured many more. The dead, as well as my son Anthony, were Jamie Gordon, a thirty-year-old asset manager who was engaged to be married; Giles Hart, fifty-five, a BT engineer who had two children; Marie Hartley, who was thirty-four and lived in Lancashire, but had come to London on a course; Miriam Hyman, thirty-one, a picture researcher who lived in Barnet, north London; Shahara Akther Islam, who was twenty, a bank cashier living with her parents; Neetu Jain, thirty-seven, a computer analyst who was planning to move in with her boyfriend; Australian Sam Ly, who was twenty-eight and came from Melbourne; Post Office worker Shyanuja Parathasangary, thirty; Anat Rosenberg, an Israeli-born charity worker, who was thirty-nine; Philip Russell, a twenty-eight-year-old finance worker from Kennington in south London; William Wise, who was fifty-four; and Gladys Wundowa, a fifty-year-old Ghanaian-born cleaner from Ilford, Essex, who had finished her shift and was on her way to a college course.

Some time after Anthony's funeral, my daughters decided they wanted to see the wreckage of the Number 30 bus. We had been thinking about it, wondering what was going to happen to it. Lauretta and Aisha felt that this was important to them. They had to go and see the vehicle in which their beloved Anthony had died. The authorities eventually made that possible, on a specified date, for all the families who wished to see it.

'What's going to become of the bus?' Lauretta asked them.

'It will be crushed,' she was told.

Lauretta and Aisha went with their dad, accompanied by the family liaison officers, to the secured site where the bus was kept, and saw what was left of it. What struck Lauretta, during this quick viewing, were two things: first the serial number was 17758, and the coincidence of the 7/7 in that number made her thoughtful. Second, the symbolism was intensified because of the very peculiar advertising slogan on its side, for a movie called *The Descent*. What was left of the slogan that Lauretta saw was 'Outright Terror – Bold and Brilliant'.

She wanted to photograph all of these things with her phone but she was not allowed to. And yet the bus was going to be crushed, and swept away: a tragic icon reduced to a lump of scrap. Everybody said after the bombing that this bus was the symbol of London's wounds, the red double-decker torn apart. But it cannot be preserved.

That bus could have been put in the British Museum, where people could gaze at it in pain and say, 'Ah . . . There's 7/7.' Beside it there could have been part of a carriage from one of the Tube trains, and people would see it and say, 'This is something that happened in our era. It's history, but it is also very much the present.'

One morning in January 2006, when I was in London,

working on this book, a whale swam up the Thames. For a day or two, Britain could talk of nothing else. It was on every front page, and rolling television news covered its every splash. When the whale died, its carcass went to the Natural History Museum. It was a beautiful whale, and I was sad when it died – but it didn't symbolise very much.

The whale is going to be immortalised. The bus is going to be crushed. It is symbolic, but maybe the government does not want us to be reminded of what it symbolises. Maybe it is being crushed for the same reason that there will be no full scale inquiry.

But I think it will take a lot longer for the image to be crushed out of people's memories. Families will never, ever forget their lost loved ones, in the same way the injured will remain in our consciousness.

14

A two-paragraph letter, the first and only official communication, came from 10 Downing Street, dated 3 October 2005, though I did not receive it until a week later, after the 'Three Months On' event. It was signed by Tony Blair, who said that he knew we had been invited to the National Memorial Service on 1 November at St Paul's Cathedral for the families bereaved by the bombings. He added that he hoped to meet us at the reception following the service.

In fact, we had not received any invitation. At the venue for the 'Three Months On' event, some of the other families told me about the ceremony, and said they had already received official notification and invitation passes.

When I arrived home, I mentioned this to my family liaison officer, Sharon, who said she would make sure that my letter arrived. She brought it over personally, with another officer, the same man who had brought back Anthony's briefcases and various other items – except for his mobile phone, which has still not been returned.

I read the letter, and saw that we were being invited to contribute our thoughts and suggestions to the running of the service. I asked the policeman. 'I want to be clear about this: you say that the families are to contribute to the service. In what form? I would like to know what areas we can bring something to bear. Because it would be very unfair, and I would be very hurt, if I suggest something and it is rejected, then you tell me, "Oh well, we didn't want to have you involved in that area." '

I want to be absolutely clear about this: I spelled out my concern at the outset. I didn't go rushing in. I asked for reassurance that my contribution was being sincerely sought, and I was given it.

The officer said: 'This is the best way. They have left it open so you are free to contribute.'

That seemed too broad a brief for me, so I said, 'Where shall I start? Is it the Mass or the songs or the order of service or the programme? If it's too open for us, we won't know what to do. Will they be able to accommodate everybody who makes a suggestion?'

The policeman insisted that we could trust the organisers to do it the right way, and that they wanted to accommodate everyone. He pointed to the letter: 'That's what it says.'

I said, 'OK, fair enough, if that's what the letter says, then fine. I will see what I can do.' So I dialled the number on the top of the letter, and my call was passed to a woman named Anna. She was very helpful, making sure that I had her fax number, and she told me that I had to forward her a list of names of Anthony's relatives who would be attending.

I said I had two requests: 'The first is that I want a particular song to be sung.'

She said, 'Sure, no problem, just fax your request to me and I will make sure it's passed on.'

'And the second thing,' I continued, 'is that I would like to give out bookmarks. Of course I will send these to you beforehand. This is my way of preaching the gospel of peace and trying to heal some of the damage. There will be 2,000 people there and I want to reach out through them to as many people as I can.' I described the bookmark and told her about the foundation, and I emphasised the aims of the organisation. At that stage it was in its infancy, but the essential mission was plainly stated: 'Recognising our common humanity and working for world peace.'

She wanted to know if I was personally responsible for this bookmark initiative, and I assured her that I was.

The song that mattered so much to me was the Magnificat, Mary's prayer: 'My soul doth magnify the Lord, and my spirit hath rejoiced in God my saviour.' I wanted it to be prayed, or spoken, or sung, but for it somehow to be in people's minds. It is a very important prayer for me.

When I faxed her the names of the people who were coming, at the bottom of that letter I put a note: 'Please remember, I request that this should be my contribution to the service: the Magnificat, sung or prayed. Please call me back if you need this to be clarified, but any priest will be able to tell you which prayer I mean. And don't forget the bookmarks.' Later I called her, just to make certain: 'Did you get my fax? Did you see my notes?' And of course she said yes, and that we would be hearing from them.

I left for Nigeria, but every day I thought about this service and I checked the mail: 'Is there anything today? No? Nothing?' I was in England a week before the memorial service on 1 November. Another letter came some time before the service, to inform us about the parking arrangements and the need for cars to be registered.

The family liaison officer confirmed that we had to make these arrangements, so we tried to register two cars. The letter said that we were to park miles away, at the Mall, on a first-come-first-served basis as parking spaces could not be guaranteed, and then take a bus that would be provided.

This might seem like a trivial thing, but on days of great emotional stress, trivial things can assume great weight.

There was a number provided, so we phoned to check we understood the arrangements – and the number didn't exist.

We tried it again; it definitely did not exist. A mechanical and automatic voice-message told me to check and try again. I was completely thrown – how could this be? This letter had come from the government, and the helpline had been set up, or so we were told, to enable us to sort out all our arrange-

171

ments. Instead, it was adding another layer of confusion.

I found another number, and called in the hope that they would be able to clear everything up. No sooner had I started to explain the problem than the voice at the other end said, 'This is a Red Cross number. We have nothing to do with the car parking arrangements, but we could give you another number where they could assist you.'

They were helpful, finding a number for 7/7 assistance, a helpline for anyone who was affected by the bombings. I called them and explained the difficulties I was having, and they said, 'It appears a digit is missing from the number on the paperwork.' And they gave me the correct number to dial. All that trouble, for one missing number.

Finally, with the new number, we were able to register the cars and make arrangements to take the bus to the cathedral. So I now asked this person: 'I am trying to find out what is happening about the inclusion of what I asked for in the programme.'

She said, 'I can't help you with that. You have to contact the organisers of the service. We're just sorting out the transport. You'll need to contact someone called Debbie.'

By now I was starting to feel like a champion hurdler. Every time I cleared one barrier, there was another set in my way, at a more awkward angle than the last. However, all my life I have respected authority. I don't cut corners, I go through the proper channels. And I don't give up. So I said, 'OK, how do I contact Debbie?'

I called her. She was a colleague of Anna and she was also helpful. I told her, 'I would have thought that by now, with just three days to go till the service, I would have had some sort of a reply, some feedback, but we don't even have a copy of the programme. We don't know how the service is going to go. I don't know anything except where I'm supposed to park.'

By now I was thinking, 'Why am I killing myself to go to this service at all?' But I like to follow everything to its conclusion. If I don't go, I won't be able to comment on it later: and it was that thought that pushed me to be part of it. But I couldn't turn up carrying those bookmarks around with me. I had to send them to someone before the service. 'I'm really worried about those bookmarks,' I told Debbie. 'I requested this in writing, and I requested that the Magnificat should be included.' But it seemed Debbie did not know about this – she asked if she could get back to me later.

The day before the service, I phoned again and Debbie said the best thing to do was to take the bookmarks along with me and hand them over to one of the ushers.

I was amazed. 'Really? How will I know which usher to hand them over to? Why would they take them from me?'

'Just look for those wearing black suits. They will all be clearly identified as ushers. They will be happy to collect the bookmarks from you, and they'll just take it from there. I'll tell them. I can't name any of the ushers to you right now but, whoever you see, they'll be happy to help.'

So on the day of the service I took a little carrier bag full of bookmarks with me to the Mall where we parked and hopped on the bus. There were quite a few of the other relatives and survivors on it – how they managed to make their arrangements, I couldn't imagine. Perhaps we had all spent the week chasing wrong telephone numbers.

When we reached the cathedral, I approached the first usher I saw, and he said, 'Oh no, not me, love! I'm not responsible for that sort of thing. Wait till you get inside and ask somebody else.'

We were shown through the doors and to our seats, and I introduced myself to another of the ushers, and made my explanation.

That seemed to fluster her. She asked me to wait while she found out what was happening from someone else. 'I don't think I'm in a position to distribute the bookmarks myself,' she said, 'but let me try to do something.'

When she came back, with the service about to start, she

said: 'Give them to me and we'll put them under the canopy outside, where the refreshments will be taken later.' And I knew at that moment that that was the last chance gone for those little bookmarks. I was not going to get anywhere. They were taken away.

There were 2,300 people there: bereaved relatives, survivors, passers-by who had been caught up in the nightmare, and emergency workers. Some families had come from as far away as New Zealand, and there were ambassadors from fourteen countries, an indication of how widely the suffering had been directly felt. In the front row were the Queen and Prince Philip, the Prime Minister and many of his Cabinet.

Dr Rowan Williams, the Archbishop of Canterbury, preached: 'Every life is a special sort of gift. When we behave as if that were true, we do what's most important for the defeat of terror and indiscriminate violence . . . It is not death itself that should be the focus of fear. Rather, we should be afraid of losing that passionate conviction about the beauty and dignity of each unique person that brings us here today.'

Later, we went outside, under the canopy in the Square. In one corner, beside all the tea and cakes, was a list of names of the people who had been involved in the bus bombing, the victims of Tavistock Square. I saw Anthony's name, typed on this white sheet.

Near to this was a small table with printed matter about the transport services, but no bookmarks. One of the organisers tried to tell me later that they had been there.

'The canopy where I was,' I told her, 'there were no bookmarks. It is better for you not to say anything, rather than to insist on what I know full well did not happen. I am the one wearing the shoes and I know precisely where they hurt.'

The Magnificat did not feature in the programme. At the conclusion of the service, four candles were carried to the altar, to represent the four bomb sites, with the relatives of one victim from each atrocity following. They were not even accorded the privilege of carrying or placing the candles themselves: those were carried by members of the emergency services and London Transport representatives. The selected family members took a bow and went back to their seats.

I remembered the service of lights we had done for Anthony, where there were fifty-two lights, one for each of the victims, and then even more were lit. That took less than an hour. For the main memorial, four months later, all they could light were four candles. The families were not even given the chance to place those lights themselves on the altar.

The government officials, of course, were in the main nave of the church. Most of the families were in a side aisle. Finally, while the officials filed out, we were expected to remain standing.

When, later, I tried to find out why the Magnificat had not been included, I was fobbed off with excuses and told the decision had been taken by officials at St Paul's, to keep the length of the service down to fifty minutes. That made me very sad. I was sad for England, that this was the best the country could do to mark this occasion. Why, after four months, would the government decide to impose such a time limit? Who asked for that? Was there someone who was in such a rush that the service couldn't be ten or more minutes longer? In that case, this person should not have been present. He should have gone straight to his next engagement, so that the families could have a service that was worthy of their loved ones.

The Magnificat, if it is sung, takes about two minutes; if it is prayed, about one minute. That was all I asked for. It was not given.

Afterwards, I said to my family, 'Let's just go.' We stayed long enough to discuss the service with the bereaved Ghanaian family, who felt as we did, and to greet the Cardinal of Westminster and the Archbishop of Canterbury, under the canopy. And then enough was enough: I wasn't there for tea and cakes. And so we left.

It was very sad. I regretted even going. I would not have gone if I had known that it was a service meant for the government officials. It wasn't done for the relatives or their loved ones. We were surplus to a state occasion.

I was touched to read later that one boy who had lost his father had refused to attend. His younger sister, Ruby, who was seven years old, presented the Queen with an autumnal bouquet, but Adam Gray, eleven, stayed away because Tony Blair was to be present. This young man, from Ipswich, told his mother that he held the Prime Minister responsible for the Iraq war which, he believed, led to the bombings and the death of his father, Richard, on the Aldgate train.

As we drove home, I reflected that, in a way, my whole life had been a preparation for the foundation which I intended to set up as my son's true memorial. Certainly in the two years before Anthony died, my studies were very much to the point: I took a masters degree in international relations. It seemed natural for me to enrol, because I've always been concerned by world issues. My degree is in French – I spent a year studying in Paris, as part of my course at the University of Ife, which is now the Obafemi Awolowo University in Nigeria. I originally went there to study law. That was quite an achievement, because the tutors were very selective.

I loved the lawyer's clothes as a child: they really looked very dignified. But gradually I realised that what I loved most was the ability to communicate in another language, and I started falling in love with the diplomatic world. I knew I had always had a flair for languages, so I changed courses, and graduated in 1978 with a BA Honours.

Alan and I began our relationship in our penultimate year of university, and it crystallised during national service. We got together simply as part of the camp life. Now he is a senior general practitioner with his own practice in Lagos, currently the president of the Society of Family Physicians of Nigeria, and a former Regional Vice President for Africa of the World Organisation of Family Doctors (WONCA). But back then he was a normal Youth Service Corps doctor, like many others I was in camp with.

Every Nigerian university graduate is expected to participate in the National Youth Service scheme. It is designed to push you out of your comfort zone. You don't stay within your territory: the idea is to see what other cultures can bring. Some people of course try to fix their postings, to engineer a cushy slot for themselves, but that's one thing I didn't do. If you're a medical doctor, you go to some village or other for eleven months; I had a degree in French, so I was despatched as a French teacher, first to a village that had only a little school with a thatched roof – and with more vultures on the premises than students who were willing to learn French! Eventually, I was re-posted as a lecturer to the College of Education in Uyo, which was then a part of Cross River state, now the capital of Akwa Ibom state. It was a long way from the cosmopolitan comforts of Lagos. I was slightly asthmatic, very tiny and fragile, and everybody said, 'Goodness gracious, you can't go there,' but I wanted to see where the posting took me.

In later years, when the children were growing up, I became very active in the National Council of Women's Societies of Nigeria. I also sat on the board of the International Council for Women, whose headquarters were then in Paris. I was part of the Nigerian Women's delegation to Beijing, and also past President of the International Women's Society of Nigeria. It is that experience that I intend to bring to bear as I build up the Anthony Fatayi-Williams Foundation for Peace and Conflict Resolution.

Its purpose is to ask grieving mothers around the world whose hearts have been maimed like mine, by war, by terror, to come together. Let's join hands, let's work for peace, because when you look back, every century has its causes and its problems. The world is like a family – there are conflicts and rows that can only be mended by tolerance and love and mutual understanding.

I think of that photograph which I held in Tavistock Square: it was taken in Lagos to mark twenty-five years of marriage. Alan and I, like every long-married couple, have had our ups and downs. Whenever we had a rough patch, things came back to being better. We were thankful for that, and when twenty-five years came round we said, 'That's an achievement. It deserves to be marked.' We had a church ceremony and then a little get-together. We realised we had become stronger, over the years, than we were when we started out. Clearly our marriage was meant to be. It's not as if it's all been a bed of roses, but, as with everything, you have got to work at it. You cannot give what you don't have, but at least give what you can.

And that is what I keep saying about the peace issue: give what you have. Work at it. It's the same for a family, the same for the world.

This book is one of the ways I intend to do that. I am telling my story to make people think. I had a good teacher: my mother was a wonderful story-teller, and she passed that gift on to her children.

I will never forget the many late evenings we spent listening to her fund of African folktales. The twist to the tales always delivered a moral lesson. There were so many of them that, looking back now, I wonder if she made some up herself as she went along. These folktales had such an impression on our young minds that my sister Teresa made a reader of some of them for each of my children, entitled 'The Singing Fish'.

One of the most intriguing things about these stories is the fact that the animal characters are always represented by the clever tortoise, the gullible dog, the greedy tiger and the foolish sheep or goat. In the human world it was always the wicked King Ogiso, the jealous, wicked queen, the barren wife and the wicked step-mother. Most of all we loved to hear our mother tell stories about the tortoise, because he seemed to be always one step ahead of the other animals – until the day she told us how he got his shell cracked in a chequerboard pattern, when the other animals finally got the better of him.

Story-telling meant that as children we spent more time with our mother, cooking, chatting and drawing from a deep source of wisdom. I have gathered a lot of those stories, told to us by our mother. My children used to want to hear the stories too, and my mum told Anthony many of them when he was growing up. As we got older – and, I think, as the store-house of my mother's stories was gradually emptied – she got us to start telling the stories ourselves. Each one of us took a turn each night and, believe me, this was talent on display!

One of my brothers (I'll spare him the embarrassment by not saying which one!) got the nickname 'Formulator' because we soon realised he was just making up the stories as he went along, looking at the things around him and drawing on them. The Formulator's stories were never-ending, carrying on from one night to the next. He would even compose a song within the story, just like my mother did.

When eventually everyone caught on to his tactics, we had to drag my father in to be the judge of the best story-teller and he always gave that extra incentive when we were lucky enough to get him to participate. When I watch *The Sound of Music* and I see the Von Trapp family's singing scene, I chuckle to myself. That could have been our family because we each had a talent to sing, act, tell stories or dream 'fairytale dreams'.

We gathered outside to tell the stories, in the courtyard. I was the youngest, so at first I was just listening, but when I was old enough to join in, when I was going to primary school, I used to tell them the stories I heard in my lessons, as I could memorise very quickly. We used to use the *Oxford English Reader*. I learnt many poems and parts of plays when I was six, seven, eight, and I still remember them. The first Shakespeare play I learned was *Julius Caesar*, and I know all of Mark Antony's speech. Some people think I am eloquent – if so, it must be a God-given gift. I loved to sit and read as a child, especially Enid Blyton – I read all of the *Famous Five* books. She was my favourite.

The ability to remember clearly, I believe, is a family trait. Anthony had a very good memory. Words and phrases spring up from when I was six years old, and I think, 'Where did that come from?'

All of us were born in West Cameroon, when it was still a part of Nigeria. There was West and East Cameroon before the reunification that gave birth to the Republic of Cameroon, completely separate from Nigeria. So we grew up in the Commonwealth of Nigeria before independence. My father was a businessman, in marketing and hotels.

I was the youngest, and they loved me to bits. I was spoilt – but not spoilt! My brother Ben was just before me in age so we had a very special relationship when we were growing up. We were buddies and we still are. I had grazes on my knees because when he climbed trees I would climb them and share every little tumble. I didn't have anyone else to play with. He would do anything for his dogs, so I had to like them too! To Ben, Anthony was like his son, and Anthony respected and loved Ben to bits.

Childhood was pleasant in spite of the fact that we had a very strict father; now, of course, we value everything he instilled in us. My memories of growing up are linked inextricably with the fun we generated for ourselves. We were content with entertaining ourselves as a family, and we certainly had very close friendships which continue to be our mainstay.

At the age of nine, going on ten, I passed the National Common Entrance exam to go to one of the best secondary schools for girls in Nigeria: St Teresa's College, Ibadan. That was exciting for me, to be at school with a mixed group of girls from all the regions (as they were then known) of Nigeria as well as Cameroon. The blend also cut across all religions, especially Christianity and Islam, even though St Teresa's College was a Catholic school. Some of Nigeria's most successful women, who have held government positions, received their education at St Teresa's.

There was never any reason for discrimination or misunderstanding because of differences in religion. In fact, there was no need for tolerance as we were not made to believe that any difference existed. All the girls, especially those in the boarding house, looked forward to the Muslim feast of Eid-el-Kabir (Sallah) and the slaughtering of rams, because that meant the parents of Muslim girls could visit them. Those who went home for the celebrations would return to school with loads of goodies for everyone else. It was then, and only then, that some of them might return dressed differently, wearing Muslim attire instead of the clothes we saw on a daily basis.

How I pray and wish that things could be this way all round the world, instead of hatred and religious intolerance. Instead, self-appointed religious leaders and elected decision-makers, as well as extremists, are politicising religion and polluting young, vulnerable minds. Even as I write, a priest and dozens of Christians have been killed and churches destroyed in an outbreak of violence that engulfed one of the northern states in Nigeria, during a street protest against the ill-conceived anti-Muslim cartoons published far away in Denmark. Why?

At St Teresa's there was not even a need for tolerance, because there was no tension. We were all just equal members of one group. It was the same when Alan and I decided to marry. My parents didn't mind at all, not for one second, that Alan was Muslim – just so long as I was happy. They wanted me to marry for love.

15

The next few weeks, leading up to Christmas, were very difficult. I was asked to appear on *Songs of Praise*, I believe in November, after a trip to Washington, though it was not broadcast until January. It's a programme I have always loved to watch, for many years. It speaks to my heart, and brings me peace and joy. So when I was asked to do it, I thought, 'This is a way for me to reach out to others and show how I am coping with grief, and what I believe we must do to talk of peace.'

The resolution had been growing stronger and stronger in me that I had to use as many means as possible, every legitimate method, to get my message across. That was the only way my suffering could bring about something positive for other mothers.

Somewhere, among the millions who would see this edition of *Songs of Praise*, there might be one person who was planning an act of violence. If they saw the suffering in my face and heard the pain in my voice, their hearts might be moved. They might say, 'Look what has been done to this woman. Is that what I want to do to another mother like her?' It might inspire them to re-examine their beliefs and look differently at what they were planning to do.

That's why I did it: I wouldn't want anyone to think there was any payment for that appearance, because there wasn't.

For Christmas, I really wanted us to go to Fatima in Portugal. I was feeling utterly out of sorts, and I wanted to disappear to somewhere that no one could find me and where I could find myself.

I really was not sure I could face Christmas without Anthony. I imagined us in the warm and him in the cold, us inside and him outside, us eating and him not eating, us at the table and his seat vacant. When I thought of this, I just wanted to disappear and hide, to go somewhere I could pray all the time, away from television and all the modern world.

I kept saying this, until my two daughters came to me and said, 'Mummy. It is not fair. It is not fair on Anthony. You know he always loved Christmas, whether in Lagos or London. Most of all he loved to come back to Nigeria for Christmas, to share a happy family time with the rest of his larger family and his friends. If we really do love him, we must do what would make him happy. Let's do Christmas the way we're used to. If he is looking down on us, the first place he will want to see us is at home. He won't want to look for us somewhere we have never been before. Why should he be happy to see that we are cutting ourselves off from the world?'

'I know I should be happy,' I said. 'I know I should be thanking God at Christmas time. But I am deeply hurt.'

'But we want to go home,' the girls pleaded. 'We want to go to Lagos, the way we do every time when Anthony is around. And if we did go to Fatima, what would happen when we left? We would still have to go home. We would still have to face that. And what about next year? Some time, we are going to have to face the first Christmas without Anthony – if not in Lagos, then in London.'

I said to myself, 'How silly can I be. It is my girls who are reminding me of how I should be. They taught me that, at Christmas, if I was not happy, then Anthony could not be happy. I am being selfish. I have to think about what my family wants.' That was their wisdom.

In the end we did Christmas properly, with all the trimmings. There was a toast to Anthony during the meal. There were lots of tears, of course, and sadness, but I have a big picture of him in the sitting-room, so he is ever-present. When we came to Christmas pudding, we pulled the crackers and sang, 'We wish you a merry Christmas'. We gathered around that photograph and sang it to him. We could see that famous smile that he had, and it was as if he were beaming back, 'Yeah, happy Christmas, guys.' We could all feel something like that. And I thought, 'We did what we could, Anthony. We're doing this the way you always liked it.'

His favourite part of the turkey was the drumstick and the thigh. I carved it and said, 'OK, this was Anthony's cut. Let's share it.' We all took a piece and put it on our plates, raised our glasses and said, 'For Anthony!'

He had always been the life and soul at Christmas. He made sure he took time off work, because it was such a good break for him – a bit of sunshine in the middle of the English winter! But he would always rush back to work as soon as Christmas was over. He loved buying presents.

I was watching a home video the other day that he shot of everybody opening their presents. Anthony isn't often in the frame, because he was always the video-man. But on a few occasions, his dad managed to get the camera out of his hands, to film him opening his own presents, before he grabbed it again. Mostly, all you can hear is his voice in the background, directing people.

Once, Christmas fell in the middle of Ramadan, the Muslim fasting season. It doesn't happen every time, but once in a while the two overlap. Anthony was about nineteen. There was Alan, with all of this Christmas food around him, and he was fasting. We said to him, 'What are we going to do? We can't all be eating this food around you. It isn't fair.'

But Alan said, 'No, that's fine.'

And you can hear Anthony's voice on the tape, saying, 'Gosh, this guy's tough, man. He's got all this food around him, and he's not eating anything.'

If he is not fasting, Alan celebrates Christmas fully with

his family, because that's the way he was brought up. His mother always celebrated Christmas. She had all the English traditions – puddings, party hats, everything. He never knew any different. And when the feast comes round at the end of Ramadan, Alan holds open house, and his friends share the food we place on the table.

The New Year came, and I remembered a Yoruba saying: you pour cold water in front of you so that you will step on cool ground. And if you have that bowl of cold water, but you don't want to pour it because you're not going to be the one who steps on it, that's very selfish behaviour. It's not going to hurt you to pour the water. You can easily get more. So why don't you pour it? But there are some people who think, 'Why should I be helpful, if I'm not going to feel the benefit?'

Anthony is gone. He has been taken away from me. He has died in a horrific way. Nothing will bring him back, nothing will give me the benefit of that cool water on the ground. But as far as I am concerned, I would be very bitter if I didn't help. I don't want to let the terrorists make me bitter and selfish. I want us to learn from this.

That's why I am asking British society, 'Are we learning from this? Have we gained from it? Are we sure that if tomorrow, God forbid, there is another 7/7, we would be able to do things differently?'

We must ask ourselves these questions every day, at every opportunity. For example, when we see a glimmer of com-promise coming from those who are labelled our enemies, a chink of light, must we close the door and shut it out, or shall we see how we can let the glimmer build into a ray that becomes bright and can reach out to the whole world? We must do this, not just for ourselves and our own children, but for all the other people who will die if we don't make peace.

After all, the people who are making the decisions either way seem to be secure. They will stop at nothing to secure their own lives and those of their families. As anyone would expect, you will not catch the Prime Minister or his children on a London bus, or see the Metropolitan Police Commissioner riding on the Tube. They will not take public transport, but what about the ones who do because they have to?

First families everywhere are secure. Same goes for families of war lords and terrorist leaders. George Bush and Tony Blair, like the leaders of most other governments, can make their decisions, knowing that whatever happens to the people they govern, their own sons and daughters will be safe. I am appealing to Mr Blair, and through him to all leaders, to look at me as a parent, with the same emotions in my heart that I know he feels for his four children. His youngest son is a little boy. Can he not look at that child and see every beloved child the world over in his place? Can he not see how vulnerable he is, just as my Anthony was vulnerable? Of course he can.

I believe that when you are in a position of power, you are duty-bound to lead the people properly; that we all have to account for what we have done in life – if not here, then somewhere else. So why not make the most of your power and position now? Instead of closing our eyes, we need to open them to the realities that stare everyone in the face; instead of stopping your ears, listen. When people are telling you what needs to be done, it's no good pretending that you are right and all of the people are wrong all of the time, because if you didn't have the voters who put you in your position, you wouldn't lead anybody. There would be nobody to preach to and you would have nobody to rule.

To that end, in January 2006, I wanted to meet Tessa Jowell. She is the minister in charge of culture and, to me, culture is much more than art and music: it is about the different ways we live and interact, and how we can embrace each other's way of life, instead of fearing it. It is about going beyond tolerance, to create that atmosphere I loved so much at St Teresa's College, where we didn't have to be taught tolerance, since we felt no difference between any of us.

I sought an appointment with Ms Jowell, to discuss issues that had been on the front burner of my mind: the polarisation of different groups, the shamefully inadequate memorial on the Embankment, the way we have been kept in the dark, the vexed issue of compensation, the unilateral decision not to have a public or independent inquiry – and then of course there was the memorial service on 1 November, which was not nearly as well put together as it should have been, because the organisers did not take into account the feelings of the families. That service was more a government affair, a pat on the back and a 'Well done, good and faithful servants'.

Tessa Jowell had always said that her doors were open to those who wanted to meet her. She arranged meetings with some of the bereaved and the survivors, all of them together, during December 2005. I didn't take advantage of that because I thought it was rather ridiculous to have open day visits, making it look as though it was a special favour. I didn't think that was the way it should go, and anyway on some of those days I wasn't in the UK.

But then I thought, 'Well, two wrongs don't make a right and you don't shake hands with two clenched fists – you have to open your hand to the other person. So as I am standing for peace here, let's find out what's going on.' I phoned her office and I said I wanted to see her, and would follow that up with a normal, protocol letter, saying I was in London and I wanted to discuss a few things. Her assistant asked when I wanted to come, and I told her precisely, because there was a small window when Alan was going to be in the UK too. Eventually, when I called back, we were able to confirm a meeting for a Thursday evening, the day before I was due to leave for Nigeria.

I made my way to her offices, though I didn't have a chance to really look at the building because it was a cold winter's night, and dark. I found my way there, and waited for Alan to join me because he was coming straight from the airport. We went up in the lift to her floor, sat in the waiting room for five minutes, and were ushered in to her office. It was quite modest and tasteful, and she was welcoming.

She had a very listening ear. She listened all through as I spoke, with a look on her face that told me she was absorbed, understanding and feeling what I was saying. She was very gentle. But it is what comes out of the meeting that will matter. I found her to be very much a feeling person, someone who kept on saying: 'I am so pleased to meet with you at last, so happy you could come.'

I said, 'I have to tell you the truth madam: it is me who is bending over backwards to make this meeting happen, because if the bereaved families do not make a move, nobody else does. We seem to be making all the first moves, but if no one moves, then no one will make peace happen. I have to do it, to swallow my hurt and pride, and do whatever it takes. That's why I'm here.'

Ultimately, however, I believe it is not the leaders, but the women, who can make a real difference. As women who grieve, who feel, who touch, who reach out, I think it's time for us to rise up and lead the world in a movement to restore what every religion preaches: peace.

All mothers instinctively know how painful the loss of a child must be. What sorrow could be more than that, to have a mother bury her own child? In traditional African society, they pray all the time that it is the children who bury the parents and not vice versa. I'm sure it's the same worldwide. I believe that we feel more of the pain as women, we grieve more as mothers, and we must bring the power of that emotion to bear upon the world. As the saying goes, the hand that rocks the cradle rules the world.

Even before Anthony's funeral, I knew I had to set up this foundation in his memory. Its aims were clear, but defining them in precise language was not so easy. My ultimate goal is to remove the word 'hatred' from the dictionary.

I had to think long and hard, to set the aims down in

words. As the weeks passed and my friends and family offered constant help and support, I was able to produce a pamphlet, setting out the foundation's 'mission statement'. One breakthrough came when I realised that there were both short-term and long-term goals to be achieved. This is a life-long mission, not something to be placed on a 'To Do' list and ticked off next week; at the same time, it is necessary to start making progress immediately.

I set out the pamphlet with these twin aims in mind. The short-term goals included giving voice to the families of the victims of terrorism, educating young people about the issues that feed violence, and strengthening bonds between divided peoples, especially people (youths) on the fringes of society and the poor.

The open-ended aims were to reach out, through the internet, conferences, concerts, documentaries, study centres and a book of remembrance, to the 'peace constituency', the unseen majority who long for an end to war. It's never easy to boil a headful of ideas down to a handful of bullet points, but when I looked at the final draft, which had been through so many rewritings, I felt it made its points.

TJ is working on one of those aims, the documentary. He told me: 'I am investigating the effects of terrorism on myself and London. My apathy to the issues before Thursday 7 July is shared by too many who will be involved in what is going to happen in the future. Through the experience of what has happened to Anthony, I decided that it was important to comment on the dynamics of terrorism on the home front, and to show how this new world war may be more devastating than any we have had in the past.'

As I finished the pamphlet, I realised that what I needed was a sentence that summarised all our intentions. I found it in the writings of an unconventional philosopher and peace activist, the American Robert Fulghum: 'Peace is not something you wish for, it is something you make, something you do, something you are and something you give away.' The guiding philosophy in all of this is recognising our common humanity and working for world peace.

Several months on, I was able to put the long-term aims into sharper focus with an appeal to the Olympic Committee, through Tessa Jowell. Anthony was killed the day after London won the prestigious right to stage the 2012 Olympic Games. That victory was soured by the 7/7 atrocities, which ran counter to everything the Olympic Games stand for. There would be an immense symbolic value in co-operation between the Olympic Committee and the Anthony Fatayi-Williams Foundation.

Young people must be the focal point for change in the world: that is why I am appealing for the establishment of a youth centre for global peace, understanding and conflict resolution.

To accept this challenge is to invite the whole world to 'sign off' on a peace initiative that will not stop and start at the igniting and dousing of the Olympic flame, but instead will live on from one Olympic season to another. This initiative will embody the principles of the Games, the spirit of London and Londoners, and will ensure that the victims of 7 July live on as the light-bearers for peace in the world.

16

Every night before the seventh of the month, I have trouble
sleeping. I go to bed thinking of Anthony, and wake up thinking of him. It is so every night, but most intensely before the
seventh day of each month.

In February, seven months after he died, I woke tired and
downhearted. Looking out of the window, I gazed across at
Anthony's favourite place in the garden, and I saw a flower
there. It was a variety of white African lily, and it was
blooming gloriously.

Going outside to investigate, I realised that this plant was
exploding with blooms. Lilies will usually have two or three
flowers, sometimes four, but almost never more than five on
the same stalk. This one looked as if there might be more.

I counted the blooms, all of them fully open. Then I
counted them again. I could scarcely believe my eyes. I am a
level-headed woman, but this extraordinary sight was too
much to be a coincidence.

There were seven blooms on the lily.

It was as if Anthony were sending me a sign: 'This is the
seventh month since I was taken from you, Mum, on the
seventh day. And I'm watching over you.'

I took the lily to Mother Benedicta in the Monastery, and
she simply said, 'Glory be to God.' What else was there to
say?

That lily was a reminder to me, a wake-up call: don't ever
stop working in Anthony's memory for the sake of others.

No matter how heavily the grief weighs on me, I have a duty to my son and I cannot fulfil that by lying in bed and heaving heavy sighs. He was a boy with infinite energy for work, and I have to get back to being like him again.

His death will not be in vain, and to make certain of that I must tell his story, to inspire people and to wake up the whole world, to wake up the larger, dormant peace constituency. We cannot pretend that we are not affected by the worsening cycles of violence, we cannot claim it is none of our business, and we certainly cannot be sure that we ourselves and our own beloved families will not fall victim to it. I once thought that way, until violence came to my doorstep and my son was killed.

Now I will use what gifts I have. Thanks to my parents' insistence on education, thanks to the importance my schools placed on poetry and reading, and thanks to the eloquent tongue God gave me, I have been able to give voice to the thoughts that were in millions of minds. I didn't think of myself as an orator when I stood up in Tavistock Square – all I knew was that I was a mother and my heart was hurting terribly. But the media were quick to draw parallels with other famous speeches. A wry smile crosses my lips when I see a national newspaper comparing me with Shakespeare, Churchill or Lincoln. I have written no great plays. I have not led nations through the valley of death to safety. I am just me, little Marie, an ordinary mother.

And then I realise that this is what makes us so strong. There are millions of ordinary mothers, perhaps a billion, perhaps more. Together we have infinitely more power than any playwright, any politician.

Because we are not part of the bureaucratic set-up, governments will try to ignore us. They dismiss our efforts. We are outsiders, and they don't want to let us in. But although I cannot influence world affairs directly, because I am not part of the machinery, I can still stand up, and point to the violence, and say simply: 'This is not right.'

I speak as a mother who has been touched by events that I never dreamt would ever happen to me; as a woman who is nobody's fool; as a daughter who does not believe in violence as a means to an end; as a wife who does respect and obey authority; as a citizen who believes in justice, fairness and the rule of law; as an educated human being who is willing to listen to all the arguments, show respect to my peers and superiors alike, show loyalty to my family, and then commit my judgement: I am all these people, and I am saying as loudly as I can, 'This is not fair. This is unjust. This is not the way the world should be, it is not the way it could be, and it is not the best we can offer, nor is it the best legacy for generations yet unborn.'

I call on all winners of the Nobel peace prize to click on the 'refresh' button of their Laureate screen and select the blinking icon that urges palpable action for peace. The season is here, and the favourable time is now. To whom much is given, much is expected.

Let's try to appeal also to those who are trying to kill and murder and spread terror, and tell them: 'We have to call a truce. There has been evil and wrong-doing on all sides. I don't believe that any people are evil or barbarians or uncivilised people – let's stop, because we are rushing headlong to destruction. Stop, and think, "We need to move forward. You say this way is forward, I have claimed that way is forward . . . but let us listen to the mothers of the world. They say that the way forward is the way that leads to peace. So let us try that road." '

The political commentators say that Osama bin Laden will never go to Camp David with George Bush and discuss peace. They said the same about Yasser Arafat and Binyamin Netanyahu, but those talks happened. It is not beyond imagination that I or someone else could broker some sort of meeting, could transmit the message from one group to the next, and bring them together. All that needs to happen, in reality, is for two men to meet and unclench their fists to shake hands. It can happen, but not if everybody adheres to their hard, straight lines.

The same is true for democratically elected leaders everywhere, especially hardline governments. Please, for the sake of our common humanity, let us come away from the brink and make our pledge to peace. Peace is the one thing that forms a common pillar for our different faiths. Peace is the common denominator.

My message to every political leader is just the same as the one that any good mother would tell her son: to take the lead and to talk to your enemy does not make you weak. It makes you even stronger.

You might be a president or a warlord, but you were once a five-year-old boy. Your advisers and your servants will whisper that you wield maximum power, crowds will acclaim you the ultimate ruler, but you are nothing if you do not have the strength and confidence to look at yourself and say, 'I am not the ultimate power because of who I am and who I was born; I have power because I represent the whole multitude of people, and most especially the ones whose voices I cannot hear, whose pain I cannot bear, and whose misery is untold. And my first duty is to protect them. I must not let them be hurt further, I must not let them die, must not let them be killed in wars and terrorist attacks. I must not let them pay the price for something they are not guilty of.'

Late in 2005, the press reported a rumour that campaigners were plotting to kidnap the Prime Minister's young son. How anyone could dream of doing a thing like that is beyond me: perhaps it was just bravado, the way stupid men will talk after a few drinks. But it was said, and the Prime Minister's response was decisive. However tiny the real threat was, the result was a huge brouhaha. He had imagined how terrible it would be to lose a son, and his reaction, or that of his aides, was furious: the campaigners were sternly warned, 'If you dare come within ten kilometres of Downing Street, you will have only yourselves to blame.'

And I looked at the Prime Minister on television, picking up his young lad, clutching the boy to his heart, his other two sons standing beside him, his daughter, his wife – they made a lovely family. They were going into their house and he looked so proud of his two strapping sons in their suits. I looked at them and I could see my own Anthony as well. They were so well presented.

I thought, if someone were to try to snatch this little boy from his hands, what would he do? Pluck the eyes out of that person and say, 'How dare you!' He would throw himself on to the floor and say, 'Take me first before you take my child.'

This is my message to Mr Blair and all leaders: put yourself in my position. Anthony is my only son. And I lost him, and even more insult has been piled on to my injury by an offer of 'compensation' from the government, which puts a value of £11,000 on his life. Is this the dividend of standing 'shoulder to shoulder'? Is this what human lives have become or should be? In the name of God and all you hold dear, act now, or others will suffer what I have suffered, and what you so dread for yourself.

I will keep saying this, in as many ways as I can, to as many people as will hear me, as long as there is breath in my body. And I will gratefully accept the help and support of those who are willing to give me a platform to plead for peace. I was delighted, then, to receive an invitation in November 2005 from Monsignor William Kerr, executive director of the Pope John Paul II Cultural Center in Washington DC, to attend a dinner and accept the Center's first Legacy Award for Leadership in the name of the late Pope, who had died earlier that year. The other recipient, of the Legacy Award for Peace, was King Abdullah II of the Hashemite Kingdom of Jordan. Monsignor Kerr had stumbled on my radio interview and the committee had decided that the award to me was in recognition of my message of 'hope to the world and commitment to fostering understanding and peace among people of different backgrounds through forgiveness.' Among the very many important personalities present were Cardinal Adam Maida, Governor Marc Racicot and the French Ambassador to the USA, Jean-David Levitte.

I was allowed the privilege of addressing the gathering. I puzzled for a long time about how best to phrase it. I couldn't imitate the style of my Tavistock Square speech: that would not have been appropriate. But I didn't want to deliver a standard, Oscars-style jokes-and-thank yous speech either. I thought about it all the way across the Atlantic, making notes and testing out phrases in my mind. In the end, I decided that my last speech had come from the heart, and my next one should too.

Amid everything else I said was this passionate appeal:

The venerable John Paul II, an advocate for world peace and understanding, said that 'war and terror is an assault on the dignity and the value of life of the other'. He preached the gospel of non-violence as a means of settling differences, as this he said demonstrated a 'recognition of the inestimable dignity and value of the human person'.

Hence my pain and the pain felt around the world by others like me, whose families have been thrown into untold grief through this lack of recognition of the value of human life. How do you justify taking away something, life that you cannot give back, even if you wished to?

I am a mother with a horribly maimed heart, maimed and forever branded by the terrorist attack in London of 7/7 which took the life of my first and only son, Anthony. For my family and for dozens of Anthony's friends, that cut across colour and creed, and indeed for millions of lovely people worldwide, who shared in my pain, it brought the reality of terror right to the doorstep . . . I vowed that Anthony's innocent blood will not be spilled in vain, I vowed that by the grace of God I will dedicate time and contribute my quota to the cause of world peace and mutual understanding in a world where the fear of 'difference' is leading to a cancerous evil growing from years of sedimented hatred, now distilling through its layers the darkest and most unimaginable evil acts and weapons for their perpetration.

Peace cannot be delivered by terrorist attacks nor by war but by seeking to burrow into the depths of our actions, in search for their humanness and justification. This search will hopefully guide us to a greater understanding of the truth of our common humanity.

I cry out for women, for mothers the world over, north, south east, west, whose hearts are bleeding as they watch helplessly over the unnecessary deaths of their children for a cause they do not know or understand. I cry out from a sorrowing mother's heart to women and mothers out there not to allow themselves to be used as bomb-fodder for the destruction of humanity which only they, with the Creator, can ensure. I cry out from the depths of my heart to the perpetrators of this pain . . . Peace is the fruit of love, not hatred and violence.

As I flew home, I thought about the city I had visited, the political hub of the world. It was in Washington that George Bush and his advisers planned the invasion of Iraq, on the trail of weapons of mass destruction that were never found, but it was there too that John Kennedy took his courageous stand during the Cuban Missile Crisis, forcing a belligerent enemy to back down. There was so much more I would have liked to say in Washington, and the themes of many speeches tumbled in my mind as I was carried across the ocean.

Most of all, I wanted to urge the wheeler-dealers and policy brokers of Washington DC to plant an acorn. An acorn is hope for the future. When you plant it, you know you might not be the one to enjoy the shade of the oak that gradually grows. An oak can take centuries to mature. That's good: that means generations yet unborn will enjoy it. We might, we pray, live to experience our dreams come true, but if we don't, that doesn't matter. Anthony planted acorns with all the love he shared. He didn't live to see them grow, but they are growing, every day.

One of those acorns has already shot up to become a sapling. It is the foundation that commemorates him, and it is focused in two areas, in London where I am getting things up and running, and in Nigeria, where I have good contacts and the widest support network of friends and family.

Anthony was a boy from Lagos, so I am working with the Lagos state government to see what we can do to get them involved with the foundation. Because Lagos is the former capital and the country's commercial base, it is a vibrant, multi-cultural city, a microcosm of the world. There are many young people in Lagos, both Muslim and Christian, which of course means it has colossal potential. It also faces tensions, and I am determined to contribute my quota.

Young people everywhere in the world feel alienated and frustrated. The story in Nigeria is no different. Youths, especially those from underprivileged backgrounds, are angry that they are being excluded and short-changed. Youths of the Niger Delta region, with its deep reserves of crude oil, are up in arms because of the glaring injustice of their human condition – one of abject poverty, even though engulfed by fumes of untouchable riches. The Muslim/Christian issue is a factor, but they are also calling for redress for years of neglect, injustice, exploitation and the devastation of the environment. This need not be so, though to address it would take me beyond the confines of this book. What matters right now is this: I am trying to see how best we can reach out to them, through the foundation.

I want to let young people know that there are other ways

of resolving differences: riots and conflict, and the even more dangerous development of hostage-taking in the Niger Delta, are not the answer. In the same vein, today's political leaders will soon find out that the underdog can fast become the top dog in the assymetric power game. Resolution can only come about by sincere, open and ethical dialogue. If leaders step into the shoes of the aggrieved for just a while, we can make progress.

Meanwhile, education is the surest path to peace. Young people who understand global politics, economics and media are far better equipped to influence their peers than the ones who know nothing but hunger, rocks and bombs.

We need to train peace ambassadors who can be exported to other West African countries as well as other parts of the world, because there are many regions of the world that are in constant friction. We are still building and bringing in as many people as possible. My intention is to get the initial projects off the ground, and then get more people in. Members of my family and others from outside – friends in the press, colleagues and a few of my husband's contacts – are helping to get patrons. And other people, complete strangers, make contact all the time, wanting to join the work. There is a lot of interest, even if I just appear on a television programme; six months on, people are still coming up to me and asking what is happening and how they can help.

It has been a lesson to me to witness the good that comes out of my anguish. When I made that now-famous speech, I was very upset, and people were touched, especially the many people who have been down the same road. And my basic philosophy rang true for many too: I was reaching out to the young people who wanted to create violence and misery, a tiny minority in society but one with the potential to damage everything we value. And the vast majority, the peace constituency, saw me reach out, when the natural instinct might have been to condemn; I was stretching out my hands instead of shaking my fists. That struck a chord. People said,

'Yes, we have to focus on the youth, to tackle their problems. How can we turn them around and make them realise they don't have to go down the path to destruction?' This is not something for governments alone. We all need to think and start discussing the issues. We must ask ourselves, what are the legacies of the older generation?

A Muslim extremist might think that Anthony's death was well deserved, even though he was the son of a Muslim, because his mother was a Christian and so was he. That made him the 'other'. They might say, 'We don't care about his death because people like him are polluting the faith. His father was a Muslim and he chose to be a Christian.'

I do feel these thoughts might be going on in people's minds. My simple retort is that marriage combines the aspects that are best in two people, and if the couple come from different religious backgrounds, then it combines the best of two faiths. That is what I want to say to the protestors who think they are expressing justifiable anger by dressing up as suicide bombers, or kitting out toddlers in machine-gun belts. When women contemplate offering themselves to be used as bomb-fodder, that is the epitome of the 'us and them' mind-set, where the enemy is not like us, where difference is paramount, and the 'other' is a creature to be hated and destroyed.

We need to get young people very focused on the idea of what religion really is and what peace is, how much peace is needed in the world. Most suicide bombers have been fairly young people. When I see the photograph of the bus bomber, who was only eighteen, I'm sure that, if I could wake him up from the dead and ask him, 'Why did you do this, why did you kill my son and other people's children?', he would not really be able to explain what cause he was serving. I suspect he was functioning wholly on a highly adulterated emotional level, without the ability to engage his rational mind. That's why education is essential: education about extremism, about terrorism, and about the futility of terror and war. It needs to be part of the curriculum.

Peace is not something that just happens – you have to work at it. It doesn't come on a platter of gold; you've got to want peace, you've got to create it, you've got to have the atmosphere for it, then you can give it out. Instead, the world's scientists are employed to work endlessly at making more efficient and more deadly weapons. Then, the world's spin doctors are paid to work ceaselessly at selling some of these new weapons to the electorate, with names like 'precision bombs' and 'daisy-cutters'. Don't daisy-cutters sound harmless, like a children's game? But there are tens of thousands of children who will never play games again because of them.

These things are evil. Evil has an opposite, and human beings are just as capable of it. It is called 'good'. Can we not find a way?

17

The first major event to be taken on by the AFW Foundation could easily have become an anti-climax. In collaboration with the Lagos state government, we were hosting a forum for young people: Martin Luther King III was due to deliver a speech on non-violence and conflict resolution, to 500 youngsters at the Nigerian Institute of International Affairs in Lagos at the end of March.

Unforeseen circumstances prevented his visit, but we didn't cancel the event, because the young people were so keen. So in a great rush we got Professor Gabriel Olusanya, the former ambassador to France, to give the lecture. He is a scholar of history and classics, and a former director general of the Nigerian Institute of International Affairs.

An interactive session with the young people was anchored by Nigeria's leading mathematician and a former university vice chancellor, Professor Grace Alele-Williams. The state governor, Bola Ahmed Tinubu, and his wife, the deputy governor and other dignatories and teachers were present, lending their voices to the clarion call for peace. I was especially proud as Lauretta and her friend Sonia sang 'Bridge over Troubled Water' and 'Make me a Channel of Your Peace'.

We are planning to launch the foundation formally in July, but when this moment came we thought, 'We can't let this opportunity pass. We have to do it.'

So even without Martin Luther King III, we achieved something special. The interactive session with the youngsters allowed them to speak out from their hearts.

One of the boys from Corona secondary school re-enacted the 'I Have a Dream' speech by Martin Luther King, and one of the girls from Vivian Fowler Memorial College wrote a piece called 'For Humanity', which warned: 'Peace is not an option.' Its theme was that we don't get to know each other enough. We don't tolerate easily and we're not ready enough to open up. We should be talking.

She ended her wonderful presentation with a quotation from Dwight D. Eisenhower: 'I believe that the common people in the long run are going to do more to promote peace than our governments. Indeed I think that people want peace so much that one of these days, governments had better get out of the way and let them have it.'

The general consensus in the end was that young people feel marginalised and unappreciated and that they don't have a future, and that this can drive them into violence.

The principal of the Muslim school, Al Furquaan, is an old schoolfriend of mine, Tawakalitu. We were classmates at St Teresa's College together. She insisted she was ready to forge a partnership with the foundation, to go out and tell the world that there is no verse in the Koran that orders people to commit violence or kill in the name of Allah. She was ready to do whatever she had to do to get that message across. 'Marie is my friend,' she told the children, 'Marie is my colleague and we went to school together. She is a Catholic and I am a Muslim, but we both believe in the same thing: peace.'

All the children, Muslim and Christian, mingled at the end of the session, and ate the same food. Our aim was to start a multi-faith dialogue, and we did that in the most literal way. In future, we hope to take it to higher levels through the AFWF sponsored project, 'Dialogue – the major road to peace'.

All my classmates who still live in Lagos were there, both

Muslim and Christian. We were a little bunch at school and we kept together. Since Anthony died we have come back together, very strongly, and we remember the old days in St Teresa's.

We had always kept in touch, and I would hear that one old friend was doing this or that, and another was getting married, but we hadn't seen a lot of each other until last year. Occasionally there were reunion meetings, but I wasn't very often able to attend them.

There was a little get-together a couple of years ago, just for my class, and we all enjoyed it – it was great to see everybody and catch up on each other's news, and of course we promised we would do it much more often. But that didn't happen, until the news was released that my son had been killed. And then every one of them has contacted me and we're like a family now.

They have been so strong for me, and so generous with their time, sitting with me and crying with and praying for me – it's like stepping back in time. Many of my university friends have made contact too, and they were at the lecture. Anthony's death came as such a terrible shock to all of them, partly because I was among the first of my peers to become a mother.

They are giving me as much support as they can, with all their love. It reminds me of what I always said, that Anthony had many mothers. We are a family of friends, with no intolerance of our differences.

Even as I write, one of Anthony's special friends, Yinka, has come to visit me. It took him this long to come because he could not understand why this had to happen to Anthony. I was worried for him, as he is quite a sensitive young man who had developed a real bond with Anthony. But ironically I found strength from him when he looked at me and said, 'Auntie, I had a dream a month or so ago, and I saw Anthony. He was just as I used to know him, happy, smiling and behaving just the way he used to do. So I know God is taking care of him and he is in a good place.'

To Yinka this was more than just a dream – it was Anthony's way of reassuring him that all is well.

Lauretta and Aisha have known love and support from their friends. Lauretta and her friends are setting out in June, with the kind support of her principal and house mistress, to swim the equivalent of the English Channel in the school swimming pool. That means 1,325 laps. Her friends in her house took the sponsorship forms home and found sponsors at 50p or £1 per lap, for however many laps. 'I'll try my best, Mummy, and do as many as possible,' she promised. The event was due to take place as this book went to the printers.

The other thing she was organising was quite ambitious – a fashion show with a peace theme. She chose that idea because, as she said, 'My brother was a very fashionable guy. He liked music and he was very into fashion, so for the first anniversary I want to do something that captures that mood, something that will celebrate his life, but with a clear message.'

She came up with the concept of a fashion show featuring musical intervals, skits and poems for year end. She wants it to appeal to younger people across race, colour and creed, as well as to Anthony's friends and her sister, friends and cousins, who will model the clothes. If all goes to plan, the outfits themselves will be loaned by the designers. Lauretta is striving to put her best foot forward for the love of her brother Anthony, in a way that would make him proud.

I am striving too. I face inner challenges every day. If you ask me what I have learned since Anthony's death, first of all I believe there is strength in love and most of all in family love. Love comes from outside and love comes from within, but most of all the strongest love is the love of your family. Whichever way I turn, their love surrounds me. I face to my front, there's love; I turn around, there's love; I go left or right, there's love. If I flop, I flop into somebody's arms. If I fall, there is something there: it's love. And then I look up, and I know that God is not an evil God. Everyone around me shows me love, and I find strength from that.

I prayed so hard for Anthony, in the days when he was missing, but if anyone should think my prayers were in vain, they are wrong. If I believed that, then I wouldn't be here today. People ask how I can still hold on to my faith and think that God heard my prayers if Anthony was not one of those who stumbled from the wreckage, if he was not one of those who got off the bus before the bomb exploded, if he was one of those who boarded it in the first place. My answer is that God did hear my prayers, and answered them in his way. He allowed Anthony to go in this way to show the world the futility of terrorism.

A day or two ago, the front page of an international daily paper carried a disturbing photo of an elderly Iraqi woman, her face contorted in distress and her arms stretching out in desolation. She was sitting on the twisted remains of a burnt-out car or bus, seeking for some lost loved one. Her pain and desolation is real and human too. After each tragedy people always ask why? Is there a God? Can I forgive and accept all this injustice and pain being exhibited with reckless abandon in the world today? Why me?

One of the questions I hear frequently is about forgiveness. People want to know if I have forgiven Anthony's killers. It is a deep complex question worthy of a book in itself. Even though this isn't that book, the question naturally provokes contemplation. It is not an easy path to tread but other paths lead to far worse places – hate, revenge and destruction.

Forgiveness is a gift that does not come 'off the peg', but we have to be able to forgive, or we will hurt ourselves doubly. Certainly I do not want to give someone who has hurt me badly already, the sardonic joy of my continued pain, brought on by my wilful extension of it through hatred. I would rather draw on the work of the long-suffering Pope John Paul II, who reached out to all peoples of the world with his message for peace and co-operation and understanding. He said peace rests on twin pillars: commitment to justice and readiness to forgive. His call to young people was that they were not to be afraid of being saints of the third millennium.

All the young, innocent victims of 7/7, of 9/11, and of all the other atrocities worldwide, must be slowly forming into a band of saints for the new millennium. It is up to us to ensure that they did not die in vain, that some good comes out of this evil, to bring about justice, understanding, tolerance, respect for human life and human dignity, and above all peace in the world.

Shakespeare wrote 'The quality of mercy is not strained, it droppeth like gentle rain from heaven upon the earth, it is twice blessed. It blesseth him that gives and him that takes.' This was a verse we were forced to memorise as kids when we read *The Merchant of Venice*. It always came in handy when you found yourself in serious trouble with a friend, for having sold out or for some other misdemeanour. You pleaded in this most elaborate manner for mercy and most times it worked. Now, as I ponder on forgiveness, it all comes flooding back. But unfortunately for the suicide bomber, he cannot partake of this blessing as he cannot put back the hands of the clock.

For my part, I am blessed as I leave him to God's justice, even as I think of what he did to my Anthony: the agony of the bomb-blast; his precious life blood spilt on the street; his perhaps tattered clothes on one who cared so much about his appearance; the abandonment of his gym-fit body in an unacceptable, temporary mortuary of canopies, all forlorn with no warm clothes or hot meal or warm bed to go to – worse off than the beggar he gave his last pound to? Then my mind takes flight and the deep wounds inflicted in my heart reopen.

I have to will myself to go against the grain of this negative slide and psyche myself to think loving thoughts. Slowly I feel the coolness of joyful recollections and cherished memories, of good times, cherished moments and true love shared. Grief gives way to faith, hope and love. I can never emphasise enough that hatred will only continue to beget even more hatred, and the vicious cycle of killing will continue for as long as we freely choose evil over good.

If you ask me what I have learned since Anthony's death, it is that above all, there is strength in love and more so in family love. This is the love and support I have received and cherished from my immediate and extended family, from Anthony's friends that cut across colour and creed, and from kind-hearted and loving individuals worldwide, religious and secular, who have reached out to me in their individual and special ways. So I am certain that the love of Anthony will forever burn bright in our hearts and so the sun will shine again and I can face tomorrow. Even though his family think Anthony left too soon, we wrote on his tombstone:

Anthony Adebayo Issa Omoregie FATAYI-WILLIAMS

> To Live in the Hearts
> Of those that Love You
> Is to Live Forever

Then on the foot slab we engraved the logo of the AFW Foundation and then extracts of the St Francis prayer for Peace:

> Lord, make me an instrument of your peace
> Where there is sadness and hatred
> Let me sow Joy and Love
> Where there is injury, pardon
> For it is in pardoning
> That we are pardoned
> It is in giving that we receive
> It is in dying that we are born to eternal life.

What is life, we may ask? We are born only to die? No: we must each try to make the most of our existence and that of others. From Anthony's friends I gathered he didn't want to talk too much about life after. He must have thought, as all of us did, that at least he would outlive his parents, but alas!

He said the present will soon become the future – there's food for thought. He left behind some practical values: he disciplined his mind and body through honest hard work, healthy eating patterns, exercise and the desire to learn. He strived to see the good in others because of his conviction that there is good in everyone and you only had to make an effort to look hard and with an open mind. He hurt very easily and loved much, always with a smile.

In a one-liner personal résumé he put up in the internet he wrote 'Our greatest glory consists not, in never falling, but in rising every time we fall'. How much more human can you get? This is my Anthony.

I hope I have been able to convey how much my Anthony was loved and how deeply he is missed. This has not been an easy task for me. What I do hope for everyone who reads this book is that Anthony's story will serve as a reminder: give all the love you can, and be glad and thankful for all the love you get. All through his life he gave love – he treated his aunties as extra mothers, his sisters and cousins as best friends, his pals as brothers and sisters, his uncles as extra fathers, even the beggars as some mother's lost son. We will carry him with us in our hearts for all of our lives, and we'll be inspired by his memory to love and be loved.

If anyone who has come to know Anthony through this book feels inspired to also reach out to friends, family and others alike, then Anthony's magical personality will still be spreading happiness. He gave us the best legacy in the world: love.

THE RUNNERS' REPAIR MANUAL

A Complete Program for Diagnosing and Treating Your Foot, Leg and Back Problems

by Dr. Murray F. Weisenfeld
with Barbara Burr

W. H. ALLEN · LONDON
A Howard & Wyndham Company
1981

To my wife Shirley who makes the sun shine.
To those runners who share their agonies and
ecstasies with me.
To Dr. and Mrs. R. O. Schuster who made it possible.

Printed and bound in Great Britain by
Biddles Ltd, Guildford, Surrey
for the Publishers, W. H. Allen & Co. Ltd,
44 Hill Street, London W1X 8LB

ISBN 0 491 02934 9

Exercise illustrations by Lori Weisenfeld
Technical illustrations by Gary Tong

Acknowledgments

We want to thank all the runners and doctors and other people who helped us write this book.

Thanks to the doctors who contributed so much—Dr. Stanley Roman, osteopath; Dr. Seymour (Mac) Goldstein, chiropractor; Dr. Richard Schuster and Dr. Dennis Richard, podiatrists; Dr. Louis Galli and Dr. Josef Geldwert, podiatrists; and Dr. Ed Colt, endocrinologist. And a special thanks to Dr. George Sheehan, who has done so much for sports medicine. He also sent my co-author to me when she had an injury—and that's how this book got started.

Thanks to Melissa Hayden for her expert help on exercises and body-training.

Thanks to Mitch Maslin for his advice on shoes, and to Bob Glover, an expert on training runners, among other things.

Thanks to our invaluable secretary, Lyn Palter.

Thanks to marathon coordinator Allan Steinfeld, who gave us valuable statistics and insights on the New York City Marathon.

Thanks to my patients who gave their time and knowledge to the book—Dick Traum, Molly Colgan, Jane Killion, Barbara Backer, Nancy Tighe, and Kathy and Bill Horton.

A special thanks to my patients/friends who posed for the cover picture—Michael Cleary, Fritz Mueller, Fred Lebow, Jane Killion, Laurie McBride, and George Klas.

Contents

Foreword About the Evolution of the Foot

The evolution of man's foot is a history of constant change in function and form. The foot as we know it is a relative newcomer in terms of evolutionary time—and that's usually the problem.

Man's foot was not originally designed for walking, much less running long distances. The modern foot evolved out of the fin of some primordial fish and these fins pointed backward. Contrary to what most believe, fins are used more for stability in the water than for locomotion. Locomotion was a function of the tail and is still partly a function of the lower spine in most creatures, including man.

These fins ultimately evolved into fin-feet of amphibians. They pointed more sideways and functioned like oars of a boat in water—and on land—and were not considered maximally efficient movers in either environment.

The reptile that evolved out of the amphibian developed the first recognizable "ankle," "knee" and "hip" joints. It was capable of lifting the body off the ground and while the leg still pointed more sideways than forward, the feet had the capability of rotating in the forward direction. Locomotion was primarily the function of the leg but this is the first time feet appear to get into the act of locomotion. In the previous amphibian stage, the feet were little more than base plates for the leg.

Out of the reptile followed the early mammal with feet and legs that pointed almost completely forward. It is the mammalian foot that is most pertinent in this context. Some authorities—especially Dudley Morton of the now famous

Morton's foot—feel that the characteristics of early mammalian feet and many mammalian characteristics for that
matter, were intimately associated with the arboreal environment—trees and underbrush. The structure of these early
mammalian feet certainly suggests some form of tree adaptation. These were probably rather generalized feet adapting
somewhat to both ground and "branch" surfaces but probably not well adapted to either.

Apparently at this time in mammalian evolution something
less than a hundred million years ago, some group of early
mammals "chose" the tree environment for permanent habitation. They adapted to the tree environment for tens of millions of years and gave rise to all manner of monkeys and
apes, including man's ancestors. During this very considerable
evolutionary time span, the foot of man's ancestors became
highly adapted to the tree environment.

Before mentioning the influence of the tree environment on
the human foot, we cannot completely dismiss those other
mammals who chose not to evolve in the trees, but adapted
to the ground instead. While they are not in man's lineage,
they have in general a much longer history of foot adaptation
to the ground and are more completely adapted to the ground
than the feet of man. Not that any of us would want to run
around on paws or hooves, but an awareness of this kind of
development and how they got there is often helpful to doctors in treating people with foot problems, particularly running foot problems.

Concerning the influence of the tree in the evolution of the
human foot: We can imagine that if we were to climb or live
in trees, it would be much easier if we had a pair of strong
hands where we now have feet. While very few of us have
reason to think this way, this is just what nature provided
our ancestors with during those tens of millions of years of
tree habitation. Anthropologists actually describe our primate
ancestors as being "fourhanded."

The grasping foot was absolutely essential for survival in
the trees. This is another way of saying that it was also one

of the elements for development in the manlike direction. The grasping foot permitted the creature to squat on branches without falling out. With this secure perch, it could begin to reach out for food. Here we see the importance of grasping feet in developing different capabilities in the fore limbs and rear limbs. Reaching led to standing and holding. This, in turn, led to the first bipedal steps on the tops of branches. There is no question that with grasping hands and feet that man's ancestors could walk four-legged quite easily on the tops of branches. However, the ability to walk on two feet had a survival advantage in liberating the arms for other uses. We are inclined to think that those primitive two-legged "first steps" might have been running steps, since it is easier to maintain balance with a bit of speed.

The freeing of the hands and the ability to reach made way for an additional mode of locomotion—swinging (brachiation). Hanging and swinging under a branch tended to straighten the basically four-legged body and was a preadaptation for development in the erect bipedal direction that followed.

It seems like a paradox that the highly specialized foot characteristics that were so essential for survival in the trees and for the continued evolution of man's ancestors were rather incompatible for the use to which they would someday be put. For example, the foot was structured for a generally round surface and for this the foot had to be extremely flexible. The four outer toes were used as "wrap around" hooks and tended to be long. The first toe (the big toe) served as "back up" for the grasp. It was not all that necessary so it remained short.

The roundness of branches induced curves, slants and twists into the foot segments. This can be visualized if the relaxed hand is placed palm down on a table. Note the slant of the four outer knuckles and the low position of the first knuckle. Notice how the fingers are curved and the fingers and fingernails seem to lay a bit on the side—and how the first finger and its nail lay in the opposite direction.

And traces of tree-adapting characteristics, as seen in the

hand for example, must be discarded before a foot can function well on the ground. Unfortunately, nature is slow to adapt structures to new function.

Authorities do not agree as to when man's ancestors came out of the trees. Estimates range from twelve million years ago to twenty-five million years ago or even more. No matter. The only thing that is reasonably certain is that there has not been enough time (plus a few other factors) to eliminate all traces of tree adaptation in the human foot. Or, as the anthropologists stated, man's foot is not yet completely adapted to the ground. Only a portion of the population has been endowed with well ground-adapted feet. These people, athletes and non-athletes alike, have less foot problems than most.

Fortunately, foot characteristics that were so useful to our tree-dwelling ancestors and such a problem to modern man, can be recognized as imbalances and properly dealt with, along with the secondary annoyances, the corns, calluses, blisters, et cetera.

Modern living is another factor that contributes to foot problems. The modern individual at work or at leisure is often apt to spend more time on his feet than primitive man. Take for instance the runners who have burst on the scene during the early 70s and show every indication of staying. It is nothing for them to run anywhere from a few miles a week to 150 miles a week, and all this is compounded by hard flat surfaces and sometimes questionable shoes.

But that is what this book is all about.

There are very few doctors who have treated as many athletes, including dancers, as the author of this book—which, in a way, speaks for itself. Besides, he's a fine gentleman.

Richard O. Schuster, D.P.M.

PART ONE

1

"I Tried Running Once and I Didn't Like It"

The Podiatrist's Pain-Free, Injury-Free Way to Start Running

If you haven't started running yet, or you sort-of-started but stopped, then you've got an advantage over a lot of people. Most people don't consult a podiatrist until after they've been running a while—running wrong—and they've got an injury. Now, by reading this book, you're "seeing a podiatrist" before you start—so you can start running right.

I'm not the least bit interested in telling you how to become the fastest runner on your block, or how to increase your mileage as quickly as possible. I just want to save you from the most common mistakes beginners make—mistakes that cause pain and delays in the first few months of running.

In running, an "injury" is not necessarily a twisted kneecap or a broken bone, as it is in other sports. A running injury could be a strained or pulled muscle. It could be a bone in the foot that's bruised from running on hard pavement. It could be a back pain you get because one leg is slightly longer than the other. Weaknesses in your body show up during running. After all, no body's perfect, and running five or six

or ten miles can bring out a problem in your feet, legs or back.

But everything in life is a trade-off. You can stay home and keep your feet comfortable. Or you can go out and run and develop a foot problem (which is probably correctable), and also develop firmer muscles, healthier complexion, more energy and stamina and a better disposition.

Bob Glover says many runner's injuries are "diseases of excellence," which I think is very apt.

What I want to do is help prevent the "diseases of ignorance"—injuries you can avoid, if you learn to run properly. You can avoid these unnecessary injuries by following a very simple four-step program that starts you running right.

First of all, I want to correct some wrong ideas you may have. A lot of people don't get started because of all the stuff their running friends tell them. For instance:

- Don't run until you've spent $175 for a stress test.
- Get yourself some $50 running shoes, before you even know if you're going to like the sport.
- Bounce out of bed at 6 A.M. and stretch your body; then go out for a brisk morning run. (Even though your body normally feels about as stretchy as an old log at that hour.)

First, what about a stress test?

In a stress test, your body's responses are measured as you jog on a treadmill or pedal a bike. Many Y's give stress tests, or you can find a local hospital that has a sports medicine division, or a cardiologist who does stress testing.

A stress test is especially recommended if you're very overweight, or have been sedentary, or if you're over forty, or if anything in your medical history indicates heart problems. The American College of Sports Medicine says you should *not* automatically take a stress test; you should ask your doctor if you need one.

But my experience is, most people won't get around to asking their doctors. They keep putting off the visit and they never start running. That's why I feel that if you're moderately out of shape, like most of us before running, you should simply start jogging/walking—the easy-does-it way (which means enjoy yourself). Listen to your body and trust yourself.

I'll give you the basic rules in four lines. Then we'll discuss them a little.

RULE 1: Wear any firm, low-heeled shoes.

RULE 2: Do ten minutes of stretching and strengthening exercises before and after your walk/run session.

RULE 3: Stay in motion fifteen to twenty minutes—jogging or walking.

RULE 4: Do this three times a week—preferably with a day's rest in between each day of running.

Follow these rules and you'll get a good start. After two or three or four weeks, your body will be adjusted to running, and you'll feel like increasing the amount of time you spend running each day. And the number of days you run each week.

At that point, you're ready to buy the right shoes. And this is very important. The right shoes are part of your injury-avoiding strategy, throughout your running career. Chapter 3 will tell you how to select the right shoes for you. And it gives you a checklist to take with you to the shoe store.

Another thing you should do, after your first few weeks, is to read chapter 2 "How to Run Right and Hurt Less." Because, as you start increasing your mileage, where you run and how you run become very important. The wrong running style can cause injuries. Running on the wrong kind of road can cause injuries. But that's not until later, when you're up to a few miles a day.

Right now, let's get back to your beginner's rules and explain them a bit more.

RULE 1: *What to wear.* Dress in layers. For instance, a light sweater with a jacket over it. You heat up when you run,

and then you can take off your jacket and tie it around your waist. Wear any firm, low-heeled shoes like sneakers, work shoes, whatever. Of course, running shoes are ideal. But for the first few weeks, you won't be running long distances—so running shoes are not absolutely essential.

RULE 2: *Exercising.* If you don't do your stretching and strengthening exercises, you'll probably get an injury. It's that simple.

Why do you have to stretch? Because running tightens up the muscles in your lower back and the back of your legs. And tight muscles become stiff, tense and painful.

Why do you have to do strengthening exercises? Because running strengthens the back-of-leg muscles much more than it does the front muscles. After you've been running a while, your front leg muscles are relatively weak and prone to injury. Also, your abdominal muscles are weak, compared to your back muscles. So you can get lower-back pains.

The Weisenfeld Workout I give you in the exercise chapter are eight basic exercises I recommend for every runner. This workout is especially important for beginners, because your muscles are more out of shape and more prone to injury. Do the complete workout before you go out to run and do it again when you get back. It takes only a few minutes, and it will protect most beginners from injuries.

A few runners will still get some pains and problems, even if they do this basic workout—because they have a foot imbalance or other physical problem. So I've also given you special exercises for special problems. If you do get a pain, read the section on your injury. It will tell you which exercises to do.

RULE 3: *Jogging/Walking.* The general rule is, just stay in motion for fifteen to twenty minutes—jogging and walking, as your body and feelings direct. For example, you can jog one block, then walk half a block. Jog another block, then walk half a block.

After a week or so, you may feel like running more. You'll want to jog two blocks and walk half a block. Then you'll be

jogging four blocks and walking half a block. Eventually, you'll be jogging easily for a full twenty minutes—always at your own pace.

While we're at it, let's talk about pace, or speed of jogging. Always jog at the speed that lets you talk without huffing and puffing. It's good to jog with a friend, so you can talk as you go along. But if one person is a faster runner, you should both jog at the slower person's pace. Or you should jog separately.

I meet so many women who run with their husbands or boyfriends, and the man pushes the woman beyond her natural pace. Don't fall into this trap. It not only ruins the woman's pleasure in the run; it can cause an injury. Not to mention a fight.

The right pace is a "talking" pace. You should be able to talk as easily as if you were sitting at home in a chair. If you start huffing, jog slower or walk. Resume jogging when you can talk without breathing hard. If you're jogging alone, talk aloud to yourself now and then, just to check your breathing.

It's nice to bring your dog along, if you can't find a friend. Then you can talk to your dog. Some people start running with a dog because they're embarrassed to be out running. They think all runners are lean and muscular, so they don't dare appear in running clothes with a potbelly. That's fine. Make it easy for yourself. Just wear your regular jeans or slacks and pretend you're taking your dog for a walk. You'll start to see other less-than-perfect bodies out running. And you'll start to get a good feeling, seeing them. You have a feeling of pride and fellowship with all these other people who are out doing something good for their lives. Just as you are.

RULE 4: *How often to run.* Run three times a week for the first two or three weeks, or longer. Add another running day to your week when you really feel ready for it—not when your ego tells you that you should. It's hard to give a rule for how quickly you should increase your running days. But it's usually better to under-do rather than over-do. I know a lot of people who've "started" running three or four times— because they overdid it and had to rest and start again.

When Do You Stop Being a Beginner?

I'd say when you can jog twenty minutes comfortably and without walking . . . and do this four times a week . . . then you're no longer a beginner.

When are you a runner instead of a jogger? It's up to you. I've heard people specify X minutes per mile for jogging and Y minutes per mile for running. I'll let someone else argue about that. If you feel like you're running, then you're running.

You'll find you pass through your beginner stage naturally, just by increasing the time you spend running, as your body feels ready for it.

Some days, you're so full of energy, you feel like you're flying. The run doesn't seem to take any energy; in fact, it gives you energy, and you're feeling good the rest of the day and looking forward to tomorrow's run. Don't be surprised if tomorrow's run is a downer. You've just hit a small peak, and after a peak, you always go down. Just rest the next day —either skip your run or take it slow and easy. And accept that this is normal. Your body will recover and you'll hit another peak. This is how you make progress.

Serious, advanced runners plan their peaks. They train toward a few big races a year and plan their training so they'll hit a peak on the day of the race. After the peak, their performance is down again for a while. Then they slowly build up to the next peak.

So just keep steadily running and resting, and soon you'll get interested in counting the miles and thinking about entering a race.

At this point, read chapter 2, "How to Run Right and Hurt Less." As I said earlier, the *way* you run and *where* you run can make all the difference in staying injury-free.

In preparing this book, I had a roundtable discussion with several of my patients. And most of them found that their injuries showed up when they started running four or five miles on a fairly regular basis. Here's where you really have to pay attention to your running style. Run with other people

—especially experienced runners—and ask them to correct any errors you're making.

Of course, you may get some injuries, no matter how careful you are and how correctly you run. As I said, no body's perfect, and running for miles a day can put stress on your muscles and structure.

So the best you can do is minimize any injury. As soon as you start feeling pain, run slower. If it doesn't go away, stop running. Go home and consult the "Injuries" section of this book, and learn how to handle the problem before it gets serious.

About the only pain you can safely run through is a side stitch. It helps if you slow down and do some deep diaphragm breathing. This helps relax the stitch. Another remedy is to shout "HA!". I mean really shout. Squeeze the air out of your lungs with a short, forceful yell.

After you've been running a few months, and increasing your mileage, it's fun to start planning for a race. For instance, one runner I know, Kathleen Jordan, started running in January. She set a goal right away—to run the L'Eggs Mini-Marathon in June. That's 6.2 miles. Kathleen is under thirty and in good health, and she did achieve her goal with no problem. She ran the race with her sister-in-law, who had been running for a year and a half but is fifteen years older. The younger woman ran a faster race, but they both had a fine time.

So let your body be your guide, as to when you want to start training for a race. Races are stimulating and sociable and a lot of fun, and I encourage you to do them. But I can't teach you how. There are a lot of books and articles in the runner's magazines that will give you tips on training for races. In this book, I just want to teach you to run properly so you'll stay injury-free.

Don't increase your mileage too soon. Your enthusiasm and your cardiovascular capacity increase faster than your muscular strength and flexibility.

Along about the third day, or the tenth or fourteenth day, you may start feeling uncontrollably good. You're delighted with your health and vigor and a love of exercise that you never knew you had. Suddenly, there's no limit to how much energy you have and how far you can run! Overnight, you've doubled your distance, and you're puffing along at high speed, your face red and your heart pounding.

Next day, your legs are too stiff to walk on when you get out of bed. You're tired, depressed, your muscles are sore and you feel like an idiot for overdoing it—acting like a kid in a candy store.

Well, lots of people make this mistake. But you don't have to. In the long run, you'll get more exercise and you'll advance faster if you increase slowly and gradually.

As I said, your cardiovascular system improves a lot faster than your muscular system. We still don't know exactly what happens, physiologically, when a person overtrains. But we do know that the body protests and you feel rotten and you hold yourself back on the road to better health.

Here's a horrible example of how not to start running.

One of my patients started running in February, 1978. The day before he started, he was a two-pack-a-day smoker and twenty pounds overweight. So he stopped smoking and started running. So far so good. Then he became a born-again runner. He was turned on by the thrill and pleasure of running, of feeling his body change and come alive. He got that glorious desire to run as much as he could. He wasn't working at the time, so he devoted all his time to running, stretching, dieting and resting. He ran from upper Manhattan down to the World Trade Center in the morning and loved every block of it. He ran to the unemployment office. He followed the Marathon Training Program a friend gave him.

Yes, he decided to run the New York City Marathon in October—having just started running in February.

He ran the marathon. That was October, 1978. Nearly a year later, he still wasn't back into running on a steady basis.

Right after the marathon, he got the "I don't wanna run"

blues that so many overstressed runners get. That lasted a few months. He ran some more and got a groin pull. His feet and legs kept bothering him. He still considers himself a runner and will probably get back to it. But look at all the months he's lost. Look at the price he's paid, just to run those glorious 26.2 miles of the marathon. He would have run more if he'd gone slower.

You probably won't overdo to this extent.

But many people do the same thing on a smaller scale. They run too far before they're ready, and then they get aches, pains and injuries and they slow down their running progress.

So be smart. Let your progress come naturally. Don't push it. As they say, don't push the river, it flows by itself. And you grow by yourself. Have you ever seen a flower pushing itself to grow faster?

It isn't necessary.

You'll probably hear the general rule that it's safe to increase your mileage 10 percent a week. This is okay as a general rule. But you may find it's too much for you, some weeks. If you're under pressure on the job, and you start putting pressure on your running—pushing yourself to increase your distance each week—you'll probably catch a cold or pull a muscle or start getting some of the other symptoms of overstress—like aching legs, lack of interest in running, irritability, tiredness without being able to sleep.

Please, be smart. Learn your own body language and listen to it, throughout your running career.

If you have tried running before, and didn't like it, it's probably because you followed the good old American way of exercise which is "go out and kill yourself." It's no good unless it hurts.

I'm not an expert on Eastern and Western philosophies, but I have taken some yoga. And I was very impressed by one thing they taught us. They told us to take the position we were practicing and stretch to the degree that was comfortable for us. Then hold it in that comfortable position.

Did you ever hear anything so revolutionary?

Be *comfortable*? In an exercise class? Don't push yourself, don't hurt yourself, let your body be your guide? I was shocked. And so relieved.

And then I realized a commonsense thing: if you enjoy your exercise today, you'll exercise again tomorrow. If you hate your exercise because you're pushing yourself, you'll eventually find a reason to stop the exercise—whether it's running or pushups or anything else.

I also discovered, in my yoga class, that if you stretch to the limit of your comfort, your comfort-limit stretches. A few classes later, you feel comfortable stretching farther.

Running is like that.

If you jog as much as is comfortable for two weeks, then at the end of two weeks your comfortable jogging-range will naturally be greater. Those yogis learned a thing or two about the human body, over the centuries. A lot more than the drill sergeant in the gym class you took as a kid or as an adult.

How do you learn to trust yourself? By listening to your body. If you're like most of us, your body has to go to extraordinary extremes to get your attention—like giving you a cold or an ulcer or a pulled muscle. Use running as an opportunity to start getting smart. Start listening to the quieter clues your body is giving you—like irritable fatigue (as opposed to pleasant fatigue)—sleeplessness—hard, brutal soreness, as opposed to pleasant soreness.

This "trust yourself" technique is the secret of remaining injury-free as you go on in running. The runner who pushes himself beyond his limit is the one who gets injuries. Say you've advanced to the point where you're comfortably running five or six miles a day. One week, you start feeling your oats and you push it up to ten miles a day, on a regular basis. That's when I'll expect to see you in my office with runner's knee or Achilles tendonitis or any one of the injuries runners afflict themselves with.

So get out, get started and enjoy. Just remember the slogan of smart runners: Easy does it. But do it.

2
How to Run right and Hurt Less

Advice for Beginning and Experienced Runners

Do you really have to learn how to run?

You ran when you were two- or three-years old and never stopped running till you were about twelve, if you're a woman, or sometime later, if you're a man.

So why don't you just go out and run now? Do you really need a podiatrist to tell you how?

Judging by all the pulls and pains and injuries I see— injuries caused by the wrong running habits—I'd say you probably do. It's worth your while to take a few minutes to learn the right way to run.

There are two differences between your childhood running and the running you do today. First, you're older. Your body doesn't have the flexibility you had as a kid—so it doesn't recover as quickly from any damage you inflict on it.

Your body *will* become stronger and more flexible as you run and exercise properly. Your muscles will be more resilient. Some of your bones will probably become thicker. Your lungs will be stronger. Your heart will be more efficient. But you've

got to run properly—or your running can hurt you instead of strengthening you.

The second difference is that as a kid you never ran the long distances you're doing now. Kids run in short spurts, then stop to hit a ball or climb a tree. Today, people run one to ten miles a day—and each foot hits the ground about 800 times in every mile. So if you're making a wrong move, you're doing it hundreds and thousands of times—until you get swollen tendons, inflamed knees, aching heels, bruised bones and a sore back.

Podiatrists see more people with running injuries than any other kind of doctor. Every day we see what the wrong running habits can do to you. And we've come to know what's the best way to run, to avoid injuries.

So learn the few simple principles involved in running right. And you'll run with more energy and less strain. Every run will benefit your body instead of hurting it.

Keep Your Spine in Line

The right way to run is to stand straight up with your weight directly over your hips. Don't lean forward. When you lean forward, you're pulling harder on the calf muscles. This can be one of the causes of Achilles tendonitis, shin splints or just sore calf muscles.

You see a lot of young runners leaning forward. They probably think it gets them there faster, or at least makes them look faster. Don't do it. Your spine should be straight, your shoulders should be low and relaxed, not hunched up.

You have to watch out for the tendency to lean forward—especially when you're tired. Sometimes you even feel like you're falling forward. This is understandable, since running and walking are done by falling forward and then putting your foot out to catch yourself. So, be aware of that "leaning" tendency, whenever you run.

How do you hold your arms when you run? Some runners

hold the forearm at a 90-degree angle to the upper arm. I think you should drop your forearms even lower. And, as I said, don't hunch up your shoulders. It makes them tense and tired. As you run, check your shoulders occasionally, to be sure they're low and relaxed.

Tuck your chin in so the back of your neck is straight.

In other words, the same straight posture your grammar school teacher tried to teach you is what you want when you run. It keeps your body well-balanced and relaxed, with the minimum of muscle pull and tension.

The Heels Hit First

When you run, you should land on your heels—not on the balls of your feet.

Your heel should hit the ground first—then your arch comes down—then the ball of the foot and toes. You take off from the ball of the foot—and you're into your next step.

Landing on the balls of the feet is bad for you because your calf muscle never gets a chance to stretch. It stays contracted. That's how calf muscles get short and tight. Any kind of running makes your calf muscle shorter and tighter, but running on the balls of the feet makes it worse.

And tight calf muscles are one of the main causes of shin splints, Achilles tendonitis and muscle pulls.

When you're doing speed work or running on hills, you're landing on the balls of the feet. So eliminate this kind of training if you're suffering from any of the injuries I just mentioned.

If you have no injuries, it's okay to run on the balls of the feet for short distances—a short sprint or a little hill work. But when you're doing five, ten, twenty miles a day and you're running on the balls of your feet, you're going to feel a strain in the Achilles tendon.

Right now, whether you're standing or sitting, put your foot through the motion of taking one running step. Put your

heel down. Then roll onto the outer side of the foot. Now lift up onto the ball of your foot. That's the right way to run. You have to stop and notice, to appreciate what a complicated job your foot has to do to keep you running. No other foot in the animal kingdom can do it, because no other foot is built like ours.

Our foot is the only one that can be both rigid and flexible. Quadruped runners like dogs and horses have completely rigid feet; all the spring and flexibility come from the legs. Apes' "feet" have all flexibility, with no rigid arch. They really have four hands. Human feet are sometimes rigid and sometimes flexible.

When you run, your weight moves from one part of your foot to another. And it travels along a very definite route. Ideally, your weight goes from the outer side of the heel to the outer side of the arch and then into an area behind the first and second toes. Look at the bottom of your shoes. The wear pattern will tell you the path that your weight is taking.

The first thing that happens in your running step is that the heel gives you a tough, rigid landing platform. Next, the foot muscles move as you go to the arch. The arch flattens out a bit. While your weight is on the arch, you're motionless for a fraction of time. The arch becomes firm and rigid, or else you couldn't stand. You'd have to drop down on your hands, the way our cousins, the apes do.

Next, your weight transfers to the ball of your foot and your toes and you bounce off into your next step. Of course, your legs are providing some of that springing action, too.

I'm describing all this, not just to make you realize what a wonderful mechanism your foot is, but to point out that you shouldn't think your feet are deficient if they get a pain or an injury now and then. I'm surprised we don't get even more injuries than we do. In running, your foot is doing such a complex job, with so many changes in where the weight falls, that almost no foot can do it—thousands of times per run—without showing signs of stress.

Every foot has some little imbalance built into it. When

you run long distances, these imbalances really become evident. And your foot needs help in doing its job—arch supports, strapping, padding, supportive shoes. I want you to appreciate your feet the way I do, and don't get mad at them when they need a little help.

Where Not to Run

The ideal running surface would be a dirt road, or grass, with no incline and no holes. This is the most injury-preventive running environment.

Obviously, you can't always get that. And you don't always need to. But, if you're having pains, problems and injuries, there are certain places you should avoid.

Sand When you run on sand, your heels are sinking in and you're giving an extra pull to the Achilles tendon. So don't do it if you have any calf problems, Achilles problems or shin splints. Also beginning runners should not run on sand because their muscles and tendons are not flexible enough for all that pulling. When you're a beginner, try to run under ideal conditions until your body has built up and stretched out.

Actually, running on sand isn't great for anyone. But it is enjoyable, so if you have no injuries and you really want to run on sand, do it for short distances. Run on the damp, firm sand near the ocean—not on the soft, deep sand.

Hills When you run on hills, you're landing on the ball of your foot and your heel has a longer way to go to reach the ground. You're pulling hard on the Achilles tendon and delivering a harder blow to the ball of the foot. If you're running on a steep hill, your heel may never reach the ground—you're just keeping your calf muscles contracted.

So if you're having trouble with bone bruises in the ball of the foot or Achilles tendonitis or shin splints or runner's knee, don't run on hills until the pain has disappeared—and then go back to hill work slowly.

Pavement   It's difficult not to run on pavement; for most people it's the most available surface. But many parks have some dirt roads you can use. If you have to run on pavement, be sure your shoes have good cushioning; try adding an extra Spenco lining or other lining if you're suffering from impact shock or heel bruise or runner's knee.

Banked Tracks; Roads with an Incline   When you run on an incline, your upper foot is twisting inward with every step. And you're giving yourself one short leg. Both these conditions can lead to injuries. Do run on flat surfaces as much as possible.

The rules for "right running" are simple and common-sensical and they'll become second nature in a short time. As you run, notice other runners' style—it will remind you to check your own posture. Run with other people, and you can watch each other's technique.

Knowing—and practicing—the right way to run can do an awful lot toward keeping you on the road and out of the podiatrist's office.

3
How to Buy Shoes

Personally, I believe you shouldn't have to have an engineering degree to buy a pair of running shoes.

Beginning runners and experienced runners sometimes get very worried about whether they'll pick out the right shoes. They see all the ads in the running magazines with diagrams of the inside of the shoe and special features like impact absorption ratings and varus wedges and rear foot stabilizers and God knows what. Then in the park where all the runners meet and do their stretching, you'll hear all the real pros talking about the different kinds of running shoes. They'll be happy to take a few hours and tell you how they went through seven pairs before they got the right shoes, and how the wrong shoes can give you muscle pulls.

Then they go into the discussions of different kinds of glues to repair their shoes and the would-be runner is about ready to quit, because it seems about as hard to buy a good pair of shoes as it is to buy a reliable car. And the price of making a mistake seems equally disastrous.

Well, there is a lot you can learn about running shoes. A lot of thought goes into their design. And as you become an experienced runner, you'll probably want to learn more about the shoes. Later in this chapter, we'll talk about special problems and advice for more experienced runners.

But you can learn, in about fifteen minutes, how to buy the right running shoes for you. And on page 31, you'll find a checklist you can take with you to the store. It gives you the eight points you have to look for in buying running shoes.

To make sure we were giving you all the information you need, we decided to take Ruth Burr, a new runner, shopping for shoes. So she had the advice of a podiatrist (me) and a shoe expert—Mitch Maslin, owner of the Athletic Attic store on Third Avenue, here in New York. Listen in on our conversation, and you'll have the same experts helping you buy your shoes.

We're sitting in the store with five shelves of shoes in front of us. I take a look at Ruth's feet.

Murray: Ruth, you have fairly narrow feet, and they're bony—not much fat padding. You definitely need shoes with good padding, especially here in the city where you run on paved roads.

Mitch: Yes, padding is one of the most important things about a running shoe for a new runner.

Ruth: Why? Doesn't an experienced runner need padding too? Do your feet change as you run?

Mitch: Well, they may—but the important thing is that your whole body changes as you run and do your stretching exercises. You become stronger and more flexible, so you often don't need so much foot padding to protect you from the shocks and jolts of running.

Murray: That's true. Running is much harder on your body when you're new. It's the beginning runner who gets the aches and pains and muscle pulls. Also, the experienced runner who suddenly tries to run beyond his capacity.

Mitch: More experienced runners often prefer lighter shoes with less cushioning, because it give them better speed. And

some runners just like the feel of the road under their feet.
Murray: But when you're just beginning, you should have
the feel of good cushioning under your feet.
Ruth: That's fine with me. It looks like most of these shoes
have good padding—especially at the heels.
Mitch: Yes, the heel cushioning should be about three-
quarter of an inch thick. The heel is where you really need
cushioning because you land on your heel when you run. And
you land with an impact equal to three times your body
weight. So that can send a real jolt up through your body if
you don't have good thick heels.
Ruth: (*Puts some shoes on*) These shoes really feel good
and comfortable.
Mitch: Yes, your running shoes are probably the most comfortable shoes you've ever put on.
Ruth: Except . . . the arch feels funny. I don't feel such
an arch in my regular shoes.
Mitch: That's probably because your regular shoes aren't
giving you any arch support. You've got to get used to the
feeling of support under your arches.
Ruth: But I don't think I have any arch problems. Does
everyone need arch support for running?
Murray: You certainly need it more than you do in your
regular shoes. Your arch tends to flatten out a bit when you
run—and you don't want it to come down on empty air. You
need some support under it.
Ruth: (*Tries on her street shoes again*) These street shoes
really don't have arch support. My arch doesn't even touch
the shoe, in some spots.
Murray: That's one reason why women's feet are so tired
at the end of the day. Even with not-too-high-heels—like the
street shoes you're wearing—you're sort of standing on the
balls of your feet all day. A lot of your weight is thrown
forward, instead of being evenly distributed.
Ruth: What about people with real arch problems? Will
these running shoes give them enough arch support?
Murray: No, if a person has fallen arches or other problems,

he'll probably need a support made from a mold of his foot.
Ruth: Okay, so the running shoes feel nice and cushiony.
And I can feel the arch support, which I'll get used to. What
else should I look for? What about the sole of the shoe? It's
made sort of like football cleats. What's the purpose of that?
Mitch: Originally, those waffle soles—they're also called
studded soles—were made to give traction on soft cross-
country surfaces—grass, dirt and changing terrain. Today,
when a lot of the running is done in cities, manufacturers
have incorporated more shock-absorbing features in the sole.
They use higher studs, so less of your foot is in contact with
the ground. And they experiment with different materials.
Of course, today's shoes are still good for cross-country runners. They still give good traction.
Ruth: (*Looking at several brands of shoes*) I notice some
of the shoes don't have studs. They just have a sort of herringbone design. Is that for some special road condition?
Mitch: Not really. The herringbone pattern gives you traction, too, as well as cushioning against paved roads. Actually,
for a beginner, the bottom of the shoe is about the last con-
sideration you should think of.
Ruth: A lot of these shoes have stripes along the side of
the sole. Is that just a design?
Mitch: No, that shows you the different layers of the sole.
Look—even in the shoes that don't have colored stripes on
the side of the sole, you can still see the layers. First, on the
bottom, is a layer made of fairly hard rubber with some ability
to absorb shock. This outer sole is made to contact the road
and stand up to the friction and burning of the road.

Next comes the midsole. This layer has the most shock ab-

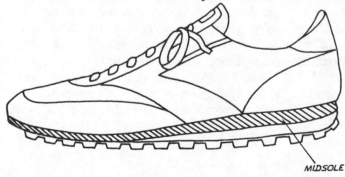

MIDSOLE

sorption. Manufacturers are experimenting with the midsole
—trying different materials and air pockets and what not. The
problem is to give cushioning without making it too soft. A
midsole that's too soft is not giving you enough support. It
would compress too much, so you'd get too much movement
in your foot and leg and knee.

Murray: And that could lead to too much action in the
leg muscles—muscle soreness—knee pain.

Mitch: But that's nothing you have to worry about. Most
good shoes have midsoles that are both shock-absorbing and
firm. Now, as you get into running, and your shoes start
wearing out, I want you to keep checking the soles and heels.
Especially the heels. Don't let them get too worn. Here's
where those colored stripes on the side can help you. You
can see when the bottom sole is worn out, because the color
of the midsole stripe starts showing through. Don't ever run
with the midsoles hitting the ground.

Ruth: The midsoles aren't tough enough for the ground?

Mitch: That's right—they're not made to stand up to the
friction of the ground.

Murray: Also, if the heels are worn down, your foot hits
the ground at the wrong angle, and this is one of the big
causes of muscle pulls and other injuries—especially knee
injuries. If you have knee pain, the first thing you should
check is heel wear.

Mitch: Later, I'll tell you how to repair worn-down heels
and how to care for your running shoes.

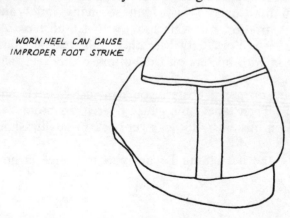

WORN HEEL CAN CAUSE
IMPROPER FOOT STRIKE

Ruth: Okay, so on the outside I can see the bottom sole and the midsole. And inside the shoe is the insole.

Mitch: Right. The insole is designed to be soft and comfortable. They use shock-absorbing material, like the Spenco insole. The insole is also supposed to minimize blisters.

Ruth: Blisters! I got a blister my first day running, in sneakers. I think the sneakers were too tight.

Murray: Let's talk about blisters a minute. You can get blisters from shoes that are too tight or too loose. If your shoes are too loose, your foot will be sliding back and forth, and that friction causes a blister.

Even socks can cause blisters. Nylon socks are abrasive, so be sure you get cotton or woolen socks. Also try to get socks that come in sizes. Those socks that say "one size fits all" can be too tight and cause pressure and interfere with your circulation.

Sometimes the counter of the shoe causes blisters. The counter is the back part of the shoe that wraps around your heel. It's got to be firm, to give support, but because it's firm, it can rub. A counter that's too loose can cause a blister on the heel.

Mitch: That's true, but you have to expect your heel to move a little in the shoe. Sometimes that will cause a blister, especially when you're just breaking in new shoes. That doesn't necessarily mean you've bought the wrong shoes. They just have to be broken in a little.

Also, your skin may be too soft, and then you'll get a blister. Or you may overdo—you run so many miles and there's so much friction on your foot, you get blisters. At the end of the New York City Marathon this year, I guarantee I'll come in with blisters on the bottom of my feet—no matter what shoes I wear.

Murray: If you do get a blister, you can just open it and let the fluid out. Then tape some gauze over it, to protect it. (See page 119 on blisters.) But let's get back to buying shoes now.

Mitch: Right—the next thing I want you to notice is how

the toes fit. Be sure your toes have plenty of room. They shouldn't hit the front of the shoe. Also, don't tie the laces too tightly over the toes, because that can cut off the circulation. Your feet swell as you run. Your foot can expand a full size during a long, hot run.

Murray: Be sure your shoes are long enough to give your toes plenty of room. But your running shoes should fit a bit more snugly, laterally, than your street shoes.

Mitch: Murray, I find a lot of my customers have one foot bigger than the other.

Murray: Yes, most people do, and it's nothing to worry about—unless one foot is a lot larger. In that case you have to fit the larger foot. Then you can put a Spenco insole, or any soft insole, in the other shoe to make it fit.

Ruth: I don't think there's much difference in the sizes of my feet. But I do have narrow feet. Do running shoes come in widths?

Mitch: Some of them do. Also, certain brands tend to be wider or narrower, although there are so many models within each brand that it's hard to make a general rule. I find that Adidas shoes tend to be narrow. Nike and Puma tend to be wide. Brooks shoes seem to be medium. New Balance comes in widths, and so do some other brands.

The thing is, each manufacturer has several models. In a running shoe store, the salesman will be familiar with the different styles, and he can bring out the models that will be best for your foot.

Ruth: I notice some of these shoes are made for women.

Mitch: Yes, they're made on a woman's last. The main difference is that women's shoes are narrower.

Ruth: Wait, my size is six-and-a-half, and you've given me a size seven.

Mitch: Don't worry about the numbers. A lot of people take a larger size in a running shoe. Sometimes they insist on getting their usual size, and they walk out with shoes that are too small for them.

I think it's smart to buy shoes in the afternoon, because

your feet can expand a full size during the day.

Ruth: Let me try a six-and-a-half anyway, since that's my usual size. . . . Mmmm, I guess it is tight—my foot's making the shoe bulge out on the side.

Murray: When that happens, the sides of the shoe can't give your foot the support it needs. That's what happens when you buy a shoe that's too narrow. Your foot won't be stable as you're running, and that can lead to muscle strain and tiredness and injuries. Also, if the shoe is too tight, you'll cut off the circulation and your foot becomes numb.

Ruth: All right, I give up. I'll take a larger size.

Mitch: Now let's check—the toes have enough room. The width is snug but not too tight. The last thing to notice about fit is the heel counter—that's the part that wraps around the heel. The counter should fit snugly, but not be so stiff that it rubs and causes irritation. The counter should be firm enough to hold your heel solidly because a wobbly heel can cause injuries in the lower leg.

Ruth: How can I tell if the counter is firm enough?

Mitch: Just squeeze it—it should feel firm. And, as I said before, don't worry if the counter does cause a blister at first. You have to give it a chance to break in.

While we're looking at the counter, here's something you should check when you buy shoes. Place the shoes on a level surface and look at them from the rear. The counter should sit straight and square on the shoe. Sometimes one of the counters is tilted in, and that could cause a wrong movement in your foot.

Ruth: Okay, so I should check to see that the counter's on straight. Now I have another question about the back of the shoe. Why are they shaped differently from the heels of regular shoes?

Mitch: They're different in two ways. One, a good running shoe will have a flared heel. The heel widens out as it goes toward the ground. This gives you a larger base to land on— because you land on your heel. This larger base makes you more solid and stable. Also, since you're landing on a larger

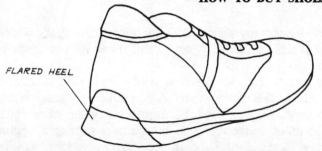

FLARED HEEL

area, you've got more shock-absorbing material underneath you.

Besides being flared, the heels of running shoes are rounded. This lets you hit the ground more smoothly.

Ruth: That makes sense. Now, what about flexibility? All my friends tell me I should be sure I get flexible shoes.

Mitch: That means the shoe should bend at the ball of the foot. Where your foot bends, the shoes should bend easily.

Murray: Your foot bends at a 35-degree angle when you toe off, so your shoe has to bend along with it. If the shoe doesn't bend easily, your muscles are working hard against the shoe. So you get soreness in the shins or the calf muscles or the Achilles tendon.

Mitch: People used to say you should test new shoes on the scale—you should put the toe of the shoe on the scale, then push down on the back of the shoe. And it should take no more than five pounds of pressure to bend the shoe. Well, I really wouldn't worry about that. If you like the shoe in other respects, the flexibility will come as you break them in, and you can help them along. Bend them back and forth several times before you wear them. And don't forget, for every mile of running, each foot is bending eight hundred times. So you're bound to increase the flexibility. You can make cuts along the bottom of the sole—at the ball of the foot—to help them bend more easily.

Murray: Or before you do that, you can try my method. When I have new shoes that are too stiff, I bend them at the ball of the foot, then tape them in that position and leave them that way overnight.

Mitch: I bend my shoes, and put them in a shallow dresser drawer overnight, so they stay bent. That makes them more flexible.

Now let's talk about the weight of the shoe. You hear a lot of talk about this from experienced runners. Racers want the lightest shoes they can get, because every gram of weight can add that much more effort to their run. But, for a beginning runner, a lightweight shoe is not that important. It's much more important for you to have good, solid cushioning under your foot.

Murray: And the heavier you are, the more cushioning you need. A lot of new runners are overweight, so they need extra-solid cushioning and support. In fact, when I get a patient who's overweight and is having problems—like pains in the heel or pains in the hips and spine—caused by the shock of hitting the ground in running—I advise them to wear work shoes, even combat boots. I got this idea from Dr. Schuster. You can't run a marathon in combat boots, but when you're first starting out, they hold you good and firm. They absorb a lot of impact. By the time you're ready to run a marathon, you'll have a lightweight body and you'll feel comfortable in lightweight shoes.

Ruth: You've told me the shoes will change as I break them in. How long does it take to break in new running shoes?

Mitch: I would say two or three weeks of gradual breaking in. I would start by wearing them around the house a few evenings or just wearing them in the street. Then go for a short run. Since you're a new runner, your runs will be short anyway. Then if you wear your running shoes on other occasions—if you just wear them like regular sport shoes— the shoes will break in as you're breaking in—getting used to running.

Murray: I tell my patients never to enter a race in brand new shoes. Your shoes and feet ought to be used to each other before you go into a race together. You should buy new shoes before the old ones are worn out. Then you wear the new shoes for a short run, or wear them every second or third

day. Break them in, the way Mitch is saying. So the new shoes are breaking in as the old ones are wearing out. And you never have to race in stiff, unfamiliar shoes.

Ruth: I notice most of these shoes are nylon on the top—part nylon and part leather.

Mitch: Yes, the nylon uppers are good because they don't need breaking in. They're nice and soft the first time you put them on. They cause less friction against your skin. And they're light in weight, so that feels good.

Also, if leather shoes get wet they often stiffen up and crack when they dry. You often go out running on rainy days, so your shoes get wet. Plus, your feet sweat a lot. Then in winter, the salt they throw on the sidewalk can make leather shoes stiff and cracked.

You shouldn't worry about getting your shoes wet, if they have nylon uppers. Just stuff them with newspapers and let them dry. But don't put them near heat. Don't try to dry them in the oven or with a hair dryer. The sole may separate from the rest of the shoe. I wouldn't even put shoes in strong sunlight to dry. Just let them dry at room temperature. They'll probably be dry the next day, and you can flex them a few times and put them right on.

Ruth: Everyone told me that running shoes are so expensive. But really, they're no more expensive than regular street shoes.

Mitch: That's true—and besides, good shoes are really the only "must" equipment in running. It's perfectly okay to run in cheap shorts and a T-shirt. I don't think cutoff jeans make good running shorts, because they're too stiff. Soft nylon shorts are better, but they don't have to be expensive.

Ruth: Anyway, if you wanted to save money on shoes, you could buy cheaper ones, right? In department stores and regular shoe stores.

Mitch: I wouldn't. The companies that make shoes for department stores and regular shoe stores have not been making running shoes for years. They're trying to make quick imitations of real running shoes. But the only thing you can count

on is that they're imitating the cosmetics—the colors and styling. You don't know what's gone into the inside of the shoe.

The companies that specialize in running shoes have years and years of experience and testing behind them, and they're constantly working on improving the running shoes. Even when running was not a big fad, Adidas and Nike were making running shoes. Brooks was making sports shoes, twenty or thirty years ago. I would trust the real running shoe companies like these—or basically, the shoes sold in stores that specialize in running equipment.

Ruth: How long do running shoes last?

Mitch: It's very hard to say. Different people wear them out at different rates. Some people are lighter on their feet. Some people drag their feet. The identical brand and model can wear out at different rates, on different runners. You may even find that one of your shoes wears out faster than the other because you come down harder on one side.

Ruth: You told me to be sure the heels don't get worn—so I don't run on the midsoles. What about that stuff people use to mend the soles? Is that any good?

Mitch: Sure, you can get Shoe Goo, or other good glues for just a few dollars and really prolong the life of your shoes. In fact, you should apply this stuff to the heels very frequently to keep them from wearing down. When your heels wear down, your foot is hitting the ground at a bad angle, and that can cause you all sorts of leg and knee and back problems.

I apply glue to my heels every three or four runs, to prevent wear.

Ruth: That sounds like a lot of trouble. Does it take much time?

Mitch: Not much more than squeezing out toothpaste. Squeeze it out and apply a thin coat. You'll get the feel of it—you'll notice that the stuff contracts a bit when it dries. So I bring the material up above the heel a little—knowing it will shrink down as it dries. The salesman in the running

shoe store will show you how to use it—or you can just experiment with it yourself.

So that's how Ruth bought her first pair of running shoes. And her experience should give most people all the guidance necessary to buy the proper shoes—whether you're a new runner or an old-timer. In fact, here's a checklist you can take with you to the store:

1. **Cushioning** Very important. You need about ¾-inch at the heel and good cushioning under the ball of the foot.

2. **Length** Should be long enough to give toes plenty of room. Toes should not touch the front of the shoe.

3. **Width** Shoes should feel snug and firm, but should not be so tight that they bulge on the side.

4. **Arch** Running shoes have good arch support—more than street shoes—and this is a feeling you'll get used to.

5. **Counter** Should feel firm when you squeeze it. Counter should be set square and straight onto the heel—not tilted.

6. **Heel** Should be wider at the base than at the top of the shoe. (Flared heel.)

7. **Flexibility** Shoe should bend easily at the ball of the foot. But flexibility will improve as you wear the shoes.

8. **Comfort** Shoe should feel good on your foot, even though it may be a bit snugger than your street shoes.

These eight points are all you have to look for—unless you have special problems.

Special Shoe Tips for Special Problems

Overweight Runners If you're overweight or have a very large frame, you need more cushioning than other people. Buy cushioning liners from the footcare stand in your drugstore, and bring them with you when you're trying on shoes.

Arthritis or Knee Damage You need extra cushioning too—so follow the procedure given for the heavy runner.

Achilles Tendonitis You need extra lift in the back of the shoe. Start with heel lifts made of sponge rubber, a ¼-

inch thick, and see if that solves the problem. Then work up to ½-inch or ¾-inch, if necessary. Victex makeup sponges are good, and they come in various thicknesses. Or buy sponge rubber on the foot care stand.

Ankle Sprains and Instability   If you tend to turn your ankle frequently and get ankle sprains, you can add something to the outside of your shoe to give you more stability. Read the section on sprained and broken ankles. It gives instructions for your shoemaker, on how to apply a strip of rubber to the outer side of your running shoes. This strip makes it almost impossible for you to turn your ankle and sprain it.

Arch Problems   You need special arch support, and a mass-produced shoe isn't designed to give you this. Read the section of this book that describes your problem—it's probably the section called weak foot—for guidance in getting the arch support you need.

Shin Splints   Be sure your shoes are flexible. And be sure you've got good heel lift. Try adding heel cushioning, inside the shoe. Be sure the toes are not too loose. If your toes have too much space, they're constantly grabbing, trying to get more stability. But they're grabbing at empty air, and that can cause shin splints.

My friend Mitch Maslin cured his shin splints when he switched to Brooks Vantage shoes. They have thick heel cushioning plus an extra-wide sole. They're wider across the arch and the ball of the foot. I think it was the higher heel that did the trick. Mitch thinks the extra width prevented excess motion in the leg and foot, and that cured the shin splints. Anyway, it worked.

Corns on Top of the Toes; Hammer Toes   You need plenty of room in the toe box. You may have to cut slits in your shoes to provide that.

Bunions   If you can't get shoes wide enough to keep your bunions comfortable, cut slits in the side of your shoes. Then cover the hole with moleskin, or glue on a piece of nylon, so the bunion doesn't get hurt.

4

The Best Anti-Injury Exercises I've Ever Found

-And The Easiest Way To Do Them

I'm going to let you in on a secret that could cut my practice by a third.

If you do the right exercises and do them regularly, you can avoid most injuries. On the other hand, if you run and don't exercise, you're almost sure to be injured. It's that simple.

Every run you take causes microscopic tears in the muscles, and when these tiny tears repair themselves, they form scar tissue. This scar tissue cannot be flexed or stretched. So every time you run, your muscles are getting tighter and tighter—and less able to stretch. A tight, inflexible muscle is a setup for injury. It can't take the shocks and jolts of running or the constant pulling of a long runner's stride. A tight muscle is one that's ready to be injured.

And, along with these tight muscles, other muscles in your body are left pretty much unexercised by running. This means some of your muscles are very tight while nearby muscles are relatively very soft. That's another setup for injury.

So save yourself some pain and money. Learn a basic group of exercises like the warm-up I'll give you here, or any good, well-balanced set of exercises.

I'm absolutely serious when I tell you that the right exercises can keep you out of the doctor's office. Here's an example. When I first got the idea for this book, I wrote up a couple of sections, including a discussion of Achilles tendonitis. I sent it to St. Martin's Press and the head of the sales force, who is a runner, read the section. He did the exercises. And he cured a case of Achilles tendonitis that had been bothering him for months. And he didn't even have to buy the book!

Here's another story. John Tesh is a TV newsman who runs in the New York City Marathon carrying broadcasting equipment. The marathon isn't tough enough—he has to talk and comment and interview other runners as he goes.

Well, in 1978 John was really suffering from runner's knee and was afraid he couldn't run in the marathon. He came to see me and I taught him exercises (standing leg lifts) to strengthen the quadriceps (thigh) muscles. John ran the marathon and tells everyone it was the exercises that got him through.

So make up your mind that you have to exercise before and after you run. And you might as well find ways to enjoy it, or at least make it a habit.

How much time should you spend exercising? I'd say twenty minutes, minimum—ten minutes before running and ten minutes after. This may sound like a lot if you're a beginner—because you may be running or jogging only twenty minutes. But beginners need the exercises more than anyone else, so don't skimp on them. They're the only way to avoid aches and pains and muscle pulls.

For experienced runners, figure your exercising time should equal one quarter of your running time. So if you run about ninety minutes, exercise a little more than twenty minutes.

Now, which exercises should you do? Which are the most effective for preventing injury?

I treat thousands of runners' injuries a year and usually the treatment involves some exercises. My patients try the exercises and report back to me—so over the years I've found out which exercises work better than others and which can actually cause harm. (I'll mention a couple of those later.)

I've refined all these exercises down to a basic group of eight that take ten minutes to do. My patients call them the Weisenfeld Warm-up. They're the most effective exercises I've found for the prevention and treatment of runners' injuries.

Some of the exercises I'll give you here include little variations on exercises you may already know. For instance, you may be doing wall push-ups for your calf muscles. Okay, now add this: After you've finished stretching your leg—stretching it out behind you, knee straight—dip your knee. Keep the heel on the floor. Feel the difference? Now you're stretching the soleus, which is another muscle in the calf that often gets injured.

Or you may be stretching your hamstrings by putting one foot on the table and holding it with your hands. Try this instead: For half of your stretching time, hold your foot with your left hand. For the rest of the time, hold the foot with your right hand. You'll feel the difference—you're reaching different muscles. Doing it this way gives each muscle a better stretch than when you hold your foot with both hands at once.

I've chosen exercises that stretch or strengthen more than one muscle group at a time. So you get more injury-prevention for your effort. And I've found an easier way to do them. Start them in bed. Do the first three exercises in bed, before you get up in the morning. It's like stretching when you first get up. (Be sure you have a firm mattress.)

Then get out of bed and continue stretching and warming up your muscles as you do the last five exercises. Now you're ready for your morning run.

If you take your run in the evening, Bob Glover recommends taking a hot bath before you start exercising—to relax the muscles. If that seems like too much trouble, lie on the

floor and do some gentle deep breathing and stretching before your workout. It's very important to be relaxed when you exercise and when you run.

Too many people come in from work full of tension and immediately start forcing their tight muscles to exercise. When they run, they're still tense. This is the way injuries start. If you're tense, relax and breathe a bit before you exercise. And start your run with a long, easy walk.

Do whatever you can to stay relaxed while exercising. Stretch with a slow, relaxed feeling and stretch just to the point where you can feel the muscle stretching—but not hurting. If you stretch too hard, the muscle will resist and contract.

The same rule applies to strengthening exercises. For instance, when you're doing sit-ups, your abdominal muscles should be making an effort, but they should not be hurting. Don't try to do the full number of repetitions I give here, if you're out of condition. Do the exercise a few times and build up slowly.

Another important tip: Never bounce when you exercise. It kills me to see how some people exercise—they bounce as they touch their toes and bounce some more as they bend to the side. It hurts me to watch. Because bouncing signals the muscle to contract, and that's the opposite of what you want.

So don't bounce. Stretch slow and easy.

Another don't: the hurdler's stretch, where you have one leg bent and you're reaching for the other leg. This is a twisting motion, which can always be dangerous. You may twist your bent knee. You may pull the inner thigh muscle.

I don't like bending over and putting the palms of the hands flat on the floor. People often throw their backs out this way. This exercise is sometimes shown with the legs together and sometimes with the legs spread. I don't advise either one.

The exercises I'm giving you here include the basic Weisenfeld Warm-up (eight exercises), plus twelve supplementary exercises. You can add an exercise from the supplementary group if you need it for the treatment of a specific injury.

If you're a new runner, I'd advise you to do the basic

warm-up before and after each run. They are a complete injury-preventive program for the great majority of runners. But, if you have a special problem and you do get an injury, you can add the exercise for the muscle group involved. As you read the section on your injury, it will tell you which exercises to do.

If you're an experienced runner and you have a group of exercises that work for you, stick with them. That's the most important thing—what works for you. But I know that runners are always looking for ways to improve their results— so take a look at these exercises. Try a few and see if they get at muscles you're not reaching now.

The Weisenfeld Warm-up

These can be done in bed, before you get up in the morning.

1. Foot Press   Strengthens quadriceps, for treatment of runner's knee. Strengthens anterior leg muscles, for treatment of shin splints.
2. Inner and Outer Thighs   Strengthens thigh muscles. For treatment/prevention of runner's knee and groin pull.
3. Knee Press   Stretches hamstrings and lower back muscles. For treatment/prevention of hamstring pull and lower back pain.

Now get out of bed and do these.

4. Three-Level Leg Lift   Strengthens abdominal and quadriceps muscles. Stretches lower back and hamstring muscles.
5. Wall Pushups   Stretches the calf muscle and soleus muscle. For treatment/prevention of Achilles tendonitis, shin splints and muscle pulls.
6. Foot on Table, Knee Up   Stretches hamstrings. Prevents hamstring pull.
7. Flying Exercise   Relaxes upper back muscles which often tense up during running.
8. Shrugs   Relaxes shoulders and upper back muscles.

Foot Press   Inner Thighs

Foot Press   Strengthens quadriceps (thigh) muscles, for treatment/prevention of runner's knee. Strengthens anterior leg muscles, for treatment of shin splints.

Can be done lying down or sitting in a chair. Put your right foot on top of your left foot. Your lower·foot tries to pull toward your body as your upper foot pushes it away from the body. Hold for ten seconds. Now switch feet—put the left foot on top of the right foot, and push/pull for ten seconds. This equals one set. Do five sets.

Inner and Outer Thighs   The turned-out position strengthens the outer thigh muscles—for treatment/prevention of runner's knee.

The turned-in position strengthens the inner thigh muscles—for treatment/prevention of groin pull.

Can be done lying down or sitting in a chair. Stretch both legs out—knees straight, feet flexed. (Toes pointed toward knees.) Tighten your thigh muscles. Now turn your feet out as far as you can and hold ten seconds. Then turn your feet

in as far as you can and hold ten seconds. Keep thigh muscles tight throughout exercise.

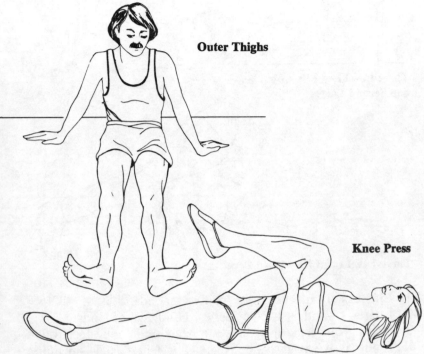

Outer Thighs

Knee Press

Knee Press   Stretches the hamstring muscles and the lower back muscles. For treatment/prevention of hamstring pull and lower back pain.

Lie on your back. Put your hands under one knee and pull your knee to your chest. Hold ten seconds. Relax.

Repeat with other leg. Do each leg five times, alternating legs. Do not wrap your arms around the outside of your knee.

Three-Level Leg Lift   Levels one and two strengthen the abdominal and quadriceps muscles. Level three stretches the lower back and the hamstring muscles.

Lie on your back, legs straight, knees firm but not locked. The small of your back should touch the floor. If it doesn't, put your hands under your buttocks.

Three-Level Leg Lift—First and Second Levels

Three-Level Leg Lift—Third Level

1. Lift legs six inches. Hold for five seconds.
2. Lift legs another twelve inches. Hold five seconds.
3. Swing your legs up over your head until your feet touch the floor above your head. Keep your feet flexed—meaning the toes pointing toward the knees. If you can't get your feet all the way to the floor, go as far as you can without strain, keeping your feet flexed. Hold five seconds.

The above equals one set. Do five to ten sets.

Wall Pushups   Stretches the calf muscle and the soleus muscle. For treatment/prevention of Achilles tendonitis, shin splints and muscle pulls. "Wall Pushups" is the name most people use for this exercise; but don't confuse it with "floor pushups." You should not pump your arms during this exercise. Just take a position and hold it.

Stand facing the wall—about two feet away from the wall. Rest palms of hands against wall. Keep both feet pointing straight ahead. Slide one foot back, with the knee straight, until you feel a burning or pulling sensation at the upper part of the calf. Your heel stays flat on the floor. This stretches the calf muscle. Hold ten seconds. After ten seconds, bend the knee of the back leg and hold five seconds. This stretches the soleus, which is another calf muscle. Now switch legs and. repeat.

Do each leg five times, alternating legs.

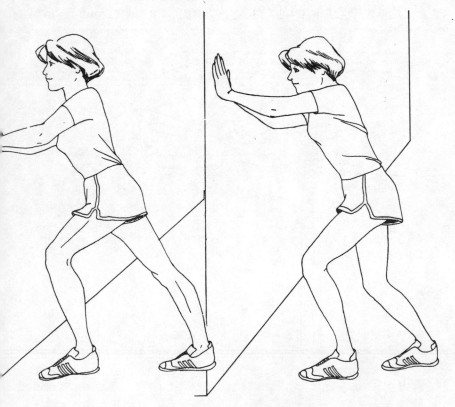

Wall Pushups for Calf Muscle   **Wall Pushups for Soleus Muscle**

Foot on Table, Knee Up   Stretches hamstring muscles, for treatment/prevention of hamstring pull.

Stand in front of a table and put one foot on the table, knee facing up. Keep both knees straight. Bend over and hold the foot that's on the table with your right hand. Bring your nose as close to your knee as possible. Don't force it. Don't strain to make your nose touch your knee. Hold ten seconds.

Now your right hand lets go of your foot, and your left hand holds it. This stretches different leg muscles. Hold ten seconds. Repeat with the other leg.

Stretch each leg five times, alternating legs.

If it's too difficult to put your leg on a table, put it on a chair.

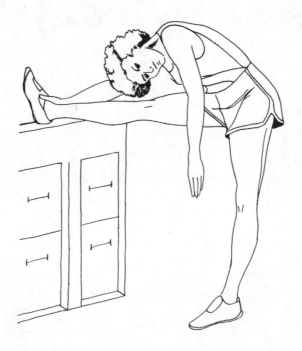

Foot on Table, Knee Up

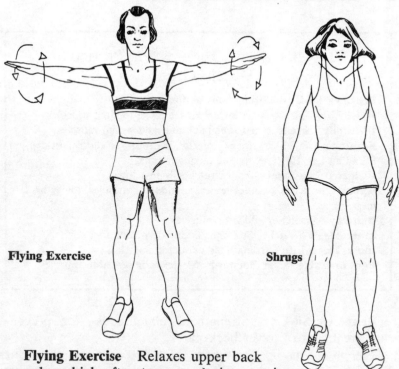

Flying Exercise   Shrugs

Flying Exercise   Relaxes upper back
muscles which often tense up during running.
Hold your arms out straight, shoulder level.
Make ten circles forward and ten circles backward.
This exercise is also a favorite with skiers—only you make
bigger circles. On a freezing day when you can't keep your
fingers warm, stop on the side of the slope (out of traffic) and
do the Flying Exercise. It brings blood to your fingers and
warms them up.

Shrugs   Relaxes shoulders and upper back muscles.
Curl your shoulders down and forward, as if you're trying
to make them touch each other in front. Next, lift your shoulders up toward your ears. Then stretch them way down in
back, as if the two shoulder blades could touch.
Then back up to the ears, and hunched forward again. This
equals one.
Do ten times.

Supplementary Exercises for Particular Muscle Groups

Bent-Leg Sit-Ups   Strengthens abdominals.
Knee Lifts   Strengthens lower back and abdominal muscles.
Hip Rolls   Strengthens lower back and abdominal muscles.
Furniture Lift   Strengthens anterior leg muscles and quadriceps.
Standing Leg Lifts   Strengthens quadriceps.
Weighted Leg Extensions   Stretches hamstrings.
Squats   Stretches Achilles tendons, adductor muscles, lower back muscles
Butterfly   Stretches adductor muscles.
Inner Thigh Stretch   Stretches adductor muscles.
Inner Thigh Lift   Strengthens adductor muscles.
Foot on Table, Knee Forward   Stretches inner thigh muscles.

Bent-Leg Sit-Ups   Strengthens abdominals—for prevention/treatment of lower back pain.

Lie on the floor, knees bent, feet flat on floor. Put your hands behind your head and sit up. Exhale and press in your stomach as you sit up. Inhale as you go down.

Start with five situps and work up to twenty per day.

If you can't sit up while holding your hands behind your head, put your hands on your thighs. As you sit up, your hands move up toward your knees.

Do not jerk your body up. Put your chin on your chest and curl your spine up off the floor.

If you're a beginner, anchor your feet under a piece of furniture. Don't try to sit up all the way. Just go as far as you can without strain.

Another don't: Don't stretch your hands up over your head while doing sit-ups. I've seen people do this, and they fling their arms forward, using the force to help them sit up. When you do this, you're jerking your body up instead of curling it up smoothly. This jerky action leads to muscle tension.

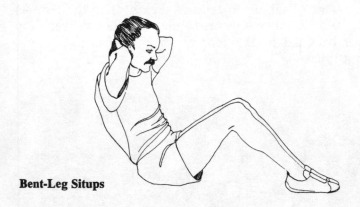

Bent-Leg Situps

Knee Lifts Strengthens lower back and abdominal muscles. For treatment/prevention of lower back pain.

Lie on your back, arms straight down at your sides. Pull your knees up to your chest, then slowly lower your feet back down again.

Do ten lifts.

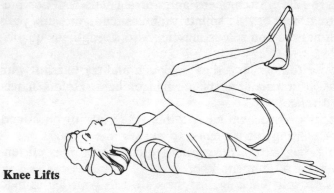

Knee Lifts

Hip Rolls Strengthens lower back and abdominal muscles. For treatment/prevention of lower back pain.

Lie on your back, arms straight out at shoulder level. Pull

your knees up to your chest. Now roll your knees over to the right side—then back up to center—then over to the left. As much as possible, move only below the waist, not above. Keep the upper back flat on the floor.

Do ten times.

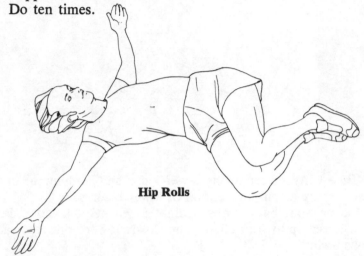

Hip Rolls

Furniture Lift   Strengthens anterior leg muscles. For prevention/treatment of shin splints, Achilles tendonitis and pulls in the calf muscle and soleus muscle. Also strengthens quadriceps.

Tuck your toes under a desk or couch and try to lift it with your toes. Your knees can be straight or bent. Hold ten seconds, then relax.

Do ten lifts. Also, you can do this while talking to boring people, or waiting for someone to answer the phone.

Standing Leg Lifts   Strengthens quadriceps. For prevention/treatment of runner's knee.

Stand with your back against the wall. Lift your leg as high as you can, holding your knee straight. Hold for the count of five. Now bend your knee to relax for the count of five. Then straighten the leg again.

Do one leg five times. Then do the other leg. Start by holding your leg straight for the count of five. Increase till you

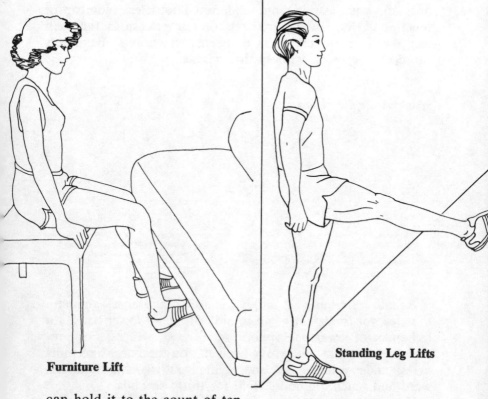

Furniture Lift

Standing Leg Lifts

can hold it to the count of ten.

Weighted Leg Extensions   Stretches and strengthens the hamstring muscles. For treatment/prevention of hamstring pull.

Attach a one-pound weight to each ankle. Lie on the floor, arms at your sides. Your knees are bent, feet flat on floor. Stretch your right leg up as straight as you can. Then put your foot back on the floor. Repeat ten times. Now repeat with your other leg.

Your aim is to straighten your leg so it's almost at a 90-degree angle to the floor. If you have hamstring pull, you will not be able to straighten it completely. Just stretch it as far as you can without causing pain. Do not extend both legs at

once, or you'll strain your abdominal muscles. Number of repetitions: Start with three sets of ten extensions for each leg. Work up to three sets of twenty extensions. Beginners can do this exercise without the weights.

Weighted Leg Extensions

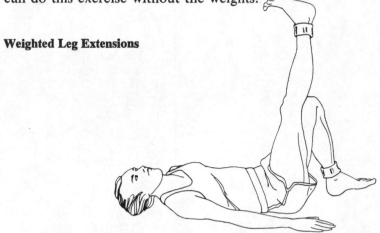

Squats Stretches Achilles tendons. Stretches adductor muscles, for treatment of groin pull. Stretches lower back, for treatment of lower back pain.

Squat down, keeping your heels flat on the floor. Your feet are shoulder-width apart, and pointed out slightly. Bend forward and touch the floor. Hold for thirty seconds.

If your leg muscles and/or Achilles tendons are very tight, you may have trouble keeping your heels on the floor. In this case, put your hands on the wall behind you.

Butterfly Stretches adductor muscles. For prevention/ treatment of groin pull.

Sit with the soles of your feet together. Bring your feet as close to your body as possible. Hold your ankles. Put your elbows on the inner side of the knees. Use your elbows to push your knees down toward the floor. Careful—only to point of stretch, not pain.

Hold ten seconds, then relax. Do five times.

Inner Thigh Stretch Stretches adductor muscles. For prevention/treatment of groin pull.

Squats   **Butterfly**

Stand with your feet slightly wider than hip width. Your left foot points forward and your right foot points toward the side. Bend your right knee and put your weight on your right foot. Hold ten seconds. Now do the other leg: point the right foot forward and the left foot toward the side. Bend your left knee and put your weight on your left foot.

This equals one set. Do five sets.

Inner Thigh Lift   Strengthens adductor muscles. For prevention/treatment of groin pull.

Position: Lie on your right side with your right hand supporting your head. Your left hand is on the floor in front of you, for support. Your left foot is flat on the floor, in front of your right leg. Your right leg should be slightly in front of your body.

Flex your right foot—so the toe points up toward the knee. Keep the knee firm and straight throughout this exercise.

Action: Lift the right leg as high as you can, then lower. Start with five or ten repetitions and work up to twenty. When you lower the leg each time, do not touch the floor with your

foot, and do not relax your leg. Keep it firm throughout the exercise.

This can also be done with a one-pound weight on your ankle.

Now turn on your left side and repeat with the left leg.

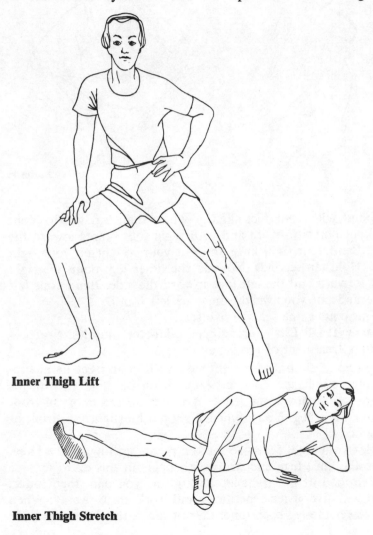

Inner Thigh Lift

Inner Thigh Stretch

Foot on Table, Knee Forward   Stretches inner thigh muscles. For treatment/prevention of groin pull. Stand in front of a table. Put one leg on the table. Both legs should be straight. Do not turn to face your leg. You should face forward, and your knees should face forward. Hold 10 seconds. This equals one set. Do five sets.

As you become more flexible, bend sideways to touch the leg that's on the table.

If it's too difficult at first to put your foot on the table, put it on a chair.

Foot on Table, Knee Forward

5

How to Be Your Own Podiatrist

-And How To Choose a Podiatrist If You Need One

Runners are not passive patients.

One day my friend and patient, Hans Hartmann, walked into my office. I had made some orthotics for Hans about six months earlier, to correct an imbalance that was causing him some ankle pain.

On this day, Hans was carrying the orthotics—but I could hardly recognize them. He had stuck bits of tape and felt and foam rubber on them to thicken them in some spots. Then he had sanded down the orthotics in other places. They were a real mess.

"Here," he said. "Now these orthotics are perfect. Can you duplicate them?" So I duplicated them, and he's been running happily on them ever since. In fact, Hans told me that if he runs for any long period without the orthotics, he feels the ankle pain returning.

Any doctor involved in treating athletes has to take his patients in as partners—because sports medicine is a new science that we're all learning as we go along. Runners, espe-

cially, have to become their own doctors to some extent—because your body changes as you run and as you increase your mileage. So if you didn't learn how to take care of yourself, you'd have to reserve a permanent seat in the podiatrist's office.

My patients have learned to become their own podiatrists. (Of course, they call me in for consultation in emergencies.) So let me give you some guidance on how you can do the same.

Naturally, if you do suffer an injury, this book can tell you how to treat it. But "injury fixing" is not the best approach to sports medicine. To take good care of yourself, you need an educated awareness of your body. You need a basic knowledge of the podiatrist's first aid procedures and the tools of first aid. You should know how to take care of your feet from day-to-day and how to keep yourself fit when injuries keep you from running. And you should know how to choose a podiatrist, if you do need one.

Here's some guidance on gaining these skills.

How to Diagnose Your Problem

You've got to be something of a medical detective to find the causes of many injuries. And since you, the athlete, are the eyewitness to the crime, you've got to become an expert at noticing what's going on in your body and in your surroundings.

George Sheehan tells of a swimmer who was beached because of "asthma," until he noticed that it was only in a certain pool that the asthma occurred. It turned out he was allergic to the chemicals in that pool.

One of my patients noticed that changing his shoes cured his shin splints. Mitch had been suffering with shin splints for weeks and we had tried everything. I loaned him my ultrasound machine and gave him heel pads and he did stretching exercises and tried whirlpool baths. Nothing worked.

Then he happened to try a different pair of shoes, and the shin splints went away. One night, when he had his seven pair of shoes turned upside down for repairing, he noticed that the new shoes had much wider soles than the others and thicker heels. So that's what did the trick.

In fact, your shoes can tell you a lot about how you run and why you get injured. Whenever a new patient phones for an appointment, I tell him to bring in some worn running shoes for me to look at.

Look at Your Shoes to See How You Run

The wear pattern on the soles of your shoes shows you how you run. Or, to put it differently, how your weight is transferred from point to point along your foot.

1. A shoe with a normal wear pattern shows that you land on the outer side of your heel. Then your weight moves quickly along the outer side of your foot (not causing much noticeable wear). Now your weight transfers to an area between the first and second metatarsal heads. You can see the wear spot—just behind the first and second toe. This is where you should be taking off into your next step. Fast runners will have a third wear spot at the tip of the shoe, because this is where they take off.
2. Look at the wear pattern for pronation. You get this when you have fallen arches (weak foot). Your arches are weak, so too much of your weight falls toward the inner side of the foot—and that's where you see a big wear spot. You're subject to pains in the arch, leg pains and back pains.
3. In the wear pattern for supination, you can see that too much of the body weight falls toward the outer side of the foot. In this case, your feet don't turn in properly. It's the opposite of pronation. If your feet supinate, you may get some knee trouble.
4. If you have a wear spot behind the big toe, you probably

have bony feet. Your first metatarsal head sticks out, and you may get a bone bruise here (sesamoiditis).

5. If your shoes show excessive wear behind the second and third toes, you probably have corns or calluses in that spot. Too much weight is going there. You have a depressed metatarsal arch.

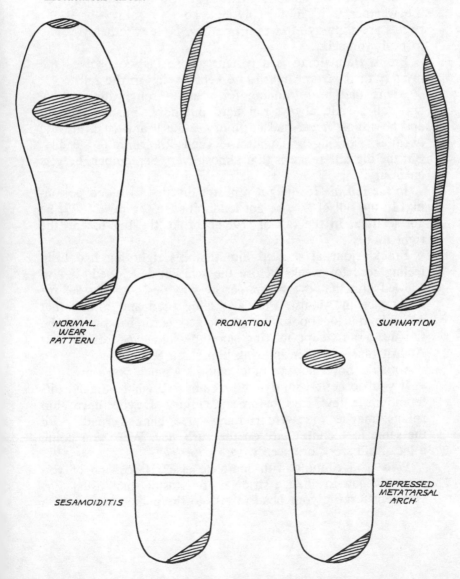

NORMAL WEAR PATTERN

PRONATION

SUPINATION

SESAMOIDITIS

DEPRESSED METATARSAL ARCH

So pay attention to your shoes and how you run and where you run. Your runner's log is a good way to keep track of these things. In your journal, record your daily mileage and speed. Note how much of the time you're doing hill work. If you ran on an indoor track—a banked track—write that down. If you ran on sand, write that down. Make a note on the weather if it's noticeably hot, cold or rainy—or if the streets are slippery after rain or snow. Note whether you had to push yourself.

Frank Handelman is a patient whose logbook solved the mystery of recurrent injuries he kept getting in the fall.

Frank had been running for years, through high school and college. He always ran hard but never pushed himself, and he almost never had an injury. Now Frank is in his late twenties, working as an attorney and still running steadily. But the big difference is that almost every September, he gets an injury.

In the fall of '75, he got a blister that led to blood poisoning. In the fall of '76, he got tendonitis. In the fall of '77, he got sciatica. In the fall of '79, he broke the big toe on the right foot.

Frank's journal showed him that his right leg had been feeling sore for weeks before the sciatica developed. It also showed him that every summer he was pushing to peak for a big race in August. He was feeling tired and jotting that down in the log book. But he trained hard, in spite of the fatigue. Frank kept making good personal records in that August race and then injuring himself in September.

So make notes how you feel, and how much you run.

If you do get an injury—check and see what you did differently the few days before the injury. If you have shin splints, maybe you were running on a banked road—with the same foot continually on the curb side. Were you doing a lot of hill work or speed work or *fartlek*?

Were you running with someone else? If so, one of you probably had to change stride or run faster than usual. Or, you kept turning your head to talk to the person next to you

or behind you. In that case, your foot was hitting the ground at a different angle.

Note when you get a pain, and when it's at its worst. If you have muscle pains during a morning run but not during an afternoon run, you may simply need more warming up.

If you get knee pain as soon as you start running, there's probably something wrong with the knee itself. If the knee pain comes after you've been running a few miles, it's probably a foot imbalance that's causing the wrong movement in the knee—and therefore the pain.

Check your logbook and see how much you were running and where you were running for the days previous to the start of the problem. You may find you've been increasing your mileage too quickly.

If you're trying a new exercise, put that in your journal.

Another way to learn about your own running habits is to have an experienced runner observe your style. Someone else can notice that you're turning your toes in too much or hunching up your shoulders or leaning forward.

Look for symptoms of overstress. For instance:

• Tiredness without being able to sleep.

• Colds, sore throat, fever blisters—any indications of lowered general resistance.

• Lack of enthusiasm for the run. This often comes the day after you've had a terrific, hard, energy-filled run. Along with this lack of enthusiasm comes a lack of interest in your work and everything else you're doing. Jobs that seem challenging and fun when you're feeling good seem just too much trouble when you've been putting too much energy into your running.

If you do get an injury, review what went on the last few days before it happened—and the last few weeks. Question yourself about your running the way a doctor would, if you went to him for treatment. Discuss the injury with a running friend—he may think of more questions to ask. This will give you a clue as to what started the problem.

As you advance in running, you'll find yourself more and more involved in observing how your body ticks. You don't

have to drive yourself crazy noticing every detail of your run. Just be an interested observer and you'll learn a lot about what makes your body hurt, and what keeps it healthy.

Your Runner's Medicine Chest

Here are some of the tools and tapes that podiatrists and runners use. Some, you'll want to buy and keep handy. Others, you may not buy right away, but I'd like you to know about them in case you ever do need them.

• Zonis Tape. A porous tape that's very protective. Runners wrap it around an area that's prone to blistering. Baseball players use it on their hands.

• Elastoplast. An elasticized adhesive tape. Many drugstores carry it, or your druggist can order it for you. Comes in one-inch, two-inch and three-inch widths. I use it for the Arch-Supporting Strapping given in the chapter on weak foot. It's good for taping down the cushioning and pads you put on your feet. Ordinary tape sometimes pulls loose when you run or pulls on your skin until the skin tears. Elastoplast stretches as your foot moves, and your padding stays in place. You can wear it in the shower—it gets wet and then dries off again.

• One-inch adhesive tape. I use it to secure the edges of the Elastoplast in the Arch-Supporting Strapping.

• I don't use Band-Aids, because they're plastic coated or lined with Telfa. Telfa and plastic don't allow the escape of liquids from a wound, so a wet wound becomes macerated and doesn't heal quickly.

• Gauze. Keep squares of gauze handy. When you have a blister you've just opened, clean it with an antiseptic, then cover it loosely with gauze. Tape down the edges of the gauze.

• Antiseptic. I like Betadine as well as anything. You can buy it without prescription. I also use Gentian Violet. Ask your podiatrist or other doctor to give you a prescription for 2 percent Gentian Violet, aqueous solution. The aqueous solution keeps it from burning. Or you can buy 1 percent

Gentian Violet without a prescription. Gentian Violet is an antiseptic, a drying agent and a mild fungicide. It's good for blisters and athlete's foot between the toes.

• Pain killers. Use aspirin if you're not allergic to it and don't have ulcers. Get buffered aspirin, so it won't upset your stomach. Ecotrin is a special coated aspirin that releases in the small intestine, so it doesn't cause stomach troubles. Ascriptin is aspirin with Maalox in it, so it coats your stomach to prevent upsets.

Now, here's a warning I give frequently in this book, but I'll give it again here, because it's important. Take aspirin with your meals and at bedtime. Never take pain killers before going out to run, because they mask pain, and pain is a symptom. It's better for you to know that something's going wrong while it's happening. Otherwise, you'll keep running and with every step you're making the problem worse. In the end, it takes longer to heal and you've lost more running time than if you had stopped running when you first felt the pain.

• Emery board for smoothing down corns and calluses. I don't recommend cutting corns with a razor blade, but it's helpful to smooth a corn down a bit with an emery board. You'll break the continuity of the dead skin and restore some elasticity to the skin. By filing the corn a bit, you're making it smaller. That means your shoe won't be so tight, and there'll be less pressure on the corn. If the pressure is taken off long enough, the corn will disappear.

• Doughnut pads for corns are fine. But don't use corn drops. And don't use corn pads impregnated with corn drops. Corn drops are salicylic acid, and it can burn good skin as well as the dead skin. It's dangerous for diabetics and other people with impaired circulation; it's dangerous for everyone.

• Lamb's wool. Curity Brand is a good one. Get the silky kind, not the uncarded lamb's wool. Lamb's wool is good for wrapping around toes that have corns—especially if the corn is on the tip of the toe or the top of the toe. It protects the whole area from pressure—more effectively than aperture pads. Wrap it around toes that are subject to blisters.

• Moleskin. Very handy for cutting out made-to-order cushioning. It's cushioned on one side and adhesive on the other. You can cut out different shapes to put behind the metatarsal heads or the ball of the foot or wherever you need them. Overlap them, double them, quadruple them—make them as thick as you want. You can roll moleskin into sticks to put under the crest of the toes where that's called for.

• Adhesive felt. Use the same way as moleskin. It's thicker than moleskin. You can double and triple the felt, cut holes in it. Trim and taper the edges so it doesn't feel like you're standing on a bump.

• Dr. Scholl's heel pads are good—for the heels as well as other parts of the foot. They can be cut and shaped to fit different parts of the foot. These heel pads are foam rubber that's covered with plastic, so they stay neater than plain foam rubber. Foam rubber sometimes gets messy—covered with tape and sweat.

• Victex Makeup Sponges. You can buy these in Woolworth's or the drugstore. They come in ½-inch and ¾-inch thickness. I like them for heel pads. I find they're just the right texture—just soft enough and just firm enough. I think the stock of Victex must have gone up since I started recommending them and I don't even own stock. One of my patients buys them by the gross. He has to wear heel pads all the time —so this way he always has fresh ones when the old ones get grubby.

• Sponge rubber metatarsal pads and cookies—you can buy these from the shoemaker. Put them in your shoe if you need some arch support. Sometimes these do the trick, and you don't even have to buy a full arch support. They're good for women, because you can put them in a high-heeled shoe, which you can't do with a regular arch support.

• Ice packs you can put in your freezer and use for inflamed Achilles tendons, runner's knees, sprained ankle or other inflamed areas. You can buy these in your runner's store.

First Aid Techniques for the Majority
of Runners' Injuries

Basic first aid for many pains and injuries includes one or more of these tools:
- ice
- elevation
- aspirin
- heat

Ice is the first thing you should use for inflammation and for muscles in spasm. You can buy an ice bag in the runners' store, and keep it in the refrigerator. Or make one by putting cubes in a plastic bag and closing the top with a twist tie.

Inflammation You know an area is inflamed if it feels warm to the touch. If your right ankle has some inflammation, it will feel warmer than your left ankle. Other symptoms of inflammation are redness, swelling, pain and limitation of movement.

Runners often get inflamed ankles, tendons, muscles and knees—and ice will help all of these. Painful heel spurs also respond to ice.

For inflammation, you should use aspirin and ice first (and elevation, where appropriate). Use the ice right after your run. In some cases heat can be used later in the day—a heating pad or hot bath. Here are some specifics.

For a sprained ankle, wrap the area in an ice pack and put the foot on a chair. Continue ice treatments—ten minutes on, ten minutes off—for the first twenty-four hours. Also keep the foot elevated, for the first twenty-four hours. Put a couple of pillows under it when you go to bed.

For knee pain, wrap the knee in an ice pack after running —ten minutes on, ten minutes off, then repeat. A heating pad can be used in the evening. Set it on low, never on high.

For hamstring pull, ice the hamstrings for a half hour after running. Dr. Seymour Goldstein, an excellent runner's chiropractor, advises icing hamstrings a half hour before running, too; but I personally don't recommend using ice before

running.

For pain in the heel, caused by heel spur or bruising of the bone, put an ice pack in a basin and rest your heels on that. Leave your feet on ice fifteen minutes—then off fifteen minutes—then repeat.

For pain on the arches or the heads of the metatarsal bones (where the toes connect to the metatarsals), rest the feet on an ice bag, fifteen minutes on—fifteen minutes off—then repeat.

For Achilles tendonitis, wrap the ice bags around the inflamed area for fifteen minutes on. Later in the evening, use the heating pad (on low) to bring blood to the area and promote healing.

For painful muscles after a run, apply an ice pack for ten minutes. Do this before attempting massage. Ice reduces inflammation, stops swelling, and anesthetizes the area. When the pain is diminished, the runner calms down—and that's very important to someone who's exhausted and hurting from a long hard race.

Aspirin—for any of these inflammations, take two aspirins at each meal and two at bedtime—unless you have an ulcer or other reason for not taking aspirin.

Relax a strained muscle before you stretch it. If you have a tight, strained muscle or tendon, you know it has to be stretched. But if it's actually painful—not just tight—wait a few days and let it relax. This means don't stretch and don't run for a few days. Then start your stretching exercises. Meanwhile, you can use a heating pad and hot baths to help your muscles and tendons relax.

Recovering from a big race. The day after a marathon—or any big race—take a few walks, to bring blood to the tight, tired muscles and help the healing process. And do some slow, easy stretching.

Basic Foot Maintenance

Use talcum powder between your toes to absorb moisture and prevent cracking. Talcum powder also reduces friction, so it's a protection against blisters.

In fall and winter, put cream on your heels to prevent cracking. Cracked skin on the heels can be very painful. All creams are about equally good. I suggest Crisco or Spry— they're cheap and they're as effective as any hand cream.

Keep your toenails cut short—long nails can jam into the front of your shoe as you run downhill. This causes black toenail or ingrown toenail. Cut the nails straight across, not curved, to prevent ingrown toenail.

Rub corns and calluses with an emery board to reduce them. It's much more effective than a pumice stone. Very thick calluses have to be removed by the podiatrist.

Alternate Exercises—When You Can't Run

If you're injured, it may console you to know that athletes heal faster than sedentary people because they have better circulation. Nutrients and healing agents are delivered faster to the site of the injury. Also, athletes have better musculature. So, if you've got a foot or leg injury, your muscles do a better job of milking the fluids up out of the swollen area.

It's very important to find some alternate exercise when you can't run. Otherwise, you'll lose endurance quickly. And emotionally, you'll be impossible to live with.

The exercise I don't recommend is jumping rope. What I do recommend is swimming, water exercises, bike riding, stretching and weight work for the upper body.

I don't like jumping rope because you're constantly landing on the balls of your feet and causing a lot of trauma. Jumping on the balls of your feet can cause Achilles tendonitis or shin splints. If you insist on jumping, use a padded mat.

Swimming is an excellent indoor or outdoor exercise. You can keep your muscles and heart in shape, without putting weight on your legs. In terms of aerobic benefit, one mile of swimming equals four miles of running.

Swimming the crawl develops the arms and chest, and that's something many runners need to work on.

Do straight swimming to keep up your cardiovascular fitness. And try a few fun exercises.

• Put a spare tire under your arm pits, and "jog" in the water. This exercises your leg muscles without strain.

• Put flippers on your feet and swim. Good exercise for the quadriceps.

• Do the frog kick. Relieves pain of the outer hip, which occurs either at leg joint or a bit higher, up toward the hip bone.

• Do stretching exercises in the water. Hold onto the side of the pool with both hands. Put your feet flat against the side of the pool and stretch.

Riding a bike is less effective aerobically than swimming or running, but it can keep your leg muscles toned up.

Weight work is good for developing the chest, arms and upper back. One of my patients, Molly Colgan, found that her upper back got tired on long runs, so she started working with weights. Molly just finished her fifth marathon, and she feels the weight work has increased her endurance.

How to Choose a Podiatrist When You Need One

I've given this a lot of thought, and I think the best way is what you'd do on your own—ask other runners. There is an Academy of Podiatric Sports Medicine that podiatrists can join, but all it means is that they've sent in their entry fee and application. A Fellow or Diplomate, however, has qualified by being tested. So I think the best thing you can do is go on the recommendation of other runners.

There are a lot of good podiatrists who don't deal with runners; so they don't learn enough about what happens to the foot in motion. A podiatrist who works with athletes learns something new every day. Before and after a marathon —or any big race—his office is filled with runners bringing him new problems and new information. That's the sort of podiatrist who's likely to know how to solve your problem.

Ask the other runners at your local "Y" or at the running store, or phone your Road Runners' Club.

How much can a podiatrist help you?

I tell my patients that I'm successful about 80 percent of the time. I don't think anyone can actually guarantee success, because every body is different. Also, some types of injuries respond better than others. Some of the injuries we have the best results with are heel spurs, runner's knee, and posterior tibial shin splints. Some problems that we don't always succeed with are groin pull and outer hip pain.

Very often your podiatrist will send you to another specialist—a chiropractor, osteopath or orthopedist. Muscle injuries sometimes need a lot of work and patience and a variety of approaches. But whatever your problem is, it can usually be helped by the teamwork of the right doctor and a knowledgeable, persistent patient.

Then, if all else fails, there's the last resort—try cutting down on your mileage.

6

The Difference Between Hard Orthotics and Soft Orthotics

Patients often ask me why I use "soft" orthotics instead of the "hard" (plastic or metal) orthotics that some podiatrists use.

If you've chosen a podiatrist—probably on the recommendation of other runners who've had success with him—I think you should trust his judgment. But I find that runners are very involved patients; they like to know what's going on, and why I'm using this treatment instead of some other one.

A lot of my patients are physicians and enjoy discussing different forms of treatment. But, no matter what line of work you're in, you're certainly concerned with your own injury and what's being done for it.

So, for your information, I'll tell you some of the differences between hard and soft orthotics; and why I almost always use the soft orthotics.

Hard orthotics are made of molded plastic or hard-hammered steel.

Soft orthotics are made of rigid leather bonded to a mixture of rubber and wood flour. Because they're made of leather,

dogs eat soft orthotics. Also, greasy substances like Vaseline separate the leather tops from the bottoms. So don't put greasy ointments on your feet when you wear soft orthotics.

Both types of orthotics are made to a mold of your foot. Here are some differences in how they work.

1. Hard orthotics do not cover the entire bottom of your foot. They stop behind the metatarsal heads (the ball of the foot). They give less control to problems in the forefoot.

For instance, your doctor may decide that the front of your foot needs to be tilted inward by a few degrees. Okay. He has an orthotic made with a wedge to tilt your foot inward.

But, if you get a plastic orthotic, which stops at the ball of the foot, your forefoot will not be tilted into the exact degree it needs. The soft tissue in the ball of your foot absorbs some of the tilt.

Another forefoot problem you may have is Morton's foot (your big toe is shorter than your second toe). To correct this problem, your podiatrist can prescribe a soft orthotic that raises the head of the first metatarsal and thereby gives better forefoot control. But a hard orthotic only raises the area behind the first metatarsal head, so you get less control.

2. Plastic orthotics can be compressed at the arch just by pressing on them with your thumb. Then the heel tilts up. Soft orthotics stay firm when you press on the arch. The heel doesn't tilt up.

What does this mean when you're running? If the arch is flattening, and the heel is tilting up, your foot may be pronating—turning inward. Excessive pronation is one of the problems we're usually trying to correct. It's a cause of many runner's injuries.

3. Now, the heel area. Your foot may need to be tilted inward or outward at the heel. We do this by putting a wedge on the bottom of the orthotics. In a soft orthotic, the wedge presses up through the leather, and your heel tilts the way it should.

But a plastic orthotic is so rigid the wedge does not press up, and your heel is not tilted properly.

4. I can fix and adjust a soft orthotic right in the office. A plastic orthotic has to be sent back to the laboratory, and you have to wait ten days.

Let me explain how this works. When you need orthotics, your doctor tests and measures your feet, makes a mold of your foot, and sends it to the lab with instructions. About ten days later, the orthotics come back, and you put them in your shoes and go out and run.

Then you start phoning your doctor's office and complaining. The arch is too high or not high enough; you need more cushioning here or less tilt there. For two weeks the doctor tells you to hang in and keep running to break in the device.

After two weeks, he wants to hear your complaints. Now you know what really needs adjustment. With soft orthotics, the doctor can sand a little material off the bottom, or glue a little on, and you're off and running. You may have to come back two or three times, for little adjustments. When you're done, you've got an orthotic device that's truly custom-made to your foot and your way of running.

This convenience is a big reason why many podiatrists and patients prefer the soft orthotics.

5. Comfort. The plastic orthotics have a rigid edge that sometimes irritates the foot. Your foot spreads out as you run, and the edge can dig into your feet. This doesn't happen with soft orthotics.

Do I ever use plastic orthotics? I use a variation—Fiberglass supports within a soft orthotic. For instance, if you have heel spurs, I may use some extra support in that area—because that's the weight-bearing area of your foot, and that painful spot needs the weight taken off it.

Or, if a patient is overweight like me, he may need extra support. So I'll use a layer of Fiberglass in the weight-bearing area of the orthotics.

These are some reasons why I—and a lot of podiatrists—use the soft orthotics. If you've found a podiatrist who uses hard orthotics, I'm sure he has good reasons for it, and he'll be happy to discuss them with you.

7
Marathoning-

A Podiatrist's Eye-View

There are no accidental running injuries.

That's what runner/coach Tom Osler says. His statement may be a little exaggerated, but I think he's basically right. It's what I've been saying throughout this book: If you get an injury, you've probably been pushing yourself—either in training or in a race.

My experience with runners in the New York City Marathon confirms this point of view. After the latest New York City Marathon (1979), I got to thinking and comparing the marathons I've worked at over the last few years—in terms of how many runners needed treatment at the finish; how they ran the race; how well they prepared and trained for this grueling effort.

Marathons are an interesting laboratory for sports medicine. We get thousands of men and women going through an incredible test of fitness, strength and endurance. It's a great place for podiatrists—and runners—to learn about what causes injuries and what keeps runners healthy.

Actually, I never get to see the New York City Marathon. I only see the bruised and blistered remains of it—the aching runners who limp in, or are carried in to our little M.A.S.H. Unit at the finish line in Central Park.

I really enjoy working at the marathon. And, judging by the growing numbers of medical volunteers every year, I'd say a lot of people enjoy it. This year, we had about 130 volunteers. Most were podiatrists or podiatry students, and we're getting more and more physicians and nurses and some very hard-working chiropractors, therapists and medical masseurs. Our medical group at the finish line is the happiest field hospital you can imagine—tents and cots and blankets spread out under the trees, vats of E.R.G. and Gookinade and cases of Perrier for the thirsty warriors, and the Red Cross contribution—the world famous doughnuts and coffee.

First, there's the Lower Extremity Treatment Unit spread out over a large lawn. Then, up on a little hill, there are ambulances and mobile oxygen units for medical emergencies. Here you can see several runners lying on cots, receiving intravenous feedings of normal saline solution. According to Dr. Ed Colt, an endocrinologist who works year-round with the Road Runners Club, most runners treated here are suffering from heat exhaustion and leg cramps—which is one of the symptoms of heat exhaustion.

Down in the Lower Extremity area, I'd have to say the most common injury we see is blisters. Now and then a runner will arrive with something serious, like a sprained ankle. And, all day long, the medical masseurs are working on people with sore, cramped muscles. Dr. Mac Goldstein, a chiropractor, was there and I noticed he often put ice packs on cramped muscles before working on the runner. Mac explained that this anesthetizes the painful muscles and helps bring down the inflammation. It's also very soothing to the suffering athlete. Once the runner is feeling less pain, the chiropractor or therapist can work more effectively. Mac is a consultant to several college track teams, so I was glad to pick up this tip from someone who's so experienced with treating

post-race problems.

Actually, we don't see all the "patients" at the finish line. This year, there were first aid stations along the whole route of the race. This innovation came from the organizers of the marathon's medical service—Dr. Louis Galli and Dr. Josef Geldwert, two very able podiatrists. So we have one first aid unit at the start of the race, one at the end, and sixteen more units all along the route—staffed by podiatrists, students and physicians and nurses from nearby hospitals. The New York City Marathon goes through the five boroughs of the city— so the local hospitals contributed volunteers.

The station at the start of the race will be expanded next year. The "patients" there are often runners who were afraid to go to a podiatrist before the marathon—because they might be told not to run.

What happens is, a runner has been working for months, all through the heat of the summer, preparing for this big race in the fall. Now, in the last week or so before the big event, he gets some aches or pains. But he grits his teeth and prays that the pain will just go away. The desire to run the marathon overcomes his common sense and he shows up, that cool October morning, wondering how he's going to get through the race and if it's really okay for him to run. Then he sees that there are some podiatrists on hand—so he rushes over for reassurance or some strapping or a pat on the head.

Basically, the volunteer medical unit is not meant to be a hospital that will treat any injury. And runners shouldn't think that it's all right to run in any condition, because there'll be doctors handy. We're simply there to give first aid and have ambulances available to send people to the hospital if necessary.

As runners check in for first aid all along the route—or at the finish line—podiatry students are there to get a few vital statistics. The point is to learn as much from this marathoning experience as possible. Information taken includes the runner's age, previous marathon experience, weekly training schedule, previous history of injury and what brand and model of shoe

he's wearing. These statistics might answer several interesting questions. For instance—is there really a "wall"? Do more runners show up for treatment at the twenty-mile mark than at any other spot? Is there anything about shoe design that can be correlated with injuries? How much does your age and sex and amount of training affect your chances of being injured? These are some of the questions we're all trying to answer, as we meet and treat and talk with hundreds of marathoners each year.

I see a lot of my regular patients at the marathon, and find out how they've fared. One of these is my friend Dick Traum, a man who runs the marathon even though one of his legs is artificial. Dick was hit by a car in a gas station some years ago, and his leg was amputated eight inches above the knee. Dick was a college student at that time, and he was involved in collegiate wrestling. Part of his training for that sport was road work to build endurance. Now Dick says he runs to keep in shape, but he just wouldn't do it, unless he had a goal. So he does about four races a year.

Dick first came to me for runner's knee. His condition improved when he started wearing an orthotic device and doing exercises for the quadriceps. But runner's knee was not his only problem—he also has some arthritis in the knee. This means he can't run as many miles per week as he'd like. So, to keep up his endurance and his aerobic capacity, he pedals as much as a hundred miles a week on his bike. This keeps his leg muscles strong, without putting strain on the knee.

Dick says he doesn't really race the marathon—he navigates it. It takes him about eight hours to finish. In order to avoid the crush of runners, he starts at five in the morning— five hours before the official starting time—so he arrives at the finish with the three-hour marathoners. Dick treasures pictures of himself being passed by Bill Rodgers in the last few miles of the race.

I didn't see Dick at the end of this year's marathon. He had a few blisters, but he's an old-time runner, so he takes care of them himself. In fact, we saw fewer of *any* runners in

the injury section this year. There were simply fewer injuries, even though there were more people running, and it was a hotter day than we had for the previous year's marathon.

The statistics aren't all together yet, but I'd say about 300 people came in at the finish line for treatment. Only a small percentage of these needed intravenous feeding or other emergency treatment. Dr. Colt estimates that ten to twenty people were sent to the hospital with heat exhaustion—fewer than last year.

My theory is that runners are getting better trained and better educated. Runners are like sponges, they soak up every bit of information they can get—on vitamin C and shoes and exercises and different ways of doing intervals. All year long, they're learning and experimenting with their running. Then they show up at the marathon with a lot more training and understanding.

This year's runners also had more specific experience in running a marathon. In 1978, 39 percent of the men had never run a marathon before and 61 percent of the women. In 1979, roughly 25 percent of the men were first-timers and 50 percent of the women. So they knew how to train and how to run the course—and they got fewer injuries.

Also, they ran slower—and that may be another reason why they got fewer injuries. Allan Steinfeld, coordinator of the marathon, looked into his statistics and told me that the peak finishing time was later this year by about a half hour. For both 1978 and 1979, the peak time is between three and a half and four hours. But, in 1979, fewer people made it at three and a half; a lot more crossed under the finish banner at four hours. At 3:30 P.M., approximately 105 people per minute were crossing the finish. At 4 P.M., about 150 people were finishing every minute. And these were experienced runners who were probably capable of going a bit faster, if they wanted to push.

What happened? Allan theorizes that this year's higher temperatures told people to run slower and not to push. So they finished later—but with fewer injuries. It's a good lesson for

all of us.

Of course, the runners who did show up with injuries have learned their lesson too. They've had it with marathons. The most frequent remark I hear in our outdoor emergency room is, "Oh my God! I'll never run another marathon!" It gives me a feeling of nostalgia. Because the same people were there last year saying the exact same thing.

PART TWO

8

How to Read Your Future in Your Feet

Or, What Injuries Mother Nature Has Set You Up For And How to Avoid Them

The best way to avoid a problem is to be prepared for it. Running is a beautiful, healthy sport—but it does put demands on your body. After a number of miles, you've got to expect some wear and tear, a little strain on some of your parts.

Yes, you may get an injury if you run a large number of miles. Does this mean that the critics are right? That runners would be better off sitting home? I don't think so. Everything in life is a trade-off. You can stay home and keep your feet comfortable. Or you can go out and run and develop a foot problem (which is probably correctable), and in exchange, you get a healthier heart and lungs, better circulation, leaner body, stronger muscles, a fresher complexion and a better disposition.

So I say run. But be prepared. If you were setting out on a long automobile trip, you'd check your car and look for weaknesses. Now you're a runner, and you're right at the start of a nice long trip. I'm hoping you've got a lot of miles ahead

of you—whether you're a beginner or an experienced runner.

So take a minute to check your feet. If you know what kind of feet you have, you'll know what injuries to expect. Virtually all running injuries start in the feet. This includes hip and back pains, as well as foot pains, knee pains, pulled thigh muscles and fractures in the legs and feet. No one was born with perfect, injury-proof feet. Even feet that have functioned beautifully for thirty or forty years suddenly start giving you problems when they're subjected to miles of pounding on hard paved roads.

But don't be alarmed—there's hope. The way I see it, running injuries are something like karma. According to certain Buddhist teachings, your karma, your life problems, are all set up before you're born. But if you make the right moves and have the right attitude, you can avoid or minimize the evil. It's the same with running injuries. If you know what to look for, you can take care of many problems before they start. And if you do get an injury, you'll know how to keep it from becoming serious.

So right now, I want you to look at your feet and start learning what kind of injury you're genetically programmed for.

Your First Toe's Shorter Than Your Second Toe

Actually, it's not your first toe that's short—it's the metatarsal bone it's attached to. You've got Morton's Foot—like so many of the athletes I see. Morton's foot contributes to many different injuries. It's one of the causes of painful knees, pain in the ball of the foot, callus under the second toe, hip pain, back pain, you name it.

Basically, your first metatarsal bone is too short to carry its share of the load. This means the weight gets shifted around, and all sorts of problems can happen. What you have to do is look up your particular problems—painful knees, hips, or whatever you're feeling—and you'll learn how to redistribute the weight and get rid of the pain.

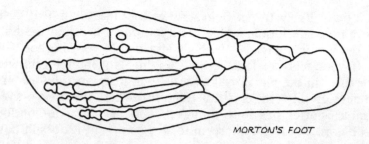

MORTON'S FOOT

Thin Feet with Prominent Bones

You may have perfectly constructed feet—arches the right height, well-proportioned bones, everything beautiful—but still have injuries because your feet don't have enough fat padding. Thin people aren't the only ones with thin feet. You could have fat padding all over your body and still have thin bony feet.

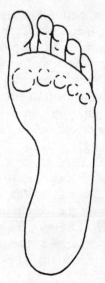

THIN FOOT WITH
PROMINENT BONES

You're likely to get bone bruises, because your feet don't have much cushioning. One bone you might bruise is the head of the first metatarsal—the bone attached to your big toe.

If your feet are long as well as thin, you might get stress fractures in the metatarsal bones. Long metatarsal bones tend to develop tiny cracks (stress fractures) where the bone curves. Frank Shorter has long thin feet, and he has a lot of foot problems. But it doesn't seem to stop him, and it doesn't have to stop you either.

Read the chapter on "How to be Your Own Podiatrist" to learn about the various kinds of padding you can use to cushion your feet. Also, the section on Sesamoiditis will be helpful to you; and the section on pain on top of the foot, along the shaft of the bone in chapter 9. This section tells you how metatarsal stress fractures are treated.

Fallen Arches (Weak Foot)

You can see this problem better when you stand on your feet and put your weight on them. Notice how the ankles turn in and the weight falls toward the inside of the foot. (In technical terms, your foot pronates.)

Here's another test. Stand up and try to lay a pencil on the floor, running from your heel to your first metatarsal head. If your arches are normal, you can do it—because there's a straight line between those two points. But if you have fallen arches, the pencil will angle out.

This condition, which used to be called fallen arches, is now known as weak foot. It can lead to knee pain, lower back pain, Achilles pain (that's pain in the back of the lower leg, just above the ankle). You may get pain in the heel and arch (Plantar Fasciitis and Heel Spurs). You're subject to pain on the inner side of the lower leg—somewhere in the area where the large calf muscle meets the shin muscle. People with fallen arches get it all.

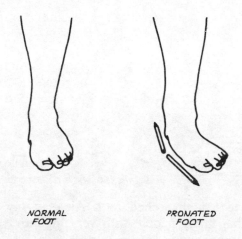

NORMAL
FOOT

PRONATED
FOOT

But don't worry—a lot of us weak-footed folks are out there running and having a fine time. You just have to know how to take care of your feet.

I was born with low arches, and I've developed fallen arches over the years. I've observed over the years that Semites (Jews and Arabs) and Blacks are more likely to have low arches than other people are. One of my patients asked me if this was because we Jews have been wandering for so many years. Another one of those interesting questions that I can't answer.

In any case, your feet are going to demand a lot of attention. Read the section on Weak Foot and read the section on each of your symptoms as it comes along.

Incidentally, you don't have to be born with low arches to get fallen arches. People who are born with high or ordinary arches have a good shot at it too.

High-Arched Foot

High arches can "fall" too—often sooner than low-arched feet. Romance people—French, Italians, Spanish—are more

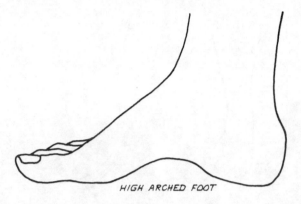

HIGH ARCHED FOOT

likely to have a high arched foot. Also, in my experience, I've found that many people with very high-arched feet tend to be thin, tense people.

If your high-arched foot starts collapsing, you too, develop the weak foot symptoms—so read the section on weak foot.

High arches are less flexible. So you may develop Impact Shock, Heel Bruise and Metatarsal Bruise. There are things you can do to treat these injuries, if you've got them. And there are ways to help prevent them. So read those sections and learn how to keep yourself running in comfort.

Extremely High-Arched Foot with Retracted Toes (Cavus Foot)

The cavus type of foot has a very high arch and high instep and the toes are a little retracted. Your foot can be good and solid—well-balanced, as far as weight distribution goes—but the high arch leads to a lot of troubles.

You can get pain on the bottom of the heel and arch (read plantar fasciitis; heel spurs in chapter 9). You may get pain and calluses on the bottom of the foot where the toes connect to the metatarsal bones (read pain and calluses on the ball of the foot). You can also get pain under the three middle toes, where they connect to the metatarsal bones (read anterior

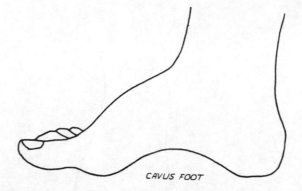

CAVUS FOOT

metatarsal bursitis). You're liable to get corns on the top of your toes. (Try slitting the tops of your running shoes to give your toes more room.) You may also get corns on the tips of the toes. Read the section on corns in chapter 9, to learn what to do—and what not to do—about corns.

Your cavus foot needs a lot of care, no question about it. But if you'll read about each symptom as it comes up, you can give your feet the intelligent care they need and keep them running comfortably.

Feet with Bunions

A bunion is an enlargement of the bone attached to your big toe. (A tailor's bunion is the same thing, only with the little toe.) If you have bunions, your big toe may be turned in toward the second toe, and tucked under or over the second toe. But people with straight first toes get bunions too.

I don't have to tell you that bunions can be painful. But what you should be aware of is that running can cause extra problems. Some doctors believe that the repeated pressure of running can cause bunions to enlarge even more. This may or may not be true. In any case, all the weight you put on the bunion by running can cause extra pain. (When you run, you come down with a force equal to three times your body

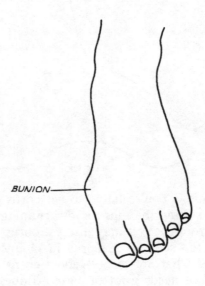

BUNION

weight.)

The right running shoes are important for everyone, but especially for people with bunions. Badly fitting shoes can make your bunions even more painful. But you didn't get them from bad shoes or anything else. You were just born to have bunions. Or at least with a tendency to bunions. Read the section on How to Buy Shoes and the section on Bunions—and learn how to take care of them.

Short Bunchy Calf Muscles

This doesn't go with any particular type of foot. But you should be aware that your kind of leg is more susceptible to certain injuries—shin splints, Achilles tendonitis, pain in the back of the knee and tight hamstrings.

Basically, you need lots of stretching and lots of attention to your running habits. Read the chapter on Exercises to

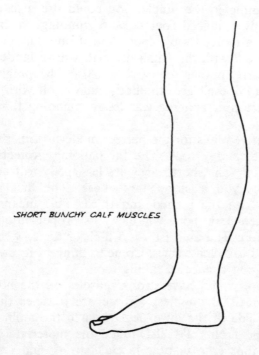

SHORT BUNCHY CALF MUSCLES

Prevent Injuries, and concentrate especially on the Wall Push-ups and Hamstring Stretches. And read the chapter on How to Run Right, and Hurt Less.

The Ideal Runner's Foot?

Nature has not yet published her plan for the perfect modern runner's foot—a foot that can run on concrete roads for the ever-increasing distances that today's runners love—and never get an injury. Since nature hasn't revealed her design, I'm not sticking my neck out either. I don't know what the perfect running foot would be. But a short, stubby, well-balanced foot —a wide foot with plenty of fat padding—would be an excellent piece of running equipment for city streets.

If you're running in the jungle, you could use a less firm and less perfectly balanced foot because running on uneven terrain requires a more flexible foot. And if one part of your foot doesn't fit well with the patch of earth you've landed on, then another part, another toe, *will* fit. Also, the jungle terrain is softer and doesn't give the body such a jolt with every step. So our ancestors' running was less demanding than our running.

But my tentative plans for the perfect modern runner's foot is a short, wide, pudgy foot. The fat padding protects you from bone bruises. The short bones are less likely to fracture. The width gives you a more stable base. The first toe is slightly longer than the second and third. This means that each toe and metatarsal bone will carry its proper amount of weight as you run. The arch isn't too high or too low. Either of these can lead to fallen arches. Come to think of it, medium arches have a good chance of falling too.

This ideal foot would have strong muscles on the bottom. And strong post-tibial muscles. (These are muscles that go from the inner side of the lower leg down to the arch. They help support the arch.) I'd also make the material on the bottom of the foot (the plantar fascia) strong and resilient —but not too resilient.

You see how easy it is to have a less-than-perfect runner's foot?

Ideally, this short fat foot should be connected to a leg with long, slender muscles. These are muscles that stay injury-free, while we less fortunate people with short, bunchy muscles get all sorts of stiffness and tightness in the lower leg.

Until the perfect foot comes along, my experience has shown me that we've all got an excellent chance at having some kind of injury. So learn what kind of foot nature gave you, and learn how to take care of it.

9
Runners' Injuries and How to Treat Them Yourself

One Leg Shorter than the Other

(Don't say no—it's the first thing you should check.)

No matter what your injury, there's a chance that it's aggravated by short-leg.

Think of a line running from the tips of your toes along your arch, then up the back of your leg and your spine. If one of your legs is shorter than the other, it can cause (or aggravate) a pain or strain anywhere along that line.

The pain can come on the shorter side or the longer side. A lot of us have one leg shorter than the other and don't even know it. It doesn't really matter, if it isn't causing you any pain. Before you started running, you may have been perfectly comfortable with one leg ¼-inch shorter. Now you start running and with every running step, you come down with three times your body weight. If you weigh a hundred fifty pounds, you're socking four hundred and fifty pounds onto a leg that's a bit unbalanced anyway because it's shorter

than the other.

To think of it another way—it's as if one leg were ¾-inch shorter, instead of ¼-inch.

So the first step for many injuries is to check your leg length. Do this if you've got arch pains, knee pains, hip or back pains, shin pains.

How to Compare Your Leg Lengths   There are two ways you should compare your leg lengths: Compare the distance from the knees to the floor; and the distance from the hipbone to the floor. In this second step, you're actually checking to see whether your hips are level. If they're not, we say you have "pelvic tilt."

To check the lengths of your lower legs (from knee to floor), get a carpenter's level and check your floor to find a place where the floor is level. Now put a straight-backed chair there. Check to be sure the chair is level.

Take off your shoes and socks. Sit with your back against the back of the chair. Put the carpenter's level on your knees and see if the bubble is in the middle. If not, you've got one short leg.

To see if your hips are level, you need a full-length mirror, a piece of string and a felt-tipped pen. Just stand in front of the mirror naked and mark each hip bone with a dot—the bone that sticks out farthest.

Now hold the string from one dot to the other, and you can see if it's level.

Next, check your hips from the rear. Very often, an imbalance shows up in the rear when it doesn't show up in front.

You'll need a helper for this. First, he takes a felt-tipped pen and puts a mark in the dimple above each buttock. Second, he draws a line across the top of your hipbone. To find where to mark, he just feels for the outline of your hipbone, and draws a line on the bone.

Now he compares: Are the two hipbone lines level? Are the dots in the dimples level? He can decide just by looking, or by using the carpenter's level.

If your hips are not level, you either have one short leg or

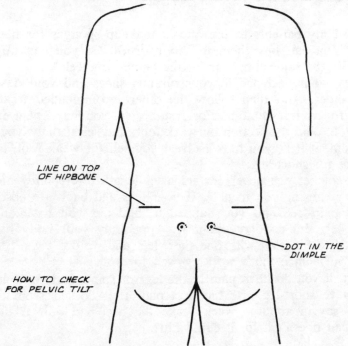

LINE ON TOP
OF HIPBONE

DOT IN THE
DIMPLE

HOW TO CHECK
FOR PELVIC TILT

there's some other reason why one hip is higher than the other. It could be that your spine curves to one side. But whatever the reason—if your hips are uneven you do have one short leg, in effect. It may be that your hip is pulling your leg up and making it short.

So you have to treat yourself for one short-leg—and that means simply putting a heel pad in one shoe.

Sponge rubber makes a good heel pad. If your leg is ¼-inch short, use padding slightly thinner than a ¼-inch. Your sponge rubber should be ³⁄₁₆-inch thick. If your leg is ½-inch short, use sponge rubber ⅜-inch thick. If your leg is ¾-inch short, use padding slightly thinner than three-quarters of an inch.

If your discrepancy is greater than ¾-inch, see a podiatrist. He'll probably give you a little padding under the sole, as well as under the heel. You can't just stick padding under your heel, if you have too great a difference in your leg lengths.

I tell my patients to use Victex makeup sponges for heel pads. You can buy them in Woolworth's. Or you can buy virtually the same thing, under the name "Jogheel."

Wear your heel pad in your running shoes and your daytime shoes. And then follow the other recommended treatment for your symptom. For instance, if you have pain in the arch, read the section on weak foot, and see if that's your problem. If it is, you have to treat yourself for weak foot, as well as for short-leg.

Of course, you never correct a leg-length discrepancy unless it's causing you trouble. If your legs and back are absolutely pain-free and you happen to find out you have one short leg, don't worry about it. Apparently your body has learned to function with one short leg, and we don't want to upset a balance that's working well for you.

But, if you do have pain in the legs or spine, and you find you have short-leg, use the heel pad. If it doesn't seem to help—say in about a week—take the heel pad out. If the heel pad doesn't help, it could hurt.

First Toe Shorter than Second
(Morton's Foot)

Actually, it's not your first toe that's short. It's the first metatarsal bone it's attached to. If you have Morton's foot, you're

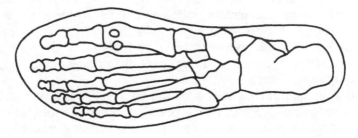

MORTON'S FOOT

in good company. A lot of the top athletes I see in my office have this kind of foot. Why do I see so many of them? Because Morton's foot causes all sorts of problems.

Here's why. When you run, you're supposed to push off on the first and second toe. Actually, between the first and second metatarsals. But a short first metatarsal can't quite carry its share of the weight; so the weight is tilted toward the inside of the foot.

This twist is sent right up the leg and spine—so it can cause knee problems, hip problems, all kinds of problems. It can cause a callus under the second toe, because the first toe is not carrying its share of weight. Your second metatarsal bone will become thicker.

Because so many different injuries can develop from a Morton's foot, we won't try to explain them all here. Just look up each problem under its symptom: painful knees, painful ball of the foot, callus under the second toe, hip pain, back pain.

Stiff Big Toe

Your big toe feels rigid or almost rigid. It's so painful, you've been cutting down on your mileage. But your toe is still painful.

If you came into my office, the first thing I'd do is take hold of your toe and move it up and down. Try it. Do you feel a grating, sandpapery feeling? If so, you may have arthritis and calcium deposits in the joint between the toe and the metatarsal.

But whether you do or not, the answer is to lift the toe up a bit from the ground so it's not getting bumped and pounded every time you run.

Your shoemaker can put a strip of Neoprene, hard rubber, on the sole of your shoe—right behind the ball of the foot. This goes on the outside of the shoe, not on the insole. Tell him to take hard rubber, about ⅛-inch thick. Cut it 1¼-inches

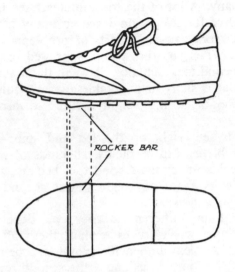

wide and long enough to go across the entire width of the shoe—right behind the widest part of the shoe. (In a shoe that fits properly, the ball of the foot comes at the widest part of the shoe.) He should taper the front and back edges of the strip, so it's not a big bump.

The strip of rubber should come just behind the metatarsal heads. The metatarsals are the bones your toes are attached to.

Now, with this addition to your shoe, your foot rocks right over the strip of rubber when you run. You've taken some of the impact off the ball of the foot and the big toe.

Pain under First Metatarsal Head, Bone Attached to Big Toe

(Sesamoiditis)

You may have increased your mileage lately, or maybe you're doing hill work or speed work—activities where you're run-

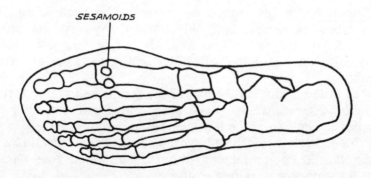

SESAMOIDS

ning on the ball of the foot.

Now, under the head of the first metatarsal bone, you have two or maybe three or four tiny bones called sesamoids. These tiny pealike bones are found at various places in the body. They're remains from our evolutionary past. One thing they do for a runner is to protect the first metatarsal head—because they get hurt before it does.

To see if you've bruised these bones, feel the bottom of your foot with your fingers. Press gently on the first metatarsal head. Look for swelling. You may or may not find any. Now press hard on the first metatarsal head with your thumb —from the bottom of the foot upward. If you feel an excruciating pain, that's it—you've either bruised or broken your sesamoids, and it doesn't matter which. The treatment is the same.

The first step is to ice them. Put some ice cubes in a plastic bag. Twist the bag closed. Then put the bag into a basin, and put your foot on it. Or, use one of the commercial ice bags sold in running stores.

Put your foot on ice for ten minutes, then take it off ten minutes, then repeat. Do this three or four times a day.

Now, second step—the long term treatment—is to correct the conditions that bruised or broke your bones in the first place.

What's happened is, running and pounding on the ball of the foot has put too much pressure on it. You may have been

running on hard pavement. Or maybe you've been doing a lot of hill work or sprinting. When you do, you're continually landing on the ball of the foot. Or maybe you just have a habit of running on the balls of the feet. You've got to correct that.

A little running on the ball of the foot, when you're sprinting for a short distance, that's okay. But if you're running for miles on the ball of the foot, you're asking for trouble.

Your heel should hit the ground first. Then the middle of the foot. Then you take off from the ball of the foot—use it as a spring, not a landing platform.

Or maybe you haven't done anything wrong in your running—maybe you've just got a bony foot. The head of the first metatarsal sticks out, and an awful lot of weight is going on that one spot.

Whatever the reason for your problem—part of the cure is to give yourself a bigger platform to take off from. The first metatarsal head is just one little knob; so pad around it and spread the impact.

I would get a piece of felt pad, about ¼-inch thick—say 3-by-2 inches in size—and cut a sort of U in it, to fit around the first metatarsal head. Don't put padding over the metatarsal head—that's got too much pressure on it already.

The way to find the right spot is, just press with your thumb until you feel that excruciating pain, and then put your pad behind that. When I say "behind," I mean in the direction of the heel. I would bevel the edges of the pad that go toward the arch—taper off the edges—so you're not standing on a lump.

For your pad you can use felt or foam rubber or Dr. Scholl's Heel Pads. These are made of foam rubber covered with plastic, so they stay neater. When you put tape on and then pull it off, the plastic doesn't pull apart the way foam rubber does. When the plastic gets too sticky, you can either buy new pads or clean off the stickiness with nail polish remover. You buy all these in any drug store.

Whatever material you use for padding, hold it over the

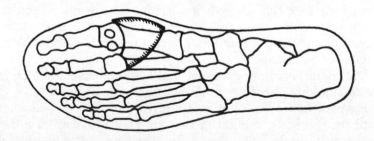

PADDING FOR SESAMOIDITIS

first metatarsal head. Now feel with your fingers and draw the outline of the bone. Then cut out the U-shape to go behind the bone. Don't pad in front of the bone (under the toes).

You can tell your padding is right when you stand and walk on it. You get a great feeling of comfort. You've got a more solid foundation. And the pressure is off that painful bone. If one pad doesn't feel thick enough, use two. You can glue or tape them together.

Whichever kind of padding you use, tape it on with the clear tape that's sold on the foot care stand. Or ordinary adhesive tape. Or use elasticized tape (Elastoplast—your druggist can order it for you if he doesn't carry it).

Wear this padding in your running shoes and in your daytime shoes. Women should stick to flat shoes until the pain is gone. You may always have to wear these pads for your running or you'll bruise your sesamoids all over again. So, once you've figured out the right position for your pads, try gluing them inside your running shoes.

You should be able to start running right away, and the pain should be completely gone in about two weeks. If it isn't, the problem is with the way your foot balances. Your foot may be putting too much weight on the first metatarsal head. It has to do with the length of the bones and the strength of the arches.

In that case, you need a corrective support for your whole

foot—an orthotic device that you wear inside your shoes. It gives your foot the strength it's lacking in certain places, so you'll stop shifting too much weight over to the ball of the foot. Your podiatrist can design a custom-made orthotic from a mold of your foot.

My co-author, Barbara Burr, and I have a special affection for sesamoiditis, because that's what brought us together.

Barbara had been running happily with no foot problems until she reached the point of running about four miles a day on a regular basis. Then she noticed the pain in her first metatarsal head and in the big toe. (Barbara has arthritis in the big toe which only flares up when the sesamoid bones are bruised.)

Like many runners, she owned a lot of running books and has a lot of running friends to consult. No book—and no other runner—came up with the answer for her mysterious aching foot. So she checked with Dr. Sheehan, who sent her to me.

I found that her foot was perfectly balanced. Her only problem was that she has bony feet without much fat padding. So the first metatarsal head sticks out sharply and bruises easily.

I corrected this with an orthotic that puts padding around the first metatarsal head and has a hollow for the bone to sit in. Barbara wears these in her running shoes and all her low-heeled shoes. For higher-heeled shoes, she sometimes tapes pads onto her foot—pads she makes herself.

Once her foot problem was solved, Barbara decided the world needed a book telling runners exactly how to care for their feet. So here it is.

Big Toe Bunions

A bunion is that enlarged bone connecting to the big toe that sticks out at the side. (The head of the first metatarsal bone is enlarged.)

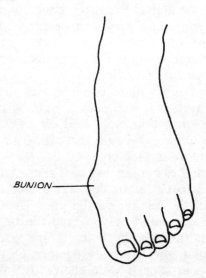

BUNION

A tendency to bunions is something that you inherited. But the size of the bunion increases—and the irritation increases —if you put too much weight and shoe pressure on it.

Why are you putting too much weight on your bunion? Very often, your big toe is angled in—it tucks under or over your second toe. This causes a weight-distribution problem. A lot of your weight drops down onto that first metatarsal head, so the bone grows bigger to support the load.

Many people think of bone as being a very hard, rigid material. Actually, it's fairly adaptable. It will get bigger in response to its surroundings—even when we're adults.

If you tied a tight bandage around your forearm, in time the bone would become narrower under the bandage, and you'd have an indentation around your arm.

With a bunion, your foot is putting extra weight on the first metatarsal head—so the bone grows bigger to handle the extra weight. But this process is not reversible. You can't shrink a bunion. You can only make it more comfortable. Or you can trim it down, surgically.

The pressure of the weight might also give you a callus

under the second metatarsal head (the bone connected to the second toe). Or you might get a corn on top of the second toe. That happens when the big toe is bent in toward the second toe. Your second toe is then crowded and pushed upward, so it rubs against your shoe.

To make your bunion more comfortable, you can buy a bunion pad. It covers the whole area, but the material that goes over the bunion is thinner. You don't want to put thick padding over the bunion, because that will cause more pressure when you put your shoe on.

Or make yourself a bunion bagel. Take a piece of foam rubber and hold it over the bunion. Now take a pencil and draw the shape of the bunion on the pad. Then cut out the shape of the bunion, so when you tape the bagel on, your bunion sticks out through the hole. If one pad isn't thick enough to give relief, glue two pads together. Of course, you'll have to be sure your shoe is wide enough to take this extra padding.

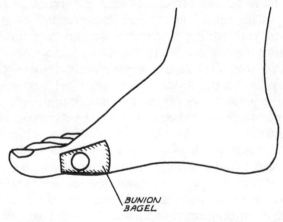

BUNION
BAGEL

If you have a bunion, and your big toe is angled in, the joint can become irritated. You can protect the joint by putting a latex jacket over the toe. This jacket covers the outside of the bunion to protect the joint. It leaves the tip of the toe uncovered.

I'll sometimes prescribe a custom-made latex jacket to protect a bunion. I make a mold of the toe and the metatarsal head, and that's used to make a latex jacket. The jacket is made with space for the bunion and any corn you may have. It's a highly sophisticated corn pad that protects the whole area and gives you a lot of comfort.

Or sometimes I'll make an orthotic device—a special lining for the shoe—that keeps pressure off the bunion. I explained that your bunion grows and becomes irritated when you put too much weight on it. So if you put some padding under your arch, the arch will take more weight, or it will redistribute the weight. Now there's less pressure on the bunion.

Try a commercial arch support. That can shift the weight load and may give you a lot of relief.

Now, check and be sure you've done these three things:

1. You've stopped wearing shoes that are too tight. You've stopped wearing extremely high-heeled shoes. (They throw too much weight forward onto the bunion and force your bunion into the narrower part of the shoe.)

2. You've tried wearing a bunion bagel or latex jacket or other cushioning.

3. You've tried wearing a commercial arch support.

If you're still having trouble with your bunions, you'd better see a sports-oriented podiatrist. You need a podiatrist who works with the mechanics of the body in motion, because your problem is probably caused by the way your weight moves along your foot as you walk and run. He may find that your foot is imbalanced in some way, and he can make an orthotic device to balance you out.

If you don't know a good podiatrist, read the section in chapter 5 on "How to Choose a Podiatrist If You Need One."

One of my patients—Barbara Backer—came to me with very painful bunions. She had always had bunions, but they never bothered her until she got up to four or five miles of

running per day and was doing a lot of hill work and speed work.

In analyzing Barbara's running style, we found that she had been taking off from her bunions. When you run, you should take off from an area between the first and second metatarsals. But Barbara's weight was rolling in, onto the bunion.

I took some Plastizote, a fairly soft, cushiony material, and made pads that fit right under her arches. I glued these into her running shoes. This gave her a more solid foundation, and her weight doesn't roll onto the bunion anymore.

Barbara now runs sixty miles a week, and her bunions are no problem.

Another way to relieve pressure on your bunion is to make a slit in your running shoes. Don't make a big hole that would let the bunion stick out entirely. If you do, your bunion will start scraping the ground as you run. That's not too comfortable.

What about surgery for bunions?

If your big toe angles in under the second toe, it is possible to straighten it out through surgery and trim down the bunion. But this would keep you out of running from six-to-ten weeks. And you're leaving yourself open to some other complication, like rigidity of the joint.

If your bunion is chronically painful and you can't live with it, you may have to resort to surgery. But if you can keep it comfortable with a little pad in the shoe, that's a lot better.

Now that you've learned to take pressure off the bunion, don't put the pressure back on with tight shoes. The key with painful bunions is to get shoes with plenty of space over the ball of the foot. That solves half the problem. Some women wear strap shoes winter and summer to let the bunion stick out. That makes sense, if your feet don't get too cold.

Some doctors think running makes bunions worse by putting extra pressure on them. I'm not so sure about that. I am sure that tight shoes make them worse, but tight shoes alone will not create bunions. If you weren't born to have bunions,

you just won't have them.

If you look back in your family history, you'll find your mother had bunions or your grandmother had them. Now they're yours; so take good care of them.

Small Toe Bunions

You can also get a bunion on the bone connecting to your little toe. This is called a tailor's bunion because tailors used to sit cross-legged and put pressure on the outside of the foot, and that would cause a bunion. So there's an exception to what I just said—if you sit cross-legged eight hours a day you can get a bunion without any help from your genes.

If you have a tailor's bunion, treat it as you would a big-toe bunion. Protect it with a bunion bagel and keep your shoes wide enough, or make a slit in your running shoes to give the bunion space.

Pain in Big Toe Tendon, Connection of Toe to Foot

Even if you have a perfectly designed foot—no bunions, toes all the proper lengths and so on—you may feel pain where the big toe connects to the metatarsal bone. The tendon that lifts the big toe may be prominent and it gets irritated if you wear the wrong shoes.

Where the shoe bends, it's hitting the tendon, and you may get a corn, a sore or an ulceration. This is a shoe problem, not a foot problem. Just figure out which of your shoes is causing the pain and get rid of them. And pay extra attention to how the shoes hit that tendon whenever you buy new ones.

Toes that Can't Straighten Out
(Hammer Toes)

Take your index finger and bend it so the joint sticks up. That's how a hammer toe looks, and generally you can't straighten it out. Some hammer toes can straighten out, but they prefer to stay bent. Any toe except the big toe could be a hammer toe.

Hammer toes are caused by shoes that are too short. The shoe forces the toe back, so the tendon on top of the toe eventually shortens. And the top of the toe really hurts when you run.

A tendon is a cord that's somewhat elastic, but not very. The tendon on top of your toe may have become so short over a long period of time that it can't stretch out again.

Hammer toes don't hurt except you often get a corn on the top. And runners with hammer toes sometimes get a corn right on the tip of the toe.

Just be sure your shoes are loose enough to keep the pressure off the toes. If you can't get running shoes that are loose enough over the toe, cut a slit in the top of the shoes.

If you already have a corn, put an aperture pad on it—a doughnut pad—or wrap lamb's wool all around the toe. I really prefer lamb's wool to a doughnut. If you wear a doughnut on a regular basis, the area all around the corn gets pressed down. So, in effect, the corn is sticking up even higher.

Wrap the lamb's wool around your whole toe three or four times, then twist and press the ends so they blend in together. Lamb's wool is waterproof, so you can leave it on when you shower. It lasts three or four days.

You can buy lamb's wool on the foot care stand in your drugstore. Get the kind that's silky, sort of like angel hair. This is different from the lamb's wool that ballet dancers use. They use uncarded lamb's wool—it's nubby, like steel wool.

If you have a corn on the front of a hammer toe, use the

lamb's wool. And also put some padding under the toe.

Your bent toes have created a big empty arch underneath. Put padding in that arch so your toes are lifted up. Then the front of your toes won't slam into the bottom of the shoe when you run. This relieves the pressure on the corn.

For padding, you can buy a crest pad in the drugstore. Another good padding is one of the cotton sticks your dentist uses. See if he'll give you some.

Or, make your own padding "sticks." Take moleskin, three-inches wide. Roll up a tube. Use enough moleskin to make the tube ¼-inch in diameter. Now wrap gauze around it to hold it together.

Cut the tube so it's long enough to fit under the three middle toes. Put the tube under the crest of the toes and wrap tape around the three toes, including the padding. Now when you run, you're not hitting the tips of the toes. Your weight is landing on the bottom surface of the toes, where it's supposed to be.

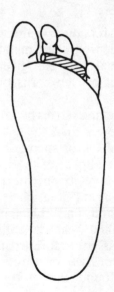

CREST PAD

Pain/Calluses on Ball of Foot

(Prominent metatarsals; bruised and inflamed metatarsals)

Feel the bottom of your foot, and find your metatarsal arch—right where the toes connect to the heads of the metatarsals. As you press along there, starting at the first metatarsal and moving along to the second and third, you should feel an arch. The second, third and fourth metatarsal heads should be higher. Then the arch goes down again, as you get to the fifth metatarsal head.

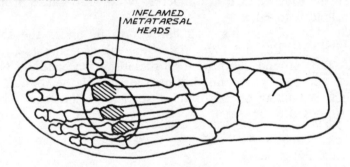

INFLAMED METATARSAL HEADS

If you don't feel an arch there—and you feel calluses on the bones—you've got a prominent metatarsal arch.

A prominent metatarsal arch can give you bruised bones. Inflammation. Calluses and even corns on the bottom of the foot.

With a prominent metatarsal arch, your second, third or fourth metatarsals are lower than they should be. So let's lift them up. Take a piece of felt or sponge rubber ¼-inch thick, and put it right behind the heads of those metatarsal bones.

How do you know where to put the padding? Bend your toes back and feel the painful area where the toes connect to the metatarsals. Press and find the spot that really hurts. Good, that's the metatarsal head. A callused, bruised or inflamed metatarsal head is going to hurt if you press on it.

You may have one or two or three metatarsals causing trouble. Once you've found the guilty parties, tape your

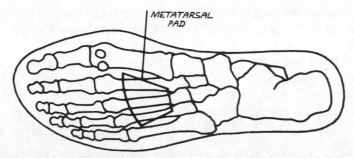

padding just behind them.

You can also buy metatarsal pads. Or you can buy a commercial arch with metatarsal pads in it. It looks like a regular arch support, but it's padded behind the metatarsal heads.

Whichever padding you use, the idea is to elevate the prominent metatarsal and take the pressure off. That will relieve the pain.

You can also do some exercises that make the metatarsal arch strong and more flexible. That may help your condition.

Pick up towels with your toes. Pick up pencils. One of my patients, ballerina Melissa Hayden, has her students pick up marbles with their toes. Then she has them pick up a marble with one toe at a time.

Also, when picking up a towel with the toes—Melissa tells her students to press on the toes as you draw them up. Don't jerk them up. Then as you flatten them out, press them down again. Always work with a slow, steady motion.

These exercises tighten up the arch and also stretch the tendons on top—the ones that help lift the toes. If you do these exercises too long, you'll get cramps in the long arch. But that's just a signal to stop and rest.

Pain under Three Lesser Toes

(Anterior metatarsal bursitis)

This is not an injury to the toes. It's the metatarsal bones that

are hurt—the bones connecting to the toes. Feel in between the toe and the metatarsal head. Press with your fingers, and you'll feel pain.

What's happened is you're coming down too hard on that area. So your body builds up a little protective cushion there —a bursa. Now, when you continue to run and put more pressure on the same area, the bursal sac gets irritated. It's swollen and painful. (You won't feel the sac with your fingers —just pain.)

The cure is to put padding behind the heads of the metatarsals. This puts some cushioning around the metatarsal heads, so you won't be slamming down on them so hard.

Where should you put the cushioning? Bend your toes back and press till you find the spots that hurt. Now tape the padding behind those spots. (Behind, meaning in the direction of the heel.)

Some good pads to use are commercial metatarsal pads. Or take a piece of sponge rubber, ¼-inch thick. Cut out a piece two- or three-inches long—long enough to go behind the painful metatarsal heads. Make the pad about two inches deep. Then tape the padding on.

Another way to take pressure off the metatarsal heads is to lower your heels. If you're a woman, stop wearing high heels until the pain clears up.

It also helps to put padding in *front* of the painful area. You can do this with a crest pad which you buy in the drugstore. It puts padding under the crest of your toes.

Another way to put padding under the crest of the toes is to get some cotton sticks from your dentist and put them under the three middle toes. Wrap tape around the three toes, including the cotton stick.

If you can't get these dental sticks, make a "stick" with moleskin. Get moleskin three-inches wide. Roll it until you make a stick that's a ¼-inch in diameter.

Doctors will often use injection therapy—steroids or Xylocaine or Novocaine—to bring down the inflammation in bruised metatarsals. I prefer padding, because any drug may

have some side effects.

Now, why did you get this bursitis? Why are you putting too much weight on that area of your foot?

Most likely there's some imbalance in your foot—so the weight isn't distributed properly. Too much weight is falling on the ball of your foot. If the pain doesn't clear up in a few weeks with your own padding, go to a sports-oriented podiatrist. He may decide to give you an orthotic, made from a mold of your foot, that will redistribute the weight. Or he can teach you how to pad your own shoes.

Exercising can help too. Pick up towels with your toes. Pick up pencils. These same exercises strengthen the long arch of your foot too, so your whole foundation is stronger and steadier. And that's something every runner wants.

Burning Sensation between Bases of Toes

(Neuromas)

You'll feel this burning sensation between the metatarsal heads and reaching out into the toes. It usually happens between the third and fourth metatarsal heads. But it can occur in the others.

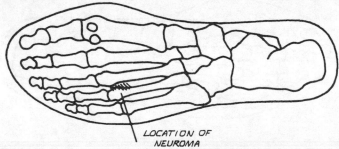

LOCATION OF
NEUROMA

Some people describe this sensation as shooting pains or electric tingling pains. But I usually hear people say they've got a burning sensation reaching out through the third and fourth toes. It's an excruciating pain and you can't bear

weight on it.

You've got a neuroma—a bundle of nerve endings whose covering or sheath has become inflamed and irritated. Very often it happens in a loose foot, a foot that's got too much movement between the metatarsals.

There's no swelling. You can't feel any bumps. You can't even see neuromas on an X ray. You know you've probably got a neuroma by the symptoms—shooting, burning pains or a numb sensation. Runners often say they had to stop running and take off their shoe to massage the foot. But the pain can come on at odd times, even when you're not running or walking.

The first thing you should do is give it ice treatment. Put some ice cubes in a plastic bag and twist the bag closed. Or, if you've got one of those ice bags they sell in running stores, use that.

Put this ice bag in a basin, and put your foot on it. Leave your foot on ice ten minutes, then take it off ten minutes. Repeat four or five times. This will bring down some of the inflammation.

Next, let's get the pressure off those nerve bundles. Put some padding right behind the spot where the metatarsal heads connect to the toes—whichever toes are hurting.

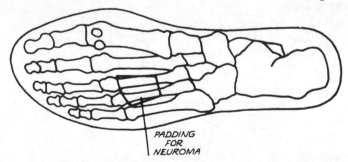

PADDING
FOR
NEUROMA

To find the right spot, bend your toes back and press on the bottom of your foot until you find the most painful spot. Put the padding behind that—in the direction of the heel.

Use ¼-inch thick padding—surgical felt or foam rubber.

Or, you can buy metatarsal pads. They're good.

Wear this padding and keep using your ice treatments two or three times a day for a couple of weeks and the pain should be relieved.

You'll probably have to keep wearing those pads all your life whenever you run, because the bones themselves are putting pressure on the neuroma and causing pain. So, why not glue the pads into your running shoes to save time. Even though the nerve bundles will always be there, they shouldn't hurt as long as you wear the padding—because there's no pressure on them.

Also, be sure that your shoes are wide enough. The tighter your shoes, the more pressure on those nerves. Another good idea is to lower your heels and take some weight off the ball of the foot. If you're a woman, try wearing lower heels.

To repeat: Your home treatment is icing and padding and proper shoes. If you've tried these for two or three weeks and you're still in pain, you'd better get professional help. In my office, the first thing I do for neuromas is make a foot support with special padding that lifts and separates the bones around the neuroma. That works most of the time.

Or your doctor might use injection therapy—steroids or maybe some vitamin B_{12} mixed with Xylocaine or Novocaine. Steroids reduce the inflammation and may even cause the nerve endings to become less sensitive.

Very often, you can solve the problem with one of these approaches. If none of these works, I would then remove the neuroma surgically, and that definitely works. It's one of the few conditions in running where we might have to resort to surgery.

This operation is not very disabling because we're just removing soft tissue, not bone, and you can stand on your feet the first day after the operation. In a couple of weeks you're out running again.

Pain on Top of Foot, Along Bone Shaft

(Could be a stress fracture of a metatarsal bone)

The metatarsals—those long thin bones that attach to your toes—can be bruised or broken under the stress of running. Soldiers and back packers do the same kind of damage when they walk for miles carrying heavy packs.

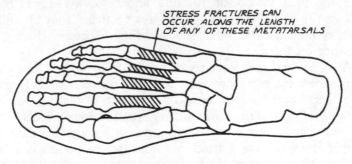

STRESS FRACTURES CAN OCCUR ALONG THE LENGTH OF ANY OF THESE METATARSALS

Stress fractures are insidious. You don't know when they're happening because there's no sudden snap. Actually, it isn't one fracture. It's many micro-fractures that occur somewhere along the shaft of the bone—usually where it bends a little.

What are the signals of stress fracture?

When you run you feel pain in a specific metatarsal. You may feel pain when you walk. There may even be a little area of redness or swelling on top of the foot. If you press right at that point, the pain will really be excruciating. Press along the shaft of the bone toward the outside and then toward the inside. You'll get a real stabbing pain.

This pain is a pretty good indication that you've got a stress fracture. But the doctor will have to x-ray to corroborate.

A stress fracture is not something you should try to treat yourself. Get an appointment as quickly as possible with a podiatrist or orthopedic surgeon. Of course, stop running. Immobilize the foot as much as possible.

Women should not wear high heels. Actually, the best thing to wear is wooden clogs to keep any motion from occur-

ring at the metatarsal area. With a clog, you lift your foot and plant it down flat. You don't bend the foot at all.

Men don't usually have clogs so the doctor may give you a wooden shoe called a Reese boot.

The doctor will probably examine your foot by feeling along the metatarsal bone in the way I described above. Then he'll take an X ray. The X ray may not show any signs of stress fractures—especially if it's soon after the injury. A stress fracture doesn't show up until about two weeks later, when some scar tissue (bone callus) has started to form. That's how you know for sure that you've had a fracture.

Even though nothing shows up on the first X ray, the doctor's clinical judgment may tell him it's a stress fracture. Now he can do one of two things.

He can put you in a soft cast. Or he can put padding around the fractured metatarsal, and give you a Reese boot to immobilize the foot.

You'll be wearing one of these two devices—the cast or the boot—for a maximum of six weeks. That's how long it takes a stress fracture to heal.

A soft cast is made of gauze impregnated with zinc oxide paste. It never really gets hard, but it immobilizes the foot somewhat, and gives it some compression.

We don't like to immobilize the foot completely, because the muscle will start to atrophy. While you're wearing the cast, be sure you do some alternate exercise, like calisthenics that don't involve your foot, or weight lifting. A stationary bike or Nautilus machine is good. You don't want the rest of your body to suffer while your foot is healing.

The second method the doctor may use, instead of a cast, is to put padding under the adjacent metatarsals. For instance, if I believe that the second metatarsal is fractured, I pad the first and third metatarsal bones.

I take ⅛-inch thick felt padding and cut it about a ½-inch wide. I tape this along the two metatarsals next to the injured one. Now the injured metatarsal has a little groove to sit in. The pressure is taken off, and that gives you some relief.

Then I give the patient a Reese boot to wear.

About two weeks after your first visit, the doctor will probably have you come back for a second X ray. Now the stress fractures show up because they're starting to heal. And you know you've got four weeks to wait before you can get out of your cast or your boot and get back to running.

The medical world got a lot of experience with stress fractures during World War II. The army took civilians that had never done much physical exercise, put heavy packs on their backs and then had them march for miles.

Soon the rookies were complaining of foot pain. The doctors would take X rays and wouldn't see anything wrong with the bone. So of course, the GI's were accused of faking it. I think they called it goldbricking in those days. But the patient would keep complaining of severe pain, so two weeks later they'd take another X ray. And now they'd see some fuzziness along the periphery of the bone. Bone callus was forming; the healing process had started. That's how they knew it was a stress fracture. They called it March Fracture.

Today, runners get fractures of the metatarsal bone when they run long distances—like a marathon.

Ron Griswold is a tall, lean, hungry marathoner in great condition. He's a labor relations specialist who found that running is a great way to forget all the settlements and strikes and disputes and demands. Ron was about twenty-eight when he ran his first marathon—the 1976 New York City Marathon. He finished in an excellent time—three hours and forty-three minutes. He also finished with a metatarsal fracture. Ron was not my patient at that time.

I first saw him after the Yonkers Marathon in March 1977—with still another stress fracture. He told me that at the twenty mile mark, he felt severe pain over the instep. This time, he knew enough—and he hurt enough—not to finish the race.

Next day, he came limping into my waiting room, which was filled with all the other post-marathon casualties. Many runners seem to finish a marathon feeling sound and healthy.

It takes a day or two or three before they realize they've been injured.

And the opposite happens too. A runner will finish in great pain. But the podiatrists working at the end of the marathon advise him to use some first aid—like ice—and wait a few days. Very often the pain goes away as the body recovers from the stress of the long run.

Anyway, Ron was definitely injured, and he knew it. I felt his foot and found that the third metatarsal was extremely tender. Interestingly enough, it turned out to be the second metatarsal that was fractured.

I put Ron in a soft cast and Reese boot.

In about six weeks Ron started slowly running again. I made a mold of his foot and got him soft orthotics. He had been running in hard orthotics, and I felt he needed a softer surface to prevent further mayhem.

To no avail. Ron quickly built up his stamina, and ran another marathon in six months. You guessed it—he got another stress fracture, on the other foot—the left foot.

This time I put the metatarsal padding onto his orthotics and let him continue to run. Why? Because I couldn't stop him. Also, the pain wasn't as bad.

At this point I sent Ron for blood work-ups and a complete physical checkup—just on the chance there was something physically wrong with him. He checked out healthy as a horse.

So I realized that Ron must need extremely soft cushioning for races. I ordered a pair of what Dr. Schuster calls his pillows. They're made of a soft, cushiony material called Plastizote. It absorbs a tremendous amount of shock, and it feels like you're walking on marshmallows.

Of course, what you sacrifice is support. The pillows don't give as much support as regular orthotics.

At first Ron wore his regular orthotics for his day-in, day-out training. Then, for the hard stress of a race, he would run in his pillows.

Lately, he's given up the pillows and wears the orthotics

for both training and racing. Last time I heard from Ron he had moved to Washington, D.C. He's still running hard. And his metatarsals are holding up fine.

Pain between Ankle and Small Toe
(Cuboid pain)

This is the area of the cuboid bone, and pain here seems to be a symptom, not an injury in itself. We don't know the exact mechanics that cause this pain. But I do know that I always find it together with an arch that's collapsing. So if you have this pain, you should read the section on Weak Foot.

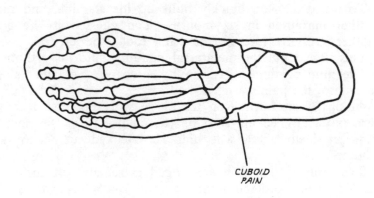

CUBOID
PAIN

You'll probably find that using a commercial arch support will help a lot. Many patients find the Arch-Supporting Strapping gives you a lot of relief. (Page 132.) Try these, and all the other techniques, exercises and running tips given for weak foot and you may be able to run comfortably.

If not, your podiatrist will have to look into what else is causing the pain.

Pain or Numbness from Instep to Toes

The subtitle to this "injury" should be "Tight Shoelaces" or "Tight Shoes." Because in most cases pain on top of the foot is caused by these two culprits.

Remember to buy running shoes in the afternoon, because your feet can swell a full size in the course of the day.

And be careful not to tie your shoelaces too tightly. This is easy to do, because your feet swell as you run—especially if you run long distances. You get interested in your speed and your mileage and very often you don't even feel the pain on top of the foot until you've stopped running.

This happened to Michael Douglas when he was in New York filming his movie, "Running." He was running a lot of miles and eventually developed neuralgia on the top of the foot. I gave him a doughnut pad to take the pressure off the painful area, and he bought looser shoes.

This may be the answer to your problem. Or you could try elasticized laces, which are sold in some orthopedic shoe stores. Or just take care to tie your laces a bit looser.

With some people, the problem is not just tight shoes. It's a bump on top of the foot—an enlarged bone, a bone spur. One of the small square bones in the middle of your foot has grown, probably because pressure was put on it.

All you do is take a foam rubber doughnut and place it over the bump before you put your sock on. Or some people like to glue the doughnut to the tongue of their running shoe, and that way they don't have to be bothered every time they put their shoes on.

If you've been putting pressure on that enlarged bone for a long time, nature may put a little padding around it—a pillow filled with liquid called a bursal sac. Pretty soon, with continued pressure, that sac will get irritated. Now you've got trouble.

Sometimes, your doctor will use injection therapy to bring the inflammation down.

The bone spur can be removed surgically, but to this day,

in twenty-seven years of practice, I've never had to remove a bone spur surgically in that area. I'd rather find a way to protect it from the shoe pressure.

Black Toenail

Runners are very prone to black toenail. It's caused by a hemorrhage under the nail.

You can get this from wearing a short shoe. Or when you run downhill, very often your shoe stops short and inertia keeps your foot going forward inside the shoe. So you're constantly jamming your nail against the end of the shoe.

You've got blocked-up blood under the nail. So you have to let it out to relieve the pressure.

If the nail is black all the way to the end of the toe, take a sharp razor blade and boil it fifteen minutes to sterilize it. Now make a small cut in the skin directly under the toenail— a slit maybe ⅛-inch long. It's absolutely painless because that skin is blistered and blistered skin is separated from the nerve endings. Don't do this if you're a diabetic or have circulatory problems.

Let the blood out, soak the toe in nice hot soapy water, then put a mild antiseptic on it. Betadine solution is probably the best. Then cover it with gauze and tape the gauze down.

If the nail is black only at the base—not all the way to the end of the toe, I'll tell you the method Bob Glover describes in his book.

You take a paper clip and heat it up till it's almost red hot and then touch the nail with the clip, being very careful not to go too deeply. This melts the nail and lets the blood out. Then you soak it in hot water.

I think Bob must have mellowed over the past few years, because he says he'd never use the Burning Paper Clip Method today. He'd go to a podiatrist.

So would I. I think it takes an awful lot of guts to put a red hot paper clip to your nail. I don't know too many people

that have the guts to do it while they're sober.

What the podiatrist does is drill through the nail with a very fine dental type drill. It allows the blood to drain out, it's painless and it usually saves the nail.

You really have to take care of black toenail, because if you wait a week or two, the nail may start to crumble. If that happens, just leave it alone unless the nail is loose.

Loose portions of nail should be clipped away with a nail clipper. Then file them smooth so there are no sharp edges. Those edges can catch on your sock and you'll tear away the good nail.

Thick Toenail

(Onychogryphosis)

Nails can thicken to the point where they're ½-inch or ¾-inch thick. If a nail is that thick, the pressure of the shoe makes it very painful.

Thick nails are usually traumatic nails—nails that have been injured time and again. Either you've dropped things on your toe or you've been jamming your toes against the front of your shoe when you run.

There's nothing you can do about it except file the top of the nail or clip it from the top with a nail clipper to thin it down. Then smooth it out with an emery board.

Nobody said nails had to be filed and clipped only at the end. Just take an emery board and file it. Go back and forth carefully across the top until it's thin enough.

If you clip and/or file your thick nail, it has to be refiled periodically because it grows thick again.

A lot of podiatrists recommend removing the nail surgically so it never grows back. This eliminates a possible future problem. But it is painful and can keep you from running for from four-to-six weeks.

Once the skin has healed, it becomes thick and tough and

it looks fine. You can even paint the skin with nail polish.

But I prefer not to use surgery unless it's necessary and in this case it usually isn't. You can take care of your problem with just a few minutes filing when the toenail gets thick.

Thick, Discolored, Crumbled Nail

(Fungus nail)

This looks a lot like the thickened nail that the runner gets. But if your nail is also discolored—yellow or white discoloration, a mottled color—you've probably got a fungus nail.

Again, the nail can be removed surgically. Or the doctor might give you a drug to take orally. But, of course, any drug can have side effects.

The treatment I prefer is a combination of doctor's care and home care. First the doctor grinds away as much of the nail as possible. Then he gives you a prescription for either fungoid tincture or Onychophytex. Three times a week you buff the nail with an emery board to create a rough surface. Then you paint on the fungicide. Each week you remove the old fungicide with nail polish remover before putting on a new coat. This treatment takes nearly a year.

If your nail doesn't hurt, I like to try this conservative care. If that doesn't work, you can always remove the nail surgically. The nail doesn't grow back, but your skin toughens up and it looks okay when done surgically.

Ingrown Toenail

Most ingrown toenails are self-inflicted. You get one when a tight shoe presses on a nail that's been improperly cut or has a jagged edge.

How do people get jagged edges on their toenails? I say it's all the fault of television. Ninety percent of ingrown toe-

nails wouldn't happen if it weren't for television.

People sit watching TV and unconsciously start picking at their toenails, sort of cleaning them. Not a very sexy sight, but what can you do? Some of the nicest people pick their toenails while watching TV.

In the process, they tear off a bit of the toenail and leave a jagged edge, like a hook. This hook is then pressed into the skin by a tight shoe, and the skin has a foreign body reaction. Your own nail becomes a foreign body to your skin.

Of course, this can also happen if you've cut your nails into V's or curves at the corners.

Once the nail is imbedded in your skin, you need professional help. Don't try to dig it out yourself. Let your podiatrist lift it up, cut it out and take care of the infection.

How to Cut Your Toenails

Cut your toenails straight across. Don't make V's in front of the nails, don't round the corners the way you do your fingernails.

How short should you cut them? Just cut them up to the end of the toe—where the toe begins.

If you keep your nails short and cut them straight across, you should have no trouble at all with ingrown toenails.

Blisters

The best treatment for blisters is to avoid them. Blisters are caused by something that's rubbing.

It could be a shoe that's too wide and moving from side to side. It could be a too-short or too-narrow shoe.

Abrasive socks can cause blisters. Nylon is often abrasive. I think you should wear only cotton or wool socks.

If you're running downhill, sometimes your shoe stops but

inertia keeps your foot moving. Then you get a blister on the tip of your toe.

You can get a blister on any prominence that sticks out and rubs against your shoe. For instance if you have a bunion, sometimes that rubs against a tight shoe and you get a blister. Or, the joints of your toes form "bumps." They can get blisters. People with hammer toes get blisters on the top of the toes and on the front end.

On the bottom of your foot, you sometimes get a blister along the arch, about a third of the way back, on the insole. This is because the first metatarsal is rolling in a bit and bearing too much pressure.

Bob Glover says rubbing Vaseline on your feet prevents blisters. Some people carry a tube of Vaseline with them on marathons to rub into their feet. That's fine, as long as you're not wearing soft orthotics. Vaseline soaks into the leather and separates the leather from the cork bottom. I think talcum powder is good. It reduces the friction and keeps your foot dry. Spenco insoles also reduce friction.

So your blister-prevention strategy has four steps: well-fitting shoes; nonabrasive socks; cushioning for any bumps on your feet; friction reducers like Vaseline, talcum powder or Spenco insoles.

If you get a blister anyway, leave it alone as long as it's small and painless. It's sterile as long as the skin isn't broken.

But if it's large and painful or it's interfering with your running, you can cut it open.

First sterilize a razor blade or nail clippers or scissors by boiling for fifteen minutes. Wash the blister with alcohol or Betadine or other antiseptic. Make a small slit in the blister and press the fluid out. This cut is painless, because blistered skin is not connected to the nerve endings.

Now clean the cut with antiseptic. Betadine solution is best. In my office, I also dry the area with 2 percent Gentian Violet, aqueous solution. The aqueous solution keeps it from burning. Your doctor can give you a prescription for this. Or you can buy 1 percent Gentian Violet without a prescription.

You want the blister to dry, so don't put ointment on it. Ointment doesn't allow for drainage; it dams up the wound. The skin can become macerated—wrinkled, white and soft.

Last, you cover the blister. I don't like Band-Aids because they're usually plastic and they don't allow air in. Use a square of gauze and put tape around the edges of the gauze.

At night take the bandage off and let the air at it.

The pain and throbbing will stop as soon as you let the fluid out. Don't peel the cap off the blister—it will flake off when it's ready.

Corns on Top and Sides of Toes

The only reason you'll ever get a corn on top of your toe is because the shoe is tight and it's rubbing. So get rid of the guilty shoe and take the pressure off the corn by using a little doughnut pad. If the shoe fits and the pressure's taken off long enough, the corn will disappear.

You can speed the process along by giving the corn a few strokes with an emery board two or three times a week. This reduces the size of the corn and therefore the pressure you get from the shoe. Also, it breaks the continuity of the hard skin and restores some flexibility to the skin.

I don't recommend cutting a corn with a razor blade. It's too easy to cut yourself. This is especially dangerous for people with poor circulation (that includes many diabetics) because the cut takes longer to heal and you're more prone to infection.

But if your circulation is good and you have nerves of steel and you're not afraid of the sight of your own blood, you can try cutting your corn. Be sure you boil the blade to sterilize it. And keep some antiseptic handy in case you cut yourself. Betadine is a good antiseptic.

One thing you should never do is use corn drops or pads impregnated with corn drops. Corn drops are basically sali-

cylic acid, and they're a very insidious way to burn good tissue along with the corn tissue. Salicylic acid can burn the skin without your realizing it and even cause a hole, an ulcer on the foot.

If you happen to have bad circulation—which many diabetics have, as well as nondiabetics—salicylic acid can have serious consequences. If it burns or ulcerates the skin, your impaired circulation means slower healing and more chance of infection. New healing blood doesn't come in as quickly, and waste products aren't carried away as quickly. As a result, you have a good chance of infection and gangrene. You can even lose a limb.

You'll notice the bottle of corn drops and the package of corn pads impregnated with drops carry a warning for diabetics and other people with impaired circulation.

So I'd say, don't use them at all, even if you have good circulation. I'm not very happy with corn drops.

Corns between the Toes

(Soft corns)

These are called soft corns or heloma molle. They're no different from any other corn except that you sweat so much between the toes—runners especially. And the sweat softens the corns.

Very often they're misdiagnosed by patients and doctors and everybody else as athlete's foot because sometimes they happen way down in the web of the toes. The difference is, with athlete's foot you've got itching and scaling, while a corn is just a painful bump of tissue.

Sometimes a corn between the toes becomes infected by causing a foreign body reaction. It's a foreign body to your own skin. Or people scratch at a corn, and that can cause infection.

The only reason you'll ever get a soft corn is tight shoes,

narrow shoes. It's true, you are more likely to get any kind of corn if you have an enlarged bone—a bone spur—or an enlarged condyle on the bone. A condyle is a bump on the bone. It's a normal thing.

But that bone spur or condyle won't itself cause a corn unless your shoe is too tight.

So put your doughnut pad on the soft corn and don't wear any shoes that aren't wide and comfortable. If the corn is way down in the web of the toes, you can cut the doughnut pad in half and stick that on.

Don't use corn drops. And don't try to cut a corn between the toes with a razor blade.

If the corn's so painful you want to get it treated right away, let your doctor remove it.

Corns on Tip of Toes

Short shoes can cause corns on the tips of the toes. But basically they're the curse of people with hammer toes and people with the cavus type of foot.

The cavus foot has an extremely high arch and high instep and the toes are somewhat pulled back. The tendons on top of the toes are pulling the toes back. If you have this kind of foot, you get a lot of calluses on the ball of the foot. Very often you get corns on the tips of the toes and also on the tops of the toes.

Just use the doughnut pad and/or a metatarsal pad. And be sure your shoes are long enough. To relieve the callus on the ball of the foot, try a Scholl's Ball-O-Foot Cushion. Try it just as it comes. And also try cutting out a hole for the callus to go through.

Warts

A wart (or verucca) is another kind of lump on your foot.

Warts are caused by a virus, and they're contagious. You can spread them to yourself—so that one wart leads to more warts on your own body. And you can spread them to other people.

Warts grow in size. Sometimes they get so large and painful you can't walk on them.

Patients sometimes mistake warts for corns or calluses. But if you look closely, you can see that the center of the wart has little dark spots. These are small blood vessels and nerve endings. Corns have no blood vessels—they're just little lumps of dead skin. If you pinch a wart, you feel pain. Pressing on it is not so painful.

A wart bleeds freely. A corn doesn't bleed. Sometimes you cut a corn and it starts to bleed—but that's because you've cut the live skin underneath or around it.

Like corns, warts sometimes occur in spots where the shoe is causing too much pressure. They can also crop up in non-pressure areas. Warts on the bottom of the foot are known as plantar warts. Plantar refers to the bottom of the foot. Plantar warts are pushed deep inside the skin because of all the weight and pressure on them.

Warts are caused by a virus and they're contagious. I remember the time a group of my patients who were dancers in the New York City Ballet came back from a tour of the Southwest. About eighteen of them came into my office to be treated for plantar's warts. So it certainly seems that these dancers spread the virus to each other.

Yet I've never had warts, although I treat them and handle them all the time. So it must be that not everyone is susceptible to the virus.

Sometimes you get a whole cluster of tiny warts, and these are called mosaic warts. They form a mosaic pattern on the skin.

Some people try to cure warts by putting copper pennies on them, or using auto-suggestion or any number of folk remedies. Some of them work, sometimes. But if your wart isn't getting better, I think you should get to the doctor before you get more warts.

Don't try to remove a wart with drops. These drops are salicylic acid, and it's dangerous to use acid on your own skin. You often burn the good skin along with the wart.

The doctor may burn the wart off with chemicals or use electrocauterization or dry ice, or he can cut it out surgically. Some doctors inject vitamin A into the area. I don't know how successful this is.

There are a dozen different ways to treat warts, which means there's no good way. If there were a good way, everyone would use that and drop all the others.

No matter what method you use, there's a chance that the wart will recur.

When it comes to mosaic warts—small warts in clusters— the most successful treatment I've found is chemical treatment. Surgery doesn't seem to work because the warts keep recurring. I treat them in the office, and then give the patient some medication—possibly a drying agent—for home treatment. The patient comes back about once a month for a checkup and re-application of the chemical. This is a long process, and the patient has to cooperate fully and use the medication religiously.

Chemicals are the least painful method—especially when the removal is done slowly in many stages.

But the wart must be kept dry between treatments, and it's almost impossible for a runner to keep his feet dry.

What I prefer to do for runners is to inject Novocaine and remove the wart surgically. I tell the runner to come into the office after a big race—he needs a rest then anyway—and I remove the wart. You only have to keep it dry for about thirty-six hours. And in four or five days, your foot has healed and you're out running again.

Cracks between Toes

Cracking of the skin between the toes can be caused by athlete's foot, but not necessarily. With athlete's foot, you've also

got itching and scaling.

Cracks can be caused simply by perspiration, and runners perspire tremendously. The moisture softens the skin and it cracks—especially during the winter months. Your feet are sweaty and suddenly they dry up in the cold and the skin cracks. It's very painful.

In the office I use 2 percent Gentian Violet on cracked skin, but you need a prescription for that. So what I recommend for home treatment is either 1 percent Gentian Violet or tincture of Benzoin compound. You can get these without a prescription. Dab the medication between your toes after you shower and powder your feet liberally after that. Also powder your feet before you go out running. The more you powder your feet, the more sweat will be absorbed and the less chance there is of cracking.

Cracks on Heels

Runners often get a lot of cracking around the periphery of the heels, especially in the winter when the skin is drier. But cracking rarely happens unless there's callus on the heel. So you may have to go to the doctor and have the callus removed. You can't really remove heavy callus with home treatment.

The doctor debrides the edges of the callus with a scalpel. Then he treats it with medication. He'll probably apply a bandage to keep the edges closed and promote more rapid healing. This treatment is painless and there's no bleeding.

If callus starts to form again after this treatment, you can use an emery board to remove some of the new callus. But don't overuse the emery board, or you'll rub your skin raw.

Stuff like Pretty Feet is nice, possibly for dry skin, but not for real callus. I don't think pumice stones do much either, except maybe exercise your arms. When a callus is really dry and hard, you'll take off a lot more with an emery board than you will with a pumice stone.

What I recommend, starting in the fall, is to rub a lot of

cream into your heels. There are a lot of good creams, and one hand cream is just as good as another. I tell all my patients to buy Spry or Crisco and rub that into the heels. It's cheaper than most creams and it works as well as anything I can think of.

Athlete's Foot

There are a few different kinds of athlete's foot. They're caused by different fungi, and they appear on different parts of the foot, and you need specific medications for each type of athlete's foot. A medication that works on the bottom of the foot may not work between the toes.

Usually you get athlete's foot between your toes—itching and scaling, sometimes even cracking between the toes.

This between-the-toes infection is usually a monillia type of infection. The powders don't do very much for it except to dry up the skin.

I would recommend you use liquids or creams. Some good products for the itching and fungus between the toes are Desenex Liquid, Lotramin and Enzactin Cream.

Athlete's foot can also show up on the bottom of the foot, again with itching and scaling and blisters. It rarely goes above the arch. A good preparation you can buy for this is Tinactin or NP27.

If the commercial preparations don't work, go to your GP, your podiatrist or your dermatologist and have him do a culture on it and find out what specific fungus is causing your problem and prescribe a medication for it.

All types of athlete's foot are contagious, and this means contagious to other parts of your own body—not only to other people. So be sure to dry your feet with paper towels, and throw the towels away, so you don't spread the infection.

Pain on Bottom of Foot, Arch and Heel

This pain could mean one or more of three injuries:
- plantar fasciitis
- heel spurs
- bursitis (inferior calcaneal bursitis)

They're all caused by the same actions on the bottom of your feet. To understand what's causing your pain, you have to know something about the materials that make up your foot.

When we started evolving our feet—transforming the ape's handlike foot into something we could stand and run on—nature looked around and came up with a variety of materials. She wanted to form a foot that would be rigid enough to stand on and flexible enough to bounce us along from one step to another.

So nature constructed the foot of hard things like bone and somewhat flexible things like tendons. And she used another interesting building material called fascia.

Fascia is used throughout the body to hold structures in place or as a separating material between muscle groups. Sometimes it's shaped into bands to connect one part to another—where you need a material that's firm but also flexible.

And that's what's needed in the arch of your foot. Fascia material is used here to make a somewhat flexible bridge from your heel bone to your toes. (Actually, to the heads of the metatarsal bones—the bones your toes are attached to.)

Okay, so this bridge—the arch of your foot—is made to flatten out a bit when weight moves across it. That's what happens when you run—the weight moves from the heel to the high curve of the arch and down to the ball of the foot. In a perfectly designed foot, the weight moves along a very specific path and the arch flattens a bit, then springs back up again as the weight moves off it.

But, if you have pain in the arch or the heel, it may be that your weight is taking the wrong lane across the bridge.

The bridge is stretched hard, and it hurts. It may even lose its flexibility, so it doesn't bounce back up again with each step. In this case we say your arch has "fallen."

Now three things can happen. Depending on just how your foot has responded, you've got one of three injuries.

First, you could have plantar fasciitis (pronounced fashee-itis.) This means the fascia has been pulled too hard, and it's inflamed. (The word plantar indicates the bottom of the foot.)

Second, you could have heel spurs. Some fascia fibers have pulled away from the heel bone, and droplets of blood were laid down. They eventually became calcified and formed an extra bit of bone, called a spur. You can see heel spurs on an X ray. They look like little points sticking out along the edge of the heel bone, where your arch starts.

Third, you could have bursitis. The heel has responded to the pressure by putting in cushioning right along the line where you've grown a heel spur. This liquid-filled cushion is called a bursal sac. If the pressure from the fascia continues, the sac itself becomes inflamed and sore, and you've got bursitis—inferior calcaneal bursitis. (The heel bone is the calcaneus.)

Very often, you've got all three injuries together. But we'll discuss them one by one.

Before we discuss each symptom, I want to give you some tips on all these bottom-of-foot problems. They're all aggravated by running on hard surfaces. By running on the balls of your feet, which you do during hill work or speed work. Or by excessive time spent running. No one can say what's excessive for you, but the foot damage is related to the amount of time you run.

Tight calf muscles and hamstring muscles make the strain on the arch even worse. Shoes that aren't flexible are another factor.

So look at your shoes. Be sure they're flexible at the ball of the foot. Then look at your way of running. Read chapter 2, "How to Run Right and Hurt Less."

And now let's look at your feet and see which injury you've got.

How to Tell Which Injury You've Got   Plantar fasciitis and heel spurs cause pain on the bottom of the heel. With both of them, you have pain after running, but not necessarily while you're running. (But some people with plantar fasciitis do have pain while running.)

With both these injuries, you have a lot of pain when you first get out of bed in the morning. Those first ten steps in the morning really hurt. I tell people with heel spurs not to try to stand the minute they get out of bed. The best way is to crawl to the bathroom and put your feet under hot water. Then you can walk.

Your feet may also hurt if you've been sitting a while and then stand up.

With plantar fasciitis, you can have pain all along the arch, or right at the front of the heel—where the heel meets the arch. Press anywhere along the arch, and it may hurt. You may feel a strain, a pull all along the arch. It may feel like the arch is tearing apart.

Here's how you tell the difference between plantar fasciitis and heel spurs.

With plantar fasciitis you feel pain when you press on the *middle* of the heel. Put your thumb there and press up—as if you could put your thumb through to the top of your foot.

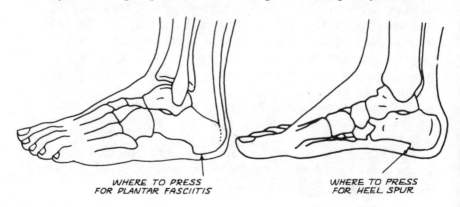

WHERE TO PRESS
FOR PLANTAR FASCIITIS

WHERE TO PRESS
FOR HEEL SPUR

With heel spurs, you feel pain when you press the *front* of the heel—where the heel meets the arch. Press backward, toward the back of the heel, and at the same time, press upward.

With bursitis, you also feel pain at the front of the heel. In fact, if you've got heel spurs, you probably have bursitis. It isn't the spur that hurts. That's bone, and bone doesn't hurt.

It's the inflamed bursa that's hurting. The treatment for these two problems is the same.

But first let's take the treatment of plantar fasciitis.

Plantar Fasciitis

This is an inflammation of the fascia—the tough, fibrous tissue that runs from the heel to the heads of the metatarsal bones.

Plantar fasciitis responds very well to home care. So try the various suggestions I'll give you here, and you can expect good results.

First step, as with any inflammation, is to ice the area. Put some ice cubes in a plastic bag and twist it closed. Then put the bag in a basin, and rest your feet on it. Ice your feet right after running—ten minutes on ice, ten minutes off, then repeat.

Also, you can take two buffered aspirins with each meal, if you're not allergic to aspirin, and don't have medical reasons to avoid it. Never take aspirin before running, because it masks pain—and pain is a symptom you should be aware of.

But to get at the cause of the injury, you'll have to change the weight distribution on your foot. As I explained earlier, when your weight moves across your arch, it's taking a wrong lane. And that misplaced weight is causing the irritation.

There are three things that can help a lot: an arch support; a heel pad to take some weight off the front of the heel; and strapping your foot to give support to the arch.

I suggest you try the Arch Supporting Strapping first. You need two materials: adhesive tape, 1½-inches wide. And Elastoplast, three inches wide. Elastoplast is like an Ace bandage with adhesive. A lot of drugstores carry it, or your druggist can order it for you.

The strapping is done in three steps. First step, encircle the outside of the foot with tape. Second step, apply tape from side to side, along the bottom of the foot. Third step, encircle the outside of the foot with tape one more time. This is to anchor the entire strapping down and keep the edges from raveling. (See illustrations for the first two steps.)

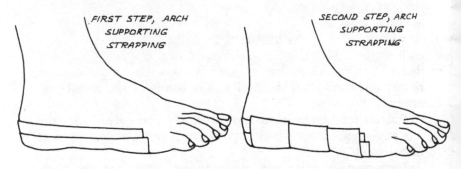

FIRST STEP, ARCH SUPPORTING STRAPPING   SECOND STEP, ARCH SUPPORTING STRAPPING

First step   Attach the adhesive tape, starting right behind the bone attached to the little toe. Bring it around to the back of the heel. Lay it on gently, with no pressure.

As you make the turn around the heel, going toward the inside of the foot, give the tape a little tug so it's pulled tighter, from the heel to the inside of the foot. Anchor the tape at the ball of the foot just behind the big toe. Make the tape smooth—no wrinkles.

Second step   Cut 3 pieces of Elastoplast, each about 4 inches long. Lay the first one along the sole of the foot, from just behind the little toe to just behind the big toe.

Overlap the second strip of Elastoplast, about ¾ of the way over the first. Then overlap the third strip. When you're putting tape across the bottom of the foot, hold the bottom of the foot to keep it smooth. The skin should not wrinkle.

Every wrinkle in the skin becomes a blister when you run.

Third step   Now take two strips of adhesive tape and tape down the edges, to anchor the entire taping down. Never wrap tape all the way around the top and bottom of your foot. This cuts off the circulation. When you run, the foot swells, and if you've cut off the circulation, the blood will be blocked in your toes, and you'll have Black Toe—not just Black Toenail. You can take a shower with this strapping—it will get wet and then dry off again. Change it after about three days. You'll only have to wear it about two weeks, and the pain should be gone by then. If the skin itches under the tape, remove the tape at once. You're probably allergic to the adhesive.

Along with the strapping, you can wear a store-bought arch support like Dr. Scholl's 610. This can be very helpful in raising the arch and taking a lot of weight off the heel. By raising the arch, you're shortening the distance between the origin and insertion of the plantar fascia, thereby taking some strain off it.

Remember, I told you there were three things that can help relieve your pain:

• strapping
• an arch support
• heel pads

You can wear the strapping alone, and see if that does it. Or you can wear the strapping and the arch support. Or you can add the heel pad and wear all three.

For a heel pad, use a piece of sponge rubber, ½-inch thick. Victex makeup sponges make good heel pads.

If you've tried all these and you're still in pain, throw away the heel pad and try a heel cup. This is a rubber or plastic cup you put in your shoe. When you wear it, your heel is falling into a trough, so again the weight is directed away from the arch. You can buy heel cups in a sporting goods store.

If you don't get relief from all these home treatments, see a podiatrist who treats athletes. He'll look at the entire weight-

support system in your foot, and see how it has to be re-balanced. He'll probably design an orthotic insert for your shoe, and that will do the job.

Plantar fasciitis responds very well once your feet are given the right support. And it's worthwhile trying to do the job yourself. These home care treatments have a good chance of success, and you've saved yourself some money.

If you have plantar fasciitis, you can be one of many good runners who are having a fine time in spite of it.

One of these is Jane Killion, who was ranked eleventh in the world for women in the marathon event by *Track and Field News* in 1978. Jane was the third woman to finish the 1978 Boston Marathon. Her time was 2:47:22. She has also won three marathons, including the 1978 Finlandia.

Jane first came to see me after the Boston Marathon in 1977. She had started to feel pain during the marathon, but finished anyway. Jane had lots of problems, all arising from strain on the arch.

She had pain at the apex of the arch; a heel spur; and a plantar fascia problem which is fairly unusual. She had developed little nodules in the fascia that hurt when she stood or ran on them. They're very painful for a runner because they rub against the bottom of the shoe.

I made some orthotics for Jane to relieve the strain on the arch. And her orthotics have a trough gouged out for the nodules to sit in. If these nodules become troublesome again, we may have to remove them surgically. But so far, the orthotics have done the job fine, and Jane is moving right along as a world-class runner.

Heel Spurs and Bursitis

These two problems usually occur together, and the treatment for them is exactly the same.

First, let me give you the bad news: You probably can't cure your heel spur problem by yourself—but I will give you

some home treatments to try. Maybe your case will respond to them.

Now the good news: Heel spurs can be treated very successfully by a podiatrist. It's one of the problems for which we can almost guarantee results.

All right, so you've read the beginning of this section. You know the symptoms and the test for heel spurs. And you've concluded that you've got them.

The first thing you should do is ice your heels after running. Put some ice cubes in a plastic bag and twist it closed. Put the bag in a basin and rest your feet on it. Leave your feet on the ice for ten minutes, then take them off for ten minutes. Then repeat.

Put heel pads in your shoes—pieces of sponge rubber, ¾-inch thick. If you can't find sponge rubber thick enough, use a couple of pieces. You can cut your own pads from a piece of sponge rubber or use Dr. Scholl's Heel Pads or Victex makeup sponges.

These heel pads will help absorb shock, and they'll help spread your weight over a greater area of the heel—so it's not all falling down toward the front where the heel spurs are.

You can try buying a running shoe with a thicker heel. Again, this gives you better shock absorption. And it puts the weight further forward on the foot; also relieves the tension on the plantar fascia.

Try Arch Supporting Strapping, or buy an arch support in the drugstore—Dr. Scholl's 610. Either of these techniques takes weight off your heel.

Now, after trying all these things, you'll probably get some relief. But in the long run, the problem will recur and become chronic, and you'll probably end up going to the podiatrist or orthopedist. I really don't think you can solve a heel spur problem yourself.

Your doctor will diagnose your problem as heel spur by pressing on the front of the heel, as I described. Then he'll probably X ray for confirmation of his diagnosis. Look again at the illustration showing you where to press for heel spur.

Notice the little point on the bone? That's how a heel spur looks on an X ray.

Some doctors may decide to use steroid injections in the heel or ultrasound. In my experience, these treatments can only give you relief for several weeks or a couple of months.

Ultimately, you're going to have to solve your weight-distribution problem, and that means an orthotic device made just for your foot and its own special problems. In our office, we make an orthotic that includes a cupped heel, a raised long arch and a redistribution of the weight so that the foot is completely balanced. The pressure is therefore taken off the spurs and shifted to other areas of the foot where it belongs.

Some doctors will do surgery and remove the spur. But I've never seen a heel spur that didn't respond to proper orthotic devices. Dr. Richard Schuster says that in his practice he has treated thousands of cases of heel spur and has never had to resort to heel spur surgery.

My experience is that after such an operation, you still have to wear an orthotic anyway. So save yourself an operation, just wear the device.

As I said earlier, heel spurs is one of the problems for which we can almost guarantee happy results—even though you may not believe it when you're hobbling along in pain.

John Pepowich was one of those unbelieving sufferers. He came to see me in January 1978, pretty well convinced that his running days were over.

John is about sixty-years old and he's secretary of the Masters Running Club. He came limping into my office and told me he had such pain in his arch and heel he could hardly walk in the morning. He virtually crawled out of bed.

X rays confirmed that he had heel spurs, and I fitted him for orthotics—doing my best to ignore the skepticism John was conveying in his eyes, his mannerisms and his voice.

The upshot of it is, I saw John crossing the finish line of a race not long ago. I assume he was wearing his orthotics. I know he was wearing a great big smile.

Weak Foot or Fallen Arches

*(Symptoms can be tired legs, pain in the arch, tiredness
in bottom of foot, low back pains)*

What used to be called flat feet is now called The Weak Foot
Syndrome or just weak foot. It can cause one or all of the
symptoms listed above.

The term "flat feet" is a little confusing because you can be
born with low arches or very high arches or "average" arches
and still develop the weak foot symptoms—because your arch
has been stretched so hard it's lost its flexibility. If you want
to understand how this happens, read the section just before
this one, "Pain on the Bottom of the Foot."

The simplest way to diagnose weak foot is simply to look
at your feet when you stand on them. With weak foot, your
weight falls in toward the inner side of your foot. Your arch
disappears to some extent. (In technical terms, the foot
pronates.)

Here's another way to tell. Stand up and put a pencil from
the first metatarsal head to the heel. If you have a normal
arch, the pencil runs straight between those two points. If you
have weak (pronated) foot, the pencil angles out from the
first metatarsal head.

Another test is to press on the arch—especially at the
highest point of the arch. That's very painful for people with
weak foot.

Another symptom of weak foot is not being able to walk
or run very far without getting sore, tired feet. Children with
weak foot tend to sit and watch, instead of running and playing. Johnny will act as second base instead of second base-
man because his feet are too tired.

Also, you can't stand very long without rolling your feet
toward the outside. I was discussing this problem with a new
patient, and she suddenly remembered seeing photographs of
herself as a child in which she was standing on the outer
edges of her feet. Her father used to tap her feet with a news-

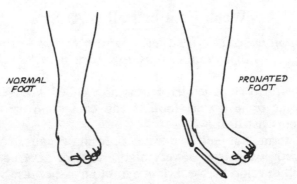

NORMAL
FOOT

PRONATED
FOOT

paper to remind her to get the weight back on the insides. But actually, she was making a right move, as children often do.

The inner side of the arch is weak, so people with this problem direct the weight toward the outside. This is a good exercise for you, by the way. And it's just what an arch support does—it tilts some of the weight toward the outside of the foot.

You can be born with high arches or low arches or "normal" arches and still develop weak foot symptoms. We've all got a pretty good shot at it.

Low arches are not an indication of problem feet. It's sort of a norr \l "abnormality" and I wouldn't think of treating someone with a low arch unless he were feeling weak foot symptoms. In fact, the low-arched foot may not show symptoms as readily as a foot with a very high arch.

Romance people—French, Italian, Spanish—tend to have high-arched feet, and these high arches can develop weak foot symptoms very readily because that high arch starts to strain under the stress of standing, walking and carrying weight.

Now you're running and maybe your arch has started to fall. But it might have fallen anyway if you're leading a normally active life.

Weak foot symptoms are helped by the Arch Supporting Strapping (page 132). Wear this strapping for a couple of weeks, until the pain is gone. At the same time, try Dr. Scholl's 610 Arch Supports. You should continue to wear these, even

after the pain is gone. You can wear them while running too.

This home treatment can very often solve your problem. If it doesn't, your podiatrist will have to analyze your whole weight-distribution problem, and probably design a custom-made orthotic for you.

And I want you to know that a lot of very strong runners have weak feet. Fritz Mueller is one of them. Fritz started running just a few years ago and he quickly became one of the world's best runners in the Master's class. (He's 43 years old.) He completed the 1978 Boston Marathon in 2:20:47.

Besides being a runner, Fritz is a chemist by profession and a bird watcher by avocation.

Fritz first came to me in 1977. His chief complaint was pain on the inner side of the ankle. I examined him and found another painful area at the highest point of the arch. Fritz felt pain while running and even when just standing on his feet.

He was wearing orthotics already, but at this point he needed more arch support. I sent his orthotics out to the lab for rebalancing, and meanwhile I gave him the Arch Supporting Strapping I just mentioned.

Fritz feels it was the strapping that solved his immediate problem, not the orthotics. He wore the orthotics only for training; for races, he ran without them. And he ran so successfully that he finished the 1977 New York City Marathon in a time of 2:27:25, setting a U.S. record for his class.

At the finish line he gave me one of the biggest thrills of my life by offering me his medal. I may not be much of a runner, but I sure love getting those medals!

Bump on Back of Heel

(Pump bump)

That bump on the back of your heel is probably something you were born with. Or maybe it developed under pressure

or friction. It's called a pump bump or Haglund's deformity.

It doesn't bother you unless your shoe keeps rubbing against it. Too much friction from the shoe can cause an irritation. The bump may even develop a bursal sac—a cushion filled with liquid. And then the bursal sac can get inflamed.

One reason why your shoe may be rubbing against the bump is that your arches are not solid when you walk and run. You may have the condition called weak foot—and you can read all about it in the preceding section.

If you do have weak foot, your foot may be giving a little twist every time you take a step. That's what's making the pump bump rub against your shoe.

Get some commercial arch supports, like Dr. Scholl's 610's, and that may solve your problem.

Another solution is to buy heel cups—cups made of rubber or plastic. You slip them inside your shoe. Next, put some cushioning inside the heel cup. To make the cushioning, get some foam rubber or felt padding and cut a U in it, so the bump sticks through the U. Put this padding inside the heel cup.

For my patients with pump bump, I make orthotics with a high padded back—it's built-up around the heel—and there's a U cut in it, so there's padding all around the bump.

Women can wear strap shoes or mules so the shoe won't press on the bump.

If it becomes very irritated, the bump can be removed surgically and this operation handles the problem very well.

Heel Bruise

Early in your running career you may get heel pains caused by inflammation of the coating on the bottom of the heel bone. Just ice your heels when you finish running. Put a plastic bag filled with ice cubes in a basin, and rest your heels on it for ten minutes. Then take them out for ten minutes. Do this two or three times.

Heel bruise seems to happen most often to new runners. The heel bone probably gets thicker and tougher as you run, and the pain gradually goes away.

Impact Shock
(New Runner's Injury)

Since long distance running has become so popular, doctors are seeing a new phenomenon called impact shock.

This problem happens most often to new runners or to experienced runners who've suddenly upped their mileage. If you're a new runner with impact shock, there are things you can do to decrease the pain. And you can also expect that it will take care of itself, as your body gets in condition.

Let's figure out just how much impact your body is absorbing.

Say you weigh 150 pounds and you run for just one mile. When you run, your heel hits the ground with three times your body weight. If you weigh 150 pounds, that's 450 pounds of impact, with each running step. And each foot takes from 800 to 1000 steps per mile. Four hundred fifty times 800 is 360,000 pounds you're socking into each heel in just one mile. And your heel is an area measuring about 1¼-inches in diameter. It's a wonder more people don't get impact shock.

The treatment for impact shock is to lessen the impact by cushioning the heel. Use sponge rubber heel pads. Victex makeup sponges are one good kind.

Try a different kind of shoe with an impact shock absorber. This is a shoe with a good deep heel. In between the outer sole and the inner sole there's a material that absorbs impact.

Shoes are very important in treating and preventing impact shock. Many runners wear heavier, better-cushioned shoes

while they're training and then switch to lighter shoes for racing. These are called racing flats. They have less heel cushioning, less sole and more flexibility. Of course, for the long miles of daily training, they don't give enough cushioning.

Naturally, the overweight person is delivering more shock to his body than the lightweight runner. Dr. Schuster sometimes recommends that the overweight runner wear work shoes or combat boots to give better support and diminish the shock. Of course, you can't run a marathon in combat boots, but by the time you're ready to run 26.2 miles, you'll probably be a lot slimmer.

If heel cushioning and better shoes don't solve your problem, Dr. Schuster makes a kind of orthotic he calls his pillow. It's made of Plastizote, a very soft cushy material. Of course, inserts made of Plastizote do not give as good support as regular orthotics do. But if your main problem is impact shock, these pillows help a lot. A sports-oriented podiatrist can design one of these for your foot.

Impact shock can be very uncomfortable when you've got it, but as you adjust your shoes and your weight and your whole body, you'll find the impact pains will gradually go away.

Bob Anastasio is a 26-year-old runner who came to me with pains in front of the knees—one of the signs of impact shock. He certainly wasn't a beginner—Bob has run a number of four-minute miles—but he had been increasing his distance quite a bit.

Bob is basically a middle distance runner, and I think he was using long distances just to build up his stamina. But he was still wearing the light racing shoes he used for shorter distances, and they just weren't giving him enough cushioning.

I made Bob orthotics to correct some imbalances; and also added Plastizote to the heel, for extra cushioning. That was back in April 1977, and Bob hasn't had any impact shock problems since then—even though he runs about 75 miles per week.

Two months after he got the orthotics, Bob was the ninth American to finish the AAU 1500-meter championship in Los Angeles. His time was 3:43:07—roughly equivalent to a 4:01 mile. I didn't see that race—but I did see him finish a 1.7 mile race here in New York, right around that time. Bob ran with no pain, and finished in 7 minutes, 51 seconds. He walked away with the first-prize trophy—which he gave to me. You can bet it has a place of honor in my waiting room.

Pain on Bottom and Back of Heel, Young Person's Injury
(Apophycitis of the heel)

This injury can happen to children, up to age nineteen. Eleven-years old is the prime time.

The pain radiates up the back of the heel. If you clasp your hands around the heel and squeeze, there's extreme pain.

The heel bone, like many other bones, is still in two pieces before the age of nineteen. If the child has been jumping and landing flat on his heels, or running very long distances, the trauma can temporarily interrupt the closure line where the heel is supposed to fuse.

In Iron Curtain countries, where they've been a lot more scientific .about studying and training their athletes, young teenagers are not allowed to run long distances.

If your child has this injury, tape his heel snugly. I'll tell you how to do the Heel Supporting Strapping I use. What you do is put one piece of tape around the back of the heel and one around the bottom of the heel—alternating tapes until you've formed a firm, supportive cup. Use 1½-inch wide adhesive tape.

1. Wrap the first piece around the back of the heel, from the inner ankle bone to the outer ankle bone.
2. Wrap the next tape around the bottom of the heel, from

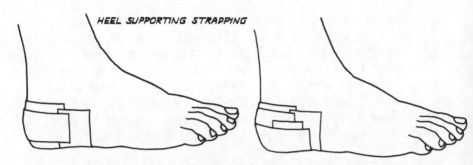

HEEL SUPPORTING STRAPPING

one ankle bone to the other. Wrap the tape snugly, as if it were helping to hold the heel bone on.

3. Put another tape around the back of the heel. Place it a bit lower than the first.

4. Put another tape around the bottom of the heel. Place it a bit more toward the back of the foot.

Use five or six pieces of tape, total. The last tape around the back of the heel should be down close to the sole.

At the same time, put sponge rubber padding in the heel of his shoes. He should wear this in all his shoes, and when you buy new shoes or sneakers, get them with well-cushioned heels. He should wear heel padding until he's nineteen.

Of course anyone who wears a heel lift in all his shoes may be shortening his Achilles tendon, and that can lead to other problems. But in this case, you have to take care of the main complaint, the heel injury. The child should do calf-stretching exercises to keep his Achilles tendons stretched out.

Another thing that can help is plastic heel cups, which you put in the shoes. You can buy these in sporting goods stores. He should wear the heel cups until he's pain free.

The separation will mend in six months, but the child should do no running or jumping during this period. This may sound impossible, but it's necessary, if the separation is ever going to heal. Swimming and bike riding are good alternate exercises during this period.

This same kind of fusion-line injury can happen in the metatarsals and shins. So I certainly would not let a youngster run long distances—no more than five miles a day.

Sprained Ankles and Broken Ankles

A sprained or broken ankle is not the sort of injury that sneaks up on you. If you've done it, you know it—because it happens suddenly.

The only question is—is it a sprain or a break?

You get one of these ankle injuries when you're running along a city street with potholes or a country road with holes and rocks and your ankle suddenly turns. The big toe and the heel turn in toward the center of the body. That's what causes an inversion sprain.

The pain radiates through the ankle joint, the foot and up the leg. There's going to be swelling, and the ankle might even be black and blue.

If you're like a lot of runners, you probably shake it off and keep on running—especially if you're in the middle of a race. You limp a little. Then when you get home, you do nothing and the ankle swells tremendously.

That's a serious mistake. The first twenty-four hours is the crucial time in caring for a sprained or broken ankle. Here's what you should do.

As soon as you feel your ankle twist and feel pain, stop running. Go right home.

Start your treatment as soon as you get home and continue it for the first twenty-four hours—or until you see a doctor. The first twenty-four hours is the crucial time for taking care of a sprained ankle.

Your treatment consists of ice and elevation. Put ice in a plastic bag and twist it closed. Put the bag on a chair and rest your ankle on it. Or put the bag on top of your ankle.

Keep your foot elevated as much as possible. In bed, put a couple of pillows under it. And keep using the ice—ten

minutes on, ten minutes off—until bedtime.

In the morning, if your ankle is still swollen and painful, it's incumbent on you to go to the doctor. The chances are the doctor will x-ray, even though you don't think it's broken and he doesn't think it's broken. An X ray is a very important part of treating an ankle problem because very often there's a fracture at the base of the fifth metatarsal (the bone connected to your smallest toe) or a slight fracture of the fibula.

If you have a sprain, this means you've torn some ligaments —the nonelastic tissue that connects bone to bone. A fracture means you've broken one of the ankle bones.

In either case there may be internal bleeding. Your ankle may turn black and blue. The toes and the inner side of the ankle may even be black and blue because the blood sometimes seeps through the joint, so both sides of the ankle look bruised.

Whether you've got a sprain or a break, the motion of the ankle will have to be restricted. In fact, that's why your ankle swells. Swelling is your body's way of restricting motion.

If there's a break, your doctor will put the ankle in a cast. If you have a fracture of the base of the fifth metatarsal— which is a common fracture site when the ankle is twisted severely—the foot will either be put into a soft cast and a walking boot or in a hard cast. Your doctor will decide which method will work best for you.

If you have a mild sprain, the doctor may just put on an adhesive strapping or an Elastoplast strapping—depending on how much he feels the movement of the ankle should be restricted. Soft casts work well too.

But don't neglect an ankle sprain. It's one of the more neglected injuries. A lot of people just suffer through it and then the ligaments become stretched or completely torn, and you've got a chronic ankle sprain. This can mean you've got a mild degree of pain for a long time. Or it can mean you keep spraining your ankle again and again.

If I have a patient who keeps spraining his ankle, I give the ankle more support—limit its movement, really—by mak-

ing an orthotic with a higher border on the outside of the foot, around the heel.

For someone who continually twists his ankle, Dr. Schuster worked out a great technique. You can get your shoemaker to do this for you. He takes a piece of Neoprene, ¼-inch thick, and glues it to the outer side of your running shoe, from the heel to behind the base of the fifth metatarsal. The Neoprene goes all the way from the upper edge of the shoe, down to the ground. Your shoemaker should taper the Neoprene so it's not so thick at the upper edge of the shoe.

Now the whole outer side of your running shoe is more solid so you can't twist in that direction. And the sole is a ¼-inch wider in that area. With this reinforcement on your running shoes, it's almost impossible for you to twist your ankle.

NEOPRENE WRAP
APPLIED TO SHOE

While we're talking about sprained ankles, I want to introduce you to one of my patients who is a typical sprained-ankle victim—she felt the pain but kept on running. Rosalie Prinzivalli is a 36-year-old runner who's been running about 3½ years and averages about 40 miles a week.

I'll let Rosalie tell her own story. This is taken from a tape of runners talking about their injuries—something runners dearly love to do.

ROSALIE: "Well, I had just recovered from my runner's knee injury and had that all solved. Then I started building up again, training for the New York City Marathon in 1978. It was my first long race in a while, so I was really looking forward to it.

My friend and I had barely started the Marathon—we were halfway across the Verrazano Bridge—when I stepped on a roll of candy and twisted my ankle.

I knew I couldn't finish the Marathon, but I didn't know where to go. If I turned around and went back to Staten Island, I thought there'd be no way to get home. (Runners always have some logical reason why they have to keep running on an injury.)

So I kept running forward, toward Brooklyn. My ankle didn't even hurt, as long as I didn't make any turns. I told my friend that when he stopped to put Vaseline on his feet, I'd ice down my ankle. They had ice at all the water stations.

So we got to Bedford-Stuyvesant, in Brooklyn, and I got some ice. When I looked at my ankle, wow, it was a mess. And once I stopped I couldn't start running again. But I'd already gone nine miles on a bad ankle. So I hitched a ride to the finish line and Murray was there working on everyone's feet. He taped my ankle and he didn't say much, but Shirley told me later (Shirley is Mrs. Weisenfeld) that he was very VERY upset that I'd run nine miles on a sprained ankle. He told me to ice it for ten minutes on, ten minutes off, for the next twenty-four hours, and I went to see him next day in the office."

That's Rosalie's story. Next day, the X ray showed that there were no broken bones. But she had torn a good many of the lateral ligaments. I put her in a soft cast for three weeks and kept her bandaged up for another two weeks. Her recovery is complete, but it kept her out of running for almost three months.

Isn't it miraculous that Rosalie was able to hitch a ride in Bedford-Stuyvesant, after she'd run nine miles—while it was absolutely impossible to find transportation back in Staten Island—a half mile away from her accident? Runners always have these very sound reasons why they have to keep running to the bitter end.

Lower Leg Pains

- Pain in Front of Leg: Anterior Shin Splints and Stress Fractures

- Pain on Inner Side of Leg: Posterior Tibial Shin Splints; Posterior Tibial Tendonitis; Stress Fractures
- Pain in Back of Leg, Just above Heel: Achilles Tendonitis
- Pain Midway Down the Calf: Soleus Muscle pain
- Sudden Pain in Back of Leg: Rupture of plantaris muscle

I can—and I will—give you a lot of bio-mechanical reasons why you're getting these various pains in the lower leg. But, for almost all these pains, there's one remedy: exercise to *stretch* the calf muscles and *strengthen* the front leg muscles. Most lower leg pains can be helped this way.

Also, you should check your running habits to see if they're contributing to your leg pains. Read the chapter "How to Run Right and Hurt Less."

First, here's a quick summary of the lower-leg pains listed above.

- Anterior shin splints are pain in front of the leg caused by inflammation of the sheath covering the bone, or by inflammation of the front-leg muscles (anterior muscles).
- Posterior tibial shin splints are felt on the inner side of the leg, between the calf muscle and the big shin bone. These shin splints are often related to fallen arches or weak foot.
- Shin fractures: Stress fractures of the shin are multiple micro-fractures of the tibial bone.
- Achilles tendonitis is a pain in the back of the leg, between the large calf muscle and the ankle bone. It's an inflammation of the tendon connecting the calf muscle and the heel bone.
- Soleus pain is a pain midway down the calf—higher up than Achilles pain. It means the soleus muscle needs some stretching.
- Rupture of the plantaris muscle is felt as a sudden sharp pain in back of the leg.

All right, now let's discuss.

What happens to your lower leg when you run? I've told you that most lower-leg pains come from a lack of stretching and strengthening—like it's all your fault. But to be fair,

nature gave some people a head start toward lower-leg pains —because of the way she designed their feet and legs.

Maybe you have feet that don't stay steady when you run —they turn in or out, trying to find a balance. Since your feet are not stable, your legs have to work harder to add some stability.

Or, maybe you were born with short, bunchy muscles that are tight to start with—instead of long slender muscles.

I think the exercises you do as a child have something to do with the way your muscles develop.

And the environment you give your feet makes a difference. If you're a man who wears high-heeled boots, or a woman who wears high-heeled shoes most of the time, your calf muscles shorten.

There are many ways your environment can affect your leg muscles. For instance, if you have to be in bed for a week, be sure the blankets are lifted up off your toes. In the old days, the blankets were allowed to weigh on the patient's toes. The toes were pulled forward so the front leg muscles were stretched and the calf muscles became relatively shorter.

When the person got out of bed and stood up after a week, he'd say, "Wow, I'm really weak—I'm falling over backward." He wasn't weak, his calf muscles were shortened, and they were pulling him backward.

That's what's happening if you have lower-leg pains—your tight calf muscles are pulling on the weaker muscles in front of the leg. Actually every time you take a step, your calf muscle is pulling your heel up and pulling the front of the foot down. And that constant pulling can cause pain.

Running can give you pain on three different aspects of your lower leg—the front, the inner side or the back. Since these pains come from the same cause (tight calf muscles and weak anterior muscles), you may have more than one of these injuries at the same time. For instance, you'll very often have both Achilles tendonitis and shin splints.

Let's discuss the front of the leg first.

Pain in Front of Leg

(Anterior shin splints/stress fractures)

Okay, we said that pain in front of the lower leg can come from overworked anterior muscles and/or because the calf muscles are shortening and pulling the front leg muscles.

Why are those front muscles getting "overwork" pains, when the back muscles may not be? Usually it's because the front muscles are weaker than the posteriors. Running doesn't exercise them as much, so you need extra exercises. Do Foot Presses and Furniture Lifts to strengthen the anterior leg muscles. Do Wall Pushups to stretch the calf muscles. They're all described in Chapter 4.

Sometimes it's because you're forcing your front leg muscles to do a lot of other jobs besides running.

For instance, you may be running on a hard concrete road, and the padding in your shoes just isn't enough to cushion the shock. So your anterior leg muscles tighten up with every step, bracing themselves against that jolt. They're keeping the shock from spreading throughout the leg, hip and spine, but they're overworking with every step.

Incidentally, this may be the origin of the term "shin splint." Generally, to splint means to put a piece of rigid material near a hurt area and wrap some bandage around it. This restricts motion. So your anterior leg muscles are doing the same thing—they're acting as a splint and restricting motion from the foot.

What else could cause your front calf muscles to overwork? It could be that nature didn't issue you The Perfectly Designed Foot. Not too many people got that number. So your foot wobbles around a little, and the anterior leg muscles again do their tightening-up movement to add some strength and stability.

Some feet, in order to add stability, clutch with the toes. But of course they're clutching empty air, and that's tiring. Again, it's the front leg muscles that do the work because they control the toes. Some people are just wearing shoes

that are too wide or too long, and that's why their toes are grasping and clutching. That one's easy to fix—just get smaller shoes.

Now you know what's causing the pain. What do you do about it?

If the pain is very bad, you should see your doctor right away to be sure you haven't got a stress fracture. A stress fracture isn't a sharp break, and you don't feel a sudden pain. It's many micro-fractures caused by continual strain, and the pain and fracturing build up gradually.

The only way to know you've got a stress fracture is to x-ray the area. Your doctor may take an X ray the first week you feel the pain and not see any sign of a fracture. Sometimes, his clinical intuition will tell him there's a fracture there anyway. So he'll have you stop running—just to be on the safe side—and ask to see you back in a week or two.

If I suspect a stress fracture of the tibia, I'll put the patient on crutches and send him to an orthopedist or an osteopath.

In about two weeks, some scar tissue starts to form along the lines of the fracture. That scar tissue does show up on a second X ray. Now the doctor knows for sure you've had a stress fracture. That means you can't run for another four weeks. If the fracture is bad enough, your doctor may decide to put you in a cast for a few weeks.

If your shin pain is moderate, you can try treating it yourself for a few days. It may simply be shin splints. But if you've stopped running, and followed all the suggestions I'll give you here for shin splints and the pain still hasn't decreased in a few days, you'd better see a doctor. Even a moderate degree of pain can mean a stress fracture, and your leg has to be put in a cast.

Now, here's the treatment for anterior shin splints.

1. First step is, bring down the pain and inflammation with an ice wrap. Before you go out to run, put a wet towel in the freezer. When you finish running, wrap the icy towel around your lower legs. Keep it there for 15 minutes. Put your feet

up on a chair while you're doing this. Or, use one of the commercial ice bags sold in running stores. They wrap around your leg and they're neater than a wet towel.

2. At bedtime, or any time during the evening, use a heating pad around the leg. Set it on low, never on high.

3. Take a couple of buffered aspirin at mealtimes and bedtime. Never before running.

4. Take a look at your feet, when you're standing on them. Are the arches flattening out? If you have painful arches, or any other symptom of weak foot, read that section and treat yourself for weak foot.

5. Cut down on your running. Cut it out for a while, if necessary. Don't try to run through the pain. You'll never get through it, you'll just make it worse.

6. Whenever you have to give up running for a while, the best exercise is swimming. And here's a good exercise while you're in the water—put an inner tube under your armpits to keep yourself afloat in a standing position. Now "run" in the water. You're using your running muscles, without putting any body weight on your legs.

7. I told you that your toes may be clutching, reaching for support, as if they were fingers. But they're clutching empty air, and that can cause strain on the anterior leg muscles. Okay, put something under the crest of the toes so they're not grabbing empty air. Get a crest pad in the drugstore. Put this padding under the three middle toes.

If you can't find crest pads, get some moleskin, about three inches wide. Roll it into a tube. Use enough moleskin to make a tube of ¼-inch diameter. Wrap this in gauze to hold it together.Now tuck it under the three middle toes and wrap tape around all three toes, including the padding.

Another good padding is the cotton sticks your dentist uses. See if he'll give you some of those.

8. Check your shoes. Sometimes a more solid shoe, with better cushioning and a better heel lift, can make all the difference.

One of my patients, Mitch Maslin, cured his shin splints by changing shoes.

Mitch is one of the "too much, too soon" school of runners who suffer all kinds of injuries because they can't resist the call of the road.

Mitch watched the New York City Marathon in 1976 and was filled with a flaming determination to be running it in 1977. In Mitch's own words: "In two months I ran myself into the ground."

So he went through many months of pains and treatments and sitting on the sideline while his various injuries healed and then going out running again. Finally, before the 1977 marathon, he was suffering with shin splints, but he insisted on running the marathon, against my advice and everyone else's advice. He finished the marathon with a stress fracture, which eventually healed.

Then, when he returned to running, Mitch discovered that just three short outings brought on a return of shin pains. He had shin splints. We tried all sorts of cures, like heel lifts and variations in the orthotics—with not much success. Finally one day Mitch decided to buy some new shoes and almost overnight the shin splints disappeared.

In comparing his shoes (like a lot of runners, Mitch has about eight pairs), he noticed that the new shoes were wider across the arch and ball of the foot. So he concluded that the greater stability is what he needed. I think the heel lift is what did it—that particular shoe, the Brooks Vantage, has a good high heel lift. Maybe it was a combination of a higher heel and a wider base.

So the right shoes are important. But another important moral I want you to learn from Mitch's story is how much of your pain can be self-inflicted. It can come from too much mileage—from not listening to your body when it first starts to hurt.

And it can come from improper running style. When you get back to running, be very aware of what could be causing your injury. Run on dirt instead of concrete. Avoid too much

hill work and speed work, because they keep you running on the balls of the feet.

Check your running posture. Your weight should be directly over your hips. Don't lean forward. That's to avoid pulling too hard on the calf muscles. Read chapter 2, "How to Run Right and Hurt Less."

This is how you work with your body and give it the conditions it needs, the strength and flexibility it needs to keep your running a pleasure.

But suppose you've done all these good things—including wearing a commercial arch support, as recommended in the weak foot section—and you've still got pain in the shins and along the outer side of the leg?

You may have a foot imbalance problem that your commercial arch supports just weren't made to handle. Your foot is about as individual as your fingerprint. A mass-produced foot support may do the job for you. Or you may need a podiatrist to analyze just how your foot is made, and how it functions when you run.

A sports-oriented podiatrist can do this, and design a support that keeps your foot from turning in or keeps the arch from flattening or keeps your toes from clutching—or any combination like that.

Pain on Inner Side of Leg

(Posterior tibial shin splints or tendonitis; stress fracture)

You feel this pain deep inside the leg. Press the inner side of your leg—the line between the calf muscle and the big shin bone. If that's painful, you've put some strain on a muscle that runs from the shin bone around the ankle and attaches behind the ball of the foot. This muscle gives some support to the arch of the foot.

Most likely, your arches "fall" when you run. Read the section on weak foot, and follow those procedures—the arch

supporting strapping, the commercial arch support and the heel pads.

You should also do stretching exercises to stretch the calf muscle. Wall Pushups is a good one. And your first aid is the same as for anterior shin splints. Wrap your leg in an icy towel after running. Take two aspirins with each meal. Don't try to run through pain. You've got to rest.

These procedures will relieve the pain of tendonitis or shin splints. They will not help a stress fracture. So, if you've strapped your foot and you've taken a few days rest from running and the pain is still not relieved very much, you have to assume you have a stress fracture. Another symptom of stress fracture is much more severe pain than you'd get with tendonitis or shin splints.

If you do suspect a stress fracture, go see an osteopath or an orthopedist and let him take care of it for you. He'll x-ray to confirm the diagnosis and probably put you in a cast and on crutches to immobilize the area.

Pain in Back of Leg above Heel

(Achilles tendonitis)

The Achilles tendon is a cord connecting the heel to the calf muscle. If you feel pain in that lower part of the calf—near where the cord is attached to the heel—you probably have Achilles tendonitis.

Here's the first thing I would do, if you came into my office. You can do it yourself, now. With your thumb and forefinger, pinch along the Achilles tendon. Start down close to the heel and continue pinching, working your way up to

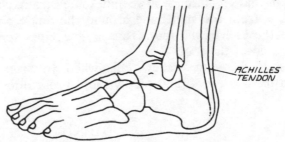

where the tendon enters the calf muscle. If you feel a little swelling there, and a lot of pain, you've got Achilles tendonitis.

Here's what's happening inside your leg. The Achilles tendon is a cord connecting your calf muscle to your heel. Actually, it's a cord inside a tube. This cord and its tube (sheath) stretch a bit, but not much. So if anything pulls too much on either end of that tendon, you're going to start feeling a lot of pain.

What happens is the fluid between the tendon and its sheath expands, and there's less space for the tendon to move in. It all feels sore and swollen.

What's pulling on this tendon? There are two possibilities: a calf muscle that's too short (running shortens the calf muscle); and a heel that's too far away from the calf muscle.

What to do About It   When you realize this, you can see that the first solution is quick and easy: Put something under your heel to lift it up so it won't be pulling down so hard.

Just stick a piece of sponge rubber, about ¾-inch thick, in your shoes. Victex makeup sponges are good. The same stuff is sold under the name JogHeel. But it doesn't have to be any particular brand—just take a piece of sponge rubber and shove it under your heel—in your running shoes and your daytime shoes. This is going to help a lot right away.

Women can wear high-heeled shoes during the day, and that's a help. But once you've corrected the tendonitis, I don't recommend high heels—they keep your calf muscle short.

The next prescription may be a little tough to take, but you've got to do it. Stop running for a few days to a couple of weeks until the pain is a lot better. Later, do the Wall Pushups described in chapter 4. That's the most important part of your cure. But don't start these right away. Don't run, don't stretch for a while. Your tendon has been pulled too much already, and your muscle can go into spasm if you pull it any more.

A quick treatment you can start right away is an ice pack —it relieves the pain and brings down the inflammation. You

can use the ice packs sold in running stores, they're probably the neatest. Or you can put a wet towel in the freezer for a half hour, and wrap that around your legs for fifteen minutes.

When you go back to running, ice the tendons after each run, but not until you've done your stretching exercises.

At other times of the day, I would put a heating pad on the area to improve circulation and bring some blood to the area. Do this while you're sitting around the house doing paperwork or watching TV. Also at bedtime. It will help get the swelling and inflammation down.

You can also take a couple of buffered aspirins to bring down the inflammation. I'd say two aspirins at each meal and two at bedtime. But don't take aspirin before running, because you deaden the pain—and that could be dangerous. Of course if you have ulcers or you're allergic to aspirin, don't take them.

Stretch Those Calves! Stretch Those Hams! Almost every famous athlete has had Achilles tendonitis at one time or another, because the more they work at their sport, the more they tighten and shorten the calf muscles and hamstrings.

The hamstrings are the muscles in the back of your thigh, between your knee and your butt.

You've got to stretch the calf and hamstring muscles. Wall Pushups will stretch the calf muscles. Knee Press and Foot on Table will stretch the hams. Squats will stretch the Achilles tendon. All these exercises are in chapter 4 and they're easy to learn. Do them before and after running. If you forget, your Achilles tendon will remind you.

Now check your shoes. If you've got Achilles problems, the two most important things to check in your running shoes are the heel lift and the flexibility at the ball of the foot. The heel should be ¾-inch thick. Read chapter 3 to evaluate your present shoes, and guide you when it's time to buy new ones.

What your foot's doing to your tendons. The structure of your feet may make you run in ways that put extra strain on the tendons. If the right shoes and plenty of stretching don't give you a complete cure, a sports-oriented podiatrist can tell

you if your foot is contributing to the problem. Orthotics made to your foot's mold can correct any imbalances and ease the strain on the tendons.

And take a good look at your running style. So far, you've learned something very valuable: too much pull on the tendon while you're running is what's causing the pain. Where you run and how you run makes a big difference in the amount of pull on the Achilles. So read chapter 2, "How to Run Right and Hurt Less," to see how you can improve your style and your comfort.

If I had to pick one running habit that's most harmful to your Achilles tendons, I'd say it's running uphill. Cut out hill work until your problem clears up and your calf muscle is elongated.

Cutting the cord. A few very rare people will still be suffering, even if they've taken all the steps discussed above. You remember, a tendon is a cord inside a tube or sheath. Well, sometimes adhesions form, and the cord gets attached to the sheath. Then the cord can't move. These adhesions can be removed surgically to allow the tendon to glide normally.

Or sometimes a bone with a sharp bump may be sticking into the tendon. Surgery can take care of this too.

But surgery on the Achilles tendon still has a lot of unknown territory. Don't consider it unless you've really done your homework—stretching, shoe adjustment and adjustment of your running conditions.

Pain in Mid Calf

(Soleus muscle pain)

Soleus pain is a dull aching pain you feel midway down the calf, rather than down low near the heel. (Pain in the lower calf, near the heel, is Achilles tendonitis.)

The soleus muscle comes between the two heads of the big calf muscle. When you use your calf muscles, the soleus

is the one that acts first. It moves maybe a thousandth of a second before the large calf muscle. So it does take a beating.

It tightens up and gets sore, and there's a good exercise for it which you should add to your regular wall pushups. After your wall pushups, keep your feet flat on the floor. Now dip one knee a little, and you're stretching the soleus muscle. Hold for 5 seconds. Repeat with the other leg. This exercise is illustrated in chapter 4.

Ice your legs after running with a wet towel you've chilled in the freezer. Use a heating pad at night—on low, never on high. Elevate your heels with heel lifts inside your running shoes and your everyday shoes. Do a lot more stretching, but don't stretch while the pain is in the acute stage. No hill work or speed work until the pain is gone.

In fact, you've got soleus pain for the same reasons you would get Achilles tendonitis. So read the section on Achilles tendonitis and follow the same treatment.

Sudden Pain in Back of Leg

(Rupture of plantaris muscle)

I can tell when a patient has ruptured the plantaris muscle because he'll say, "I was running along, and I thought someone hit me with a rock." Golfers will say they thought they were hit with a golf ball, and a tennis player will think that her doubles partner hit her with a tennis racket.

You get a sudden, excruciating pain, and it's difficult to bear weight on the heel. You have to walk on the ball of the foot. You may get a black and blue mark running down the back of the leg from internal bleeding.

The plantaris muscle is a thin muscle, about as thick as a rubber band. It runs down the middle of the calf and attaches near the Achilles tendon.

This muscle doesn't seem to do very much so a rupture is nothing to worry about. Either the muscle repairs itself or

you get along without it.

Just keep your leg comfortable for a couple of weeks. Use a heating pad in the evening to bring healing blood to the area. Women should wear high-heeled shoes to relieve the strain, and men can wear some of those fancy high-heeled boots that are popular now.

Or you can put padding under your heels, in your regular shoes. (Put the padding in both shoes, or you'll give yourself some of the problems that go with Short Leg Syndrome.) Use sponge rubber makeup sponges or heel pads that you can buy on the foot care rack. You can go to your podiatrist and he can strap your foot to keep it in an extended position. That gives relief.

But usually all you have to do is raise the heel and of course don't run until the pain is gone, which is about two weeks.

Knee Pains

The most common knee pain among runners—in fact, one of the most common runner's injuries—is runner's knee. The symptom is pain on either side of the knee.

A less common knee problem—but it does happen to athletes—is pain and swelling in the back of the knee, toward the inner side of the leg. This is a growth called Baker's cyst.

Let's take runner's knee first.

Pain on Either Side of Knee
(Runner's Knee)

I don't believe in predicting injuries for my patients, but if you're going to get any injury, runner's knee is a great possibility. This injury is very common with all kinds of "running" athletes—runners, tennis players, basketball players. One of

the running magazines polled its readers and found that 23 percent of them had been put out of the running by knee problems.

Runner's knee can happen to beginning runners. But very often, the symptoms start when you reach thirty-eight or forty miles a week. One day, when you're three or four miles into your run, you feel pain either on the inner side or the outer side of your knee.

Maybe you stop running and rest for a couple of days. Next time you go out, you've only run a mile or two, and your knees start hurting again. And the pain has increased in intensity.

Some runners feel pain, not during the run, but later that day or next morning.

You may find that the pain is worse running downhill than it is when you run uphill. And it's worse when you walk down the stairs than it is walking up the stairs.

Or, after sitting a while in a movie or in a car, you find that your knee is stiff and painful when you walk on it again.

Take your own "running history" just as a podiatrist would do if you went to see him to see if you've been having symptoms like this. A good way to review your recent running is to talk it over with a friend. That often helps you remember the details.

One question you should ask yourself: Have you been running on a banked surface? If so, you're giving yourself one "short leg" and one "long leg." This often leads to runner's knee symptoms. In fact, you may really *have* one short leg— so compare your leg lengths, following the instructions on page 88.

Some more questions to ask yourself: Did you increase your mileage drastically just before you started feeling knee pains? Had you been doing a lot of hill work or speed work? All these questions will help you find the reasons for that knee pain.

After you've taken a good look at your running history, here's an examination you can do. I always use it when I

suspect runner's knee. You'll need a friend to do my part in this examination.

Sit down in a chair and stretch one leg out straight, supporting your foot on another chair or low table. Your "podiatrist" now squeezes your leg just above the knee. At the same time, he uses his other hand to push on the kneecap. He pushes on the outside of the kneecap, pushing it toward the center. At the same time, the patient should tighten up his thigh muscle. If this test causes pain, you've got runner's knee.

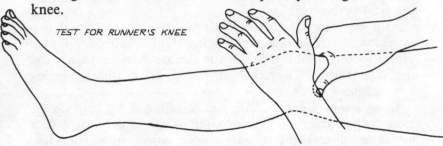

TEST FOR RUNNER'S KNEE

And now that you know it, you can stop worrying and start working—because runner's knee can be treated very successfully—and most of the treatment comes from you. Your own body causes the problem, and you've got to make the changes in your body that will cure it.

Not too many years ago, runner's knee was treated by surgery—taking out some of the rough, inflamed cushioning material around the knee (the cartilage), or by smoothing it down. This didn't work too well, since you need that cushioning when you run. So the pain would return soon after you resumed your sport.

But no sports-oriented podiatrist or orthopedist would think of surgery for runner's knee today. Because the simple and encouraging truth is, if your feet and thighs are doing their job right, you'll have no trouble at all with your knees.

We'll explain more about that later. But first let's give you some quick relief and reassurance.

First Aid   Ice the knee for fifteen minutes after running. Prepare your ice pack just before you go out to run by putting

two wet towels in the freezer. After you run, wrap these towels around your knees for fifteen minutes. The pain is numbed, and the inflammation is decreased. One of my patients decided to be very efficient and leave the wet towels in the refrigerator (not the freezer), all day long so he could use them more frequently. This causes a very smelly refrigerator, so I don't advise it.

At bedtime, you can use heat on your knees for a half hour —a heating pad is fine, or warm wet towels. Wet heat and dry heat both work fine.

You can also take two aspirins with each meal and two at bedtime to decrease the inflammation. Please don't take aspirin before running because it can deaden the pain. And that's dangerous. I'd rather have you know what's hurting you and how much.

Long Range Cure   Okay, you've brought the pain down. Now let's get to the cause of your pain and get rid of it. I mentioned before that runner's knee comes from your feet and thighs. So you've got to do two things: Support your feet; strengthen your thighs.

Support your feet.   If you've got runner's knee, your foot is probably built in such a way that it makes a wrong movement every time it hits the ground. And it hits the ground very frequently when you run—with a lot of impact. Your foot may flatten out when you run—or turn out too much—or rock from side to side. This makes your shin bone move wrong and your knee move wrong. Those wrong moves are what's causing the pain.

Incidentally, you don't have to have "flat feet" or "fallen arches" to get this problem. When you run, you're asking your foot to do a highly complicated job. It has to take the impact of landing on the heel with three or four times the weight of your body. Then it must support you in a stable position for a fraction of a second. Then it must propel you off the ball of the foot with a bounce. With so many different demands put on it, there are lots of ways your foot's structure can fail.

So you've got to keep the foot from making these wrong moves. How? With a corrective foot support.

Try a commercially made foot support, which you can find in your drugstore. There are lots of good ones—Dr. Scholl's 610 is one. If this gives you some relief, you can be pretty sure your knee problem starts with your foot structure.

Here's another way to tell whether your knee pain is starting in the knee itself or in the foot: If the pain started almost as soon as you began running, it's probably a problem in the knee itself. If the pain started after you'd been running a while, it's probably caused by a foot imbalance.

Okay, so you've got your foot supports from the drugstore. And now you add the exercises I'll give you for strengthening your front thigh muscles. And that may be the end of your knee problem.

If not, you may need a better correction of your foot-balance problem, and you can get that with custom-made orthotics. A sports-oriented podiatrist can make a pair for you, from a mold of your foot.

Will the proper foot support cure your runner's knee? Absolutely not—not by itself.

Strengthen your thighs. You've got to strengthen your thigh muscles so they can hold the kneecap in place—not let it twist to the side—when you're running. Turn to chapter 4, and learn the Quadriceps Exercises. We give four or five exercises, but pick two and do them conscientiously and that will do the job.

Runner's Knee—How Did It Happen to Me? Nature gave the knee cap a very precise path to follow in life—a nice little

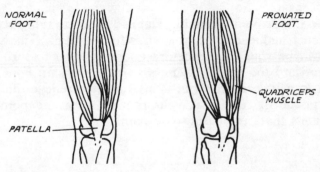

NORMAL FOOT

PRONATED FOOT

QUADRICEPS MUSCLE

PATELLA

groove in the thigh bone where it can move up and down smoothly and comfortably. You've got runner's knee because your kneecap moves out of its groove.

It twists and moves at an angle over the knob of the thigh bone. This twisting and bumping happens about 800 times in a mile of running. That hurts.

Soon the cushioning material (cartilage) around the kneecap gets worn and uneven. The medical name for runner's knee is chondromalacia of the patella (chondro—cartilage; malacia—softening; patella—kneecap).

And that wrong movement starts with your foot, as I explained earlier.

Now, how does the thigh contribute to your troubles? As you run, the four muscles in the front of the thigh (the quadriceps) should be supporting the kneecap so it rides up and down in its groove (not at an angle). But weak quadriceps allow the kneecap to pull and twist to the side, and irritate the cartilage.

How could I accuse a healthy, athletic person like you of having weak quadriceps?

I'll tell you. There must be a *balance* of strength among your thigh muscles, or the whole thing doesn't work right. If the muscles in the back of your thigh become a lot stronger than those in the front, you're in trouble. Those front muscles become the weak link. And this is just what you've done, with all that healthy running.

Running develops the back thigh muscles more than the front. So now you've got (relatively) weak quadriceps. And the more you run, the more you've got to strengthen the quadriceps.

Now Check Your Running Habits   Your running style is very much influenced by how your foot is built. That's natural. Maybe your foot structure is causing you to turn your toes outward too much, giving a twist to the shin bone. Try toeing in a little as you run—this can help relieve the pain. Your podiatrist can check your running style and point out any habits that are causing you pain.

Another thing is, where do you run?

If you're running on the side of the street—where it slopes —you're automatically giving yourself one leg that's shorter than the other. This "short" leg—the upper leg—is turning in and down (pronating) and is more likely to get runner's knee symptoms. So if you must run on a slope, be sure that your legs take turns being the "short" leg. Better yet, run on a flat surface.

Indoor tracks are the worst. On a short track, you may be circling thirty to forty times a mile, and you're constantly turning one foot down. Even if you alternate directions frequently, it's not the best place to run. I know it's hard to run outdoors in the middle of a Chicago snowstorm, but if you've got knee problems, an indoor track is not the place for you. Try it, and if your knee problem flares up, consider some other sport for the winter.

Some runners are getting interested in rope-jumping, but I don't recommend it. You're pounding down on the metatarsals, and causing a lot of trauma. And jumping on the balls of the feet can cause Achilles tendonitis or shin splints. If you really love rope-jumping, do it on a padded mat. That helps.

An aerobic sport I do recommend is indoor swimming. Try that until the weather or your knees clear up, whichever comes first.

There used to be a saying among athletes that knee problems were almost incurable. "You think you've got it licked, and it comes back next season!" Well, this may be true of some knee injuries. But runner's knee can definitely be licked, if you do your quadriceps exercises with massive determination.

Some of the most energetic runners I know are lazy about doing their quadriceps exercises.

On the other hand, some patients become fanatic about doing their exercises. One of my runner's knee patients is Dr. Enrique Loutsch, a psychoanalyst who started running because he felt it would help him give up cigars.

The first few days he would run just a few yards on the beach and then he'd feel his heart pounding and he thought he was about to die. But day by day his heart started pounding easier, the urge for cigars went away, he was happy as a clam—and his knees started killing him.

Enrique is like a lot of runners—I think many of them are males—who have a great belief in will power. He felt pain in his knees, so what should he do? Run through it! Use will power! He kept running and walking up and down flights of stairs.

The pain got worse and he couldn't sleep and his knees hurt even when he was sitting down. So he rested a few days and then went out to the country and ran a mile—up and down hills. The worst thing he could have done. He was heartbroken because he believed in the great myth of Incurable Knee Injuries, and he thought he would have to give up running.

Finally a friend persuaded him to come see me, and he came—early in 1978—with great skepticism. Enrique has weak foot, and he had been wearing arch supports for years —but they didn't happen to do the job for running. I prescribed some orthotics for him and told him to write himself a prescription for Butazolodine and taught him the quadriceps exercises.

He went home full of pain and skepticism. But then the idea of curing his pain through exercise seemed to appeal to his will power. He became a quadriceps-exercise fanatic and today he's in heavy training for this year's marathon.

Pain and Swelling behind the Knee

(Baker's Cyst)

This is an athlete's injury. Runners and tennis players get it. You feel pain at the junction where the upper leg meets the lower leg in back. It's fairly painful when you're running.

Reach back and feel it, and you can feel a lump, like a little ball of gelatin.

This is a non-malignant growth, and it's not something you can treat yourself. Go to an orthopedic surgeon, and have him take care of it for you.

Pain in Upper Inner Thigh Muscle
(Groin pull)

You get this pain from tensing up the inner thigh muscle (the adductor muscle). The adductor muscle is involved with turning the toe in, which is something you normally do when you run. Stretch your leg out and put your hand on the inner thigh muscle. Now turn your toe in. You can feel the movement in the adductor muscle. When you overwork that muscle, it can become tense and painful.

If you've been running on slippery streets—after the snow or rain or on wet leaves—you may feel pain on the inner thighs. You've been tensing up, trying to keep your balance. A friend of mine got groin pull in the right leg after spending a Sunday playing soccer with his son. He kept turning his toe in and tensing up the inner thigh muscle every time he kicked the ball.

Some people tense up this muscle because their feet are not balanced properly. If there's not enough lateral movement of the heel and ankle, the adductor muscle tightens up to help balance the body. The answer to this problem is to help the ankles and heels turn out. We do this by putting a wedge under the inner side of the heel. With this artificial eversion, the heels turns out the way it's supposed to, and there's no special strain on the thigh muscles.

If you have a groin pull, the shoes you wear can make a difference. Don't wear shoes with a very flared heel. That's a heel that's a lot wider at the bottom. The wide base may re-strain the lateral movement of the heel and ankle.

Before I tell you how to treat groin pull, I want to mention another type of pain in the groin area that women sometimes get. I see about four cases of this a year. The pain starts high up on the inner thigh, so the patient thinks it's groin pull. But then, after a few days, the pain appears right under the groin— in the bottom of the pelvic bone. In this case, you may have an ischeal fracture (the ischeum is part of the pelvis), and you should see an orthopedist and have an X ray to check on it.

Now let's discuss the treatment of groin pull. If you're in pain now, cut down on your running or stop running for seven to ten days. When the pain has subsided, do some stretching and strengthening exercises. Two good ones for stretching are Foot on Table, Knee Forward and the Butterfly. For strengthening the adductors, do the Inner Thigh Lift. You'll find all these in the Exercise chapter.

After seven days of doing these exercises and not running, you can start running gently. Just a mile or so a day. Keep up the exercises and increase your mileage gradually.

If the pain persists, take a few days off from running. Continue your exercises. Then try running again. You may cure your problem with this treatment. Or you may have to go to a podiatrist for orthotics. He may decide you need the inner heel wedge I described earlier.

Curing groin pull takes a lot of persistence on your part and a real devotion to your exercises. One runner who did beat this problem is my friend and patient, Nancy Tighe.

Nancy is a tall, slim forty-eight-year-old who helps run her husband's ad agency for a living and then goes out and runs marathons for fun. Except, it got to be less and less fun because she kept getting pain in the adductor muscles.

The first time Nancy got a clue as to the cause of her problem was when she attended a lecture by Dr. Schuster. He said that groin pulls can happen when we run on slippery pavement and Nancy had just completed a thirty kilometer race in the snow (over eighteen miles).

But Nancy's problem did not come only from slippery streets. The groin pull kept recurring as she upped her mileage

in training for marathons. She would have to cut her mileage—sometimes to nothing. Twice she had to skip marathons she had been training for. Once she completed a marathon, but had to jog the whole thing. It took her four hours and thirteen minutes to finish.

Nancy kept talking to people, trying to find an answer to her problem. Some of the suggestions were disastrous and actually made the pain worse. Finally she wound up in my office, and I ordered orthotics for her with the inner-heel wedge described earlier. These seemed to do the trick—along with stretching and strengthening exercises. She does the Inner Thigh Lift with one pound weights on her ankles. I spoke to Nancy this afternoon, and she told me she's hard at work training for a marathon—doing sixty miles a week, pain free.

Back Thigh/Back Knee Pains

(Hamstring pull or sciatica)

Seymour Goldstein, D.C.

To advise you on this subject, I've called on a man who's a genius at hamstrings—Dr. Seymour (Mac) Goldstein, a chiropractor who is doctor and advisor for the Olympic Invitational Meet and for many track teams, such as the Brooklyn Atoms. He's consultant to coaches at NYU, Fairleigh Dickinson, Brown and many other East Coast colleges that are involved in track. Here's Dr. Goldstein's advice for runners with pain in the back of the thigh.

If you feel pain in the back of the thigh, you may have pulled your hamstring muscle. Or you may have sciatica.

It's important for you to find out which it is—because sciatica is a problem you really can't treat yourself. Take it to a doctor—a GP, chiropractor, orthopedist or osteopath.

Here are a few ways to tell the difference between sciatica and hamstring pull.

• Exactly where is the pain located? If the pain is centered

down the back of the thigh, it's probably hamstring pull. If it's toward the outer side of the thigh, it's probably sciatica. With sciatica, you may also feel pain in the hip and lower back, and the pain may extend down to the foot.

• If you have hamstring pull, you'll find it very painful to extend your leg. Your knee wants to stay bent.

• Lie on your back. Raise one leg, knee straight. Have someone flex your foot—that is, bend your toe toward your knee. This will be very painful if you have sciatica. You'll feel a burning sensation or electric shock down the back of your leg or in the small of the back or in one buttock.

Repeat the test on the other leg.

If you have hamstring pull, you won't even be able to complete the test, because you won't be able to stretch your leg out straight.

• Feel the back of your thigh with your fingertips. Look for a lump. This is a contraction in the muscle. If you find this lump, you have hamstring pull. Sometimes you'll even see a black and blue mark that looks like a bruise—as if someone had punched you. That's because, in hamstring pull, the muscle fibers may tear. That's what causes the black and blue mark.

As I said, sciatica must be treated by your doctor. With hamstring pull—or a hamstring cramp—there are some things you can do to help yourself. The treatment for these two hamstring problems is the same, but the cramp will clear up in a few days, while the pull takes at least a few weeks.

The hamstring is a muscle extending from the back of the knee to the buttocks. It has contracted and become painful because you've overextended it or given it a number of quick extensions.

That's what you do when you're sprinting, and when you're running downhill. Sprinters often get hamstring pull because they're always stretching their legs to the limit. Joggers don't get it very often, because they keep their knees bent. A sprinter with hamstring problems has to become a Long Slow Distance runner until his muscles ease up.

Hamstring pull is more common in cold weather, because runners don't warm up their muscles enough.

It's also a pre-marathon injury. Say you've been running gently for months, building up your distance at a fairly comfortable pace. Now the time for the marathon comes close and you decide you want to break three hours—or whatever your goal is. So you start doing intervals, pushing for speed—and extending your legs more than usual. That's when you may get hamstring pull.

You may complete a marathon with hamstring pull, but you won't set a new personal record. You have to use a short stride and a high knee lift, because it's painful to extend the leg. You may even have trouble walking—but you can still jog.

So sprinting is one way you may overextend your legs. Another way is running on a banked track. When you do this, you're giving yourself one "short leg." For instance, say your right leg is on the upper side of the slope. It becomes the short leg—so it has to overextend itself, to keep up with the "long" leg. The solution is to reverse directions.

Or, you may really have one short leg. That's another cause for overextending. Be sure to read the section in this book that tells you how to check your leg lengths, and how to treat yourself for Short Leg. In that section, Dr. Weisenfeld tells you to check to see whether your hipbones are level—because "short leg" is often caused by hipbones that are not level. This is called pelvic tilt. Correcting pelvic tilt is one way that chiropractors and osteopaths correct hamstring pull.

There are some things you can do to treat hamstring pull yourself. How long should you try home treatment before seeing a doctor? I'd say if you just have a cramp in the muscle, it will ease up in about three days. If you have hamstring pull, work with it for a week to ten days. In that time you should have enough relief so you know you're doing the right thing. If you don't have much relief within ten days, see a chiropractor or osteopath. Because the longer your problem continues, the longer it will take to relieve it.

Now, here's your treatment.

• Keep running—or I should say, jogging. Take short steps so you don't have to extend your legs.

• If you've been running on a banked track and have hamstring pull in one leg only—reverse directions.

• Do exercises to stretch and strengthen the muscles. The two I recommend are Weighted Leg Extensions and Bent-Leg Sit-ups. They're both in the Exercise chapter of this book.

• Use ice before and after running. Put an ice pack on the sore muscle for a half hour before running, and a half hour after. This is one point on which Dr. Weisenfeld and I disagree. He never advises runners to use ice before running. Of course, we've all heard that you should never run with "cold" muscles. I'll tell you why I make an exception in this case.

When you have hamstring pull, your muscle is tight and inflamed—it hurts to extend it. But extending is just what it needs. So the ice anesthetizes the pain and brings down the inflammation. Now you're able to get out and jog—extend the leg to some degree—and this is part of your cure.

So, to sum up—your treatment for hamstring pull is:

• Treat yourself for short leg if necessary.

• If you've been running on a banked track, reverse direction.

• Don't stop running. Jog with short steps.

• Exercise

• Ice

If you haven't made much progress in about ten days, I'd advise you to see a chiropractor. He may use electrical stimulation to relax the muscle. And, if you have a short leg caused by pelvic tilt, he'll certainly work on straightening that out—so you can get rid of the basic cause of your hamstring pull.

Varicose Veins

If you've got varicose veins, you've chosen the right sport.

Running can't reverse the varicosities you've got now, but it will probably help prevent or diminish further varicosities.

You see, the heart sends fresh, oxygen-filled blood to various parts of the body. But once the blood has been stripped of its oxygen and nutrients, the heart needs help in pumping the used blood back up again for refilling and reconditioning. The veins themselves, with the help of the muscles, perform a milking action that presses the blood back up.

What keeps that used blood from trickling back down again? You've got a series of valves in your veins. These valves let the blood through as it flows upward, but don't let it flow down again.

People with varicose veins have inherited a tendency to weak valves. The used blood is allowed to flow back down and pool in the legs.

By running, you're supplying extra muscular contractions to push the blood back up in the right direction. Running develops the musculature and supportive tissue in the legs. So keep on with your running.

Incidentally, when you've finished a run, it's very important not to make a sudden stop. While you're running, you're pumping blood hard. Now when you cross the finish line, if you stop suddenly, the pumping stops suddenly and the blood can pool in your legs. So keep on walking till your heart slows down and you stop huffing and puffing. This is important for everyone, not just for people with varicose veins.

Other ways you can help yourself: Don't sit for too long at a time. You're sitting on the veins and keeping the blood from moving. Get up and walk around during the day. Also, don't stand in one place for a long time. When you're standing in one place, your blood stands in one place and gravity pulls it down. Your whole aim is to keep it moving.

People with varicose veins have a tendency toward clotting —thrombophlebitis—if they're very inactive. That's why, in hospitals, people who've had surgery for varicose veins are kept moving. The nurse tries to get the patient out of bed right after surgery. They put elasticized stockings on the patient and elevate the legs to keep the blood moving.

Don't wear pants that tie tightly around the ankle. In the

old days, women were warned against wearing elastic garters around their thighs—but I don't think this is a problem now. Panty girdles that compress the thighs are harmful too.

Any pressure on the veins makes it hard for them to pump the blood up. That's why women with an inherited tendency toward this problem develop varicose veins during pregnancy. The weight of the uterus is putting extra pressure on the veins.

For veins that are severely distended, women can get some relief by wearing support pantyhose while running. If the pantyhose have elasticized feet, cut the lower part of the feet off because your feet swell when you run.

Men can wear support socks while running. I have varicose veins, and I never buy anything but support hose. It's worth paying a few cents more to get that extra relief.

If varicose veins become very painful, your best solution is injection therapy or surgery by a physician trained in the treatment of varicose veins.

Hip and Back Pains

Stanley Roman, D.O.

Dr. Roman is an osteopath who treats a lot of runners with hip and back problems. Sometimes patients come to me with these problems and I can help them with podiatry, but often, they also need a specialist for their particular injury. I send them to Dr. Roman because he is well-known for his success in getting those aching backs comfortable again and getting those nervous runners back on the road.

• Your feet may be giving you a pain in the back.
• That ache in your hip could be coming from your legs.
• A nerve in your spine may be causing a pain in your foot.

Back pain can be a tough mystery to solve. And I gave you those little clues to suggest something to you: If you have a hip or back pain, you have to look at the whole picture. No one can say ah ha! For that pain in the left hip, you should

do such and such an exercise.

Your spinal column, hips, legs and feet all affect each other. So it's especially important for you, a runner, to know what's going on with your pelvis and spine.

Runners know a lot about their feet and legs. But their interest seems to stop there. They don't pay nearly as much attention to what happens north of the quadriceps until they get some back pain.

When you're running, every shock and jolt that happens to your feet is transferred right up to the hips and spine. If you're reading this chapter, I'll assume you've got some kind of pain in the back or hips. But, before we discuss your individual symptoms, you'll have to look at your overall body, and I'll outline a fifteen-minute checkup you should take. It will give you a pretty good first acquaintance with your skeleton. After that introduction, we'll discuss your individual symptoms and you'll be better able to understand them. The problems we'll discuss are the ones I see most in runners:

- Sciatica (Some symptoms of sciatica are pain in the lower buttock; pain down one leg; pain in lower back, on one side.)
- Low back pain.
- Side-of-hip pain.

But before you start your examination, let me give you some reassurance about your back problem. I'm sure you had a grandfather or a great aunt who always had to be "careful not to throw my back out." They treated themselves like invalids, thereby turning themselves into invalids.

These days, we're learning better. We've learned that, if you've got a back problem, there's probably nothing wrong with the way your back is made. But there probably *is* something wrong with the way you treat your back. Specifically, you've allowed your back muscles to get weak or tense through lack of exercise.

So your back problem can very likely be cured.

These days, we don't tell people with back problems to *avoid* exercise. We tell them to follow a carefully graded pro-

gram of exercise. We'll give you some exercises here to handle the problems I see most often in runners. But if you have a chronic back problem that these exercises don't relieve, I suggest you get Dr. Han S. Kraus's book, *The Cause, Prevention, and Treatment of Backache.*

Another reassurance—this time about arthritis. Patients sometimes ask me whether the pounding action of running would trigger arthritis or make it worse. A Finnish study indicated that long distance runners have a lower incidence of arthritis—in fact, half as much—as compared to non-runners. Of course, the Finns don't run on paved roads as much as we do. So if you are worried about arthritis, try running on dirt roads. But by all means keep running—and keep up your supplementary exercise. They are especially important for the runner with arthritis.

You have to exercise the affected area to keep the joints mobile. If arthritis affects your back, be absolutely faithful about doing your back exercises. If it's your knees or hips that get arthritis, keep them well-exercised. Swimming is a good exercise to keep your whole body moving smoothly. Anyone with arthritis should keep his doctor informed on his condition, and he should keep active.

All right, enough discussion. Now you're ready to start your examination. I've included a checklist for you to fill in as you do your checkup. You'll be checking the straightness of your spine and shoulders; whether your pelvis is level or tilted. Whether your legs match in length. You'll find out if your abdominal muscles and lower back muscles are strong enough. You'll take a test for sciatic pain. And you'll check your feet, for balance.

Make notes on the checklist as you go along.

It may seem like a lot of trouble to give yourself this examination, but it's the only way to get at the cause of your back problem.

First, check your overall symmetry. You'll need a mirror or mirrors that give you a front-and-back view. You should not have to twist around to see your back, because then you

won't be standing straight.

Okay, set up your mirrors and then stand in front of them, naked.

Checklist

1. Spine—any curves above or below waist? _____

2. Shoulders level? _____

3. Swayback—can you get back almost flat against wall, without bending knees? _____

4. Pelvis level, front view? _____

5. Pelvis level, back view? _____

6. Leg length equal, lying down? _____

7. Sciatica test: pain in either leg? _____

8. Sit-up: strain in abdominal muscles? ____✓____

9. Lower back test: can you hold leg lift for ten seconds? ___✓___

10. Feet: Fallen arches? _____ Long first toe? _____

---

1. *Spine.*   Your spine should run straight down your back. There should be no curves toward the left or right sides. Look for the bumps of the vertebrae, and follow that line down to see if it's straight. Look for curves above the waist or below the waist. They could be a reason for back pains, hip pains, leg pains.

Look at your shoulder blades—see if they're level.

2. *Shoulders.*   Stand straight in front of the mirror, and see whether your shoulders are level.

3. *Check for swayback.*   Stand with your back against the

wall and try to get your back as flat as possible without bending your knees. Your waist should be close to the wall in back. You should not be able to slip a flat hand between the wall and your back.

4. *Pelvis, front view*   Take a felt-tipped pen and put a dot on each hip bone. Now hold a string between the two dots and see if the string is level.

5. *Pelvis, back view.*   You'll need a helper for this. He or she should put a dot in the dimple above each buttock. He should put the dot close to the spine, not toward the side of the body. Now he should draw a line across the top of each hipbone. To do this, he feels for the outline of the bone, and draws the line there. Now he looks at the dots. Are the hipbones level or is one higher than the other? Are the dots in the dimples level?

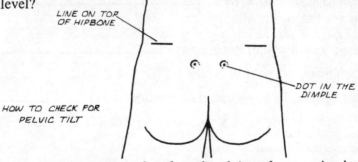

LINE ON TOP
OF HIPBONE

DOT IN THE
DIMPLE

HOW TO CHECK FOR
PELVIC TILT

6. *Compare your leg lengths, lying down.*   Again, you need someone to help you. Lie on your back. Your helper makes sure you're lying flat, with your pelvis even—you're not hitching one leg up. Now he holds both ankles and pulls on them to straighten your legs. Then he compares the ankle bones on the inner side of the leg. If the two ankle bones are not on the same level, then one leg is short.

7. *Sciatica.*   While you're lying on your back, do the test for sciatica. Lift your right leg up, with the knee straight. Now your helper holds your foot and bends the toe toward the knee. If this causes a pain in the leg, you have sciatica. Anyone will feel some degree of tightness and resistance to this foot-flexing. But if it's a definite pain, you should suspect

sciatica. Lower your leg and repeat the test with the other leg. Sciatica is not something you can treat yourself. Go to your family GP or an osteopath or an orthopedist.

8. *Abdominal muscles.*   Test your abdominal muscles by doing a bent-leg sit-up. Lie on your back, with your feet on the floor and your knees bent. Your feet should be as close to your body as possible. Put your hands behind your head. Your helper holds your feet down. Try to sit up to a full sitting position. If you feel strain in the abdominal muscles (not just effort, but real strain), then you have weak abdominal muscles. They could be a cause of your back problem. If this exercise is hard for you to do, don't force it. You'll have to work gradually on your abdominal exercises until you're ready to do the complete sit-up.

9. *Lower back muscles.*   Test your lower back muscles. Lie on your stomach with a pillow under your hips. Fold your arms under your head. Your helper holds your shoulders down as you lift your legs. Keep your knees straight. You should be able to get your thighs off the floor and hold this position for ten seconds. If you can't, then weak lower-back muscles may be causing your back pain.

10. *Fallen arches—weak foot.*   Check your feet for fallen arches. Stand up and look at the arches on the inner side of the foot. See if your arch flattens out—so it almost disappears. This is called "pronating"—the weight shifting to the inner side of the foot. This weight shift could be a cause of back pain.

Now, notice your toe lengths. If the second toe is longer than the big toe, this could cause a weight imbalance. This condition is called Morton's foot.

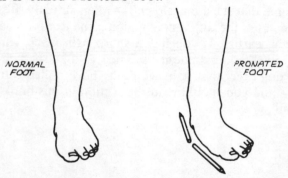

NORMAL
FOOT

PRONATED
FOOT

If you have either of these problems, you should take care of them because they're likely to cause you some aches and pains—in the back or elsewhere.

For Morton's foot, you should probably go to your podiatrist and let him check out your whole foot for imbalances. If you have fallen arches (weak foot), you'll probably end up going to the podiatrist, too. But there's a section in this book on weak foot which will give you some ways you can help the problem by yourself.

Now we've completed the examination that everyone should take for back pain. So we're ready to discuss your individual problems. The three most common back problems I see in runners are sciatica, low back pain and side of hip pain.

Sciatica   Symptoms could be pain in the lower buttock, on one side; or pain down one leg, sometimes all the way to the foot; pain in lower back on one side.

As I said, sciatica is not something you can treat yourself.

The sciatic nerve is the longest nerve in your body. It's formed by nerve roots at the end of the spine. From there it passes through the pelvis and into the legs. Its branches go all the way to the foot. If you feel pain anywhere along the sciatic nerve, there could be a pinching somewhere along the nerve. This could be caused by a pelvic tilt or by pressure on a disc.

A disc is a small package of jellylike material that separates one vertebra from another and gives the spine some cushioning. For various reasons, some of the disc may protrude out—so it's not all centered between its two vertebrae. This might happen because a pulled muscle is causing pressure. A tight, spasmodic muscle could do it.

Runners sometimes feel a pain down the back of the thigh and assume that it's a muscle pull—when actually, it's sciatica.

You can tell the difference by doing the test for sciatica that I gave you earlier. If you feel a sharp pain when your foot is flexed, you should assume it's sciatica, and go see your doctor. (If you don't feel that pain, you may have pulled a hamstring muscle—and you should read the section in this book on hamstring pull.)

Sciatica is something that may linger for months. And that means you can't run for months. Or it may just flare up and disappear again.

There's an old belief that once you've had sciatica, it will probably come back. Actually, there may be years between incidents. You may always have the tendency, but you should not be nervously expecting the next attack. Just follow your doctor's instructions and assume that you'll be out running again soon.

Make an appointment with your family doctor or an osteopath or an orthopedist and meanwhile, stop running. Take hot baths or go to the steam room. Take aspirin to reduce the inflammation. Don't do leg-stretching exercises, because that could make the inflammation worse.

Low Back Pain   This is the most frequent back problem I see in runners.

If you have low back pain, or pain in one hip, you may have found one or two things in your examination: uneven pelvis (it's called pelvic tilt) or unequal leg lengths.

It's easy to understand why either of these would cause pain.

If your pelvis is tilted, it means the muscles on one side are pulled; they're under tension. This is enough to cause pain. Now add the jarring motion of running—and the muscles may go into spasm.

The first aid treatment for low back pain has 3 steps:

1. Rest—cut down your running.
2. Two aspirins with each meal to reduce inflammation and pain.
3. Moist heat. Take hot baths or go to the steam room. I find these more effective than heating pads or heat rubs.

The long-term treatment has two steps: First, treat yourself for short-leg. Second, strengthen the muscles in your lower back and abdomen.

First, treat yourself for short-leg.   Why should you treat

yourself for short-leg? Because pelvic tilt and short-leg go together. It works like this: If you have one short leg, your pelvis may tilt to compensate for it. Conversely, if you have a pelvic tilt, your pelvis is pulling one leg up. So that leg *is* shorter, in effect.

The reason I had you compare your legs lying down was to see if you really have a short leg—or if it's just the pelvis that's pulling it up, so it seems shorter when you're standing.

In any case, treat yourself for short-leg by putting a heel pad in one shoe. Start with a pad ¾₁₆-inch thick—even if your leg is ½-inch or 1-inch short. Don't try to correct for the full inch.

To make your heel lift, get surgical felt and layer it until it's ¾₁₆-inch thick. Or, some shoemakers have hard rubber heel lifts you can wear inside your shoe.

I never use sponge rubber for heel lifts because they compress down when you stand on them. I know that Dr. Weisenfeld does recommend sponge rubber lifts because he feels the cushioning gives you good shock absorption. Since the sponge rubber does press down, Dr. Weisenfeld will tell you to use almost a ½-inch of sponge rubber for ½-inch difference in leg lengths. But in my practice, I use the less compressible material.

Use your heel lift and do your exercises, and you should get relief in about a week. If you get NO relief, the heel lift may not be helping you, so you should remove it. My feeling is, if a heel lift isn't doing you any good, it's better not to wear one. Your body may be used to functioning with two different leg lengths. And if it's working okay, let's not disturb it.

For the same reason, a person with a short-leg but no pain should not use a heel lift.

Second, strengthen your back and abdominal muscles. You'll have to do exercises to strengthen the abdomen and the lower back. You've probably heard that the abdominal muscles support the lower back, and this is true. But if you have lower-back pain, it's safe to say you should strengthen your lower back muscles too.

Bent-Leg Situps strengthen your abdominal muscles. Hip

Rolls strengthen the lower back. Knee Lifts strengthen the lower back and the abdominal muscles. You'll find all these in the Exercise chapter.

Side-of-Hip Pains   Some people feel this pain at the joint of the hip and thigh. Some people feel it up a bit higher—toward the hip bone.

Side-of-hip pain is an overuse injury. It's an inflammation of the fascia, a fibrous, somewhat flexible material that's found in the hips, legs and many other places in the body. The inflammation may start with the tendons that attach the muscles to the bones; then the inflammation spreads to the fascia.

If there's something wrong with your lower back—like weak back muscles—the problem can be passed along to the fascia at the side of the hip.

If you're using your legs incorrectly when you run, that error can be passed along to the side-of-hip fascia.

You can probably get rid of this pain—but it takes some persistence on your part. The fact is, some exercises and techniques help some people and others help other people. I'll give you some techniques that both Dr. Weisenfeld and I use on our patients. These remedies do work—but I can't tell you which will work for you.

1. If you like swimming, swim on your back and do the frog kick.

2. In running, shorten your stride.

3. If you're running on a hard surface, switch to a soft surface. If you're running on a soft surface, switch to a hard surface.

4. Change the kind of shoes you're wearing. Don't just get another pair of the same style—get a different style. Get one with a higher heel or a lower heel. Get one that's broader at the ball of the foot, or narrower. Get a shoe with a higher counter, or a lower one.

5. Do Hip Rolls and Knee Lifts to strengthen your lower back. These are described in the Exercise chapter.

Index

Abdominal muscles, back pain and, 181, 184–85
Achilles tendon, 15, 17, 144
Achilles tendonitis, 15, 17, 159–69
  exercises for treatment/prevention of, 40–41, 46, 157, 158
  first aid for, 62
  jumping rope and, 63
  shoes and, 32, 158
Adductor muscle, 169
  See also Groin pull
Adhesive felt, 60
Adhesive tape, 58
Ankles:
  broken, 145–47
  shoes and, 32
  sprained, *see* Sprained ankles
Anterior metatarsal bursitis, 105–7
Antiseptic, 58–59
Apophycitis of the heel, 143–45
Arches, 16, 62
  fallen, *see* Fallen arches
  fascia material of, 128
  high, 81–83
  low, 138
  metatarsal, 104–5
  pain in, 128–34
  plantar fasciitis, 129–34
Arch support, 135
  for bunions, 99
  for cuboid pain, 114
  for plantar fasciitis, 133

for shin splints, 155
of shoes, 21–22, 31, 32
sponge rubber metatarsal pads and cookies, 60
for weak foot symptoms, 138–39
See also specific injuries and foot problems
Arch-Supporting Strapping, 132–33, 135, 138
Arms, position for holding, 14–15
Arthritis, 91, 178
Aspirins, 131
  for inflammation, 61, 62
  for pain, 59
Athlete's foot, 122, 125–27
  medications for, 127

Back muscles:
  lower, 181
  upper, 43
Back pains, 176–85
  examination for, 178–81
  See also Lower back pains; Upper back muscles
Baker's cyst, 168–69
Ball of foot, 16
  jumping rope and, 63
  landing on, 15
  pain and calluses on, 104–5
  running on, 93–94
Band-Aids, 58
Banked tracks, running on, 18, 162, 167, 173

Betadine, 58
Beginner's rules, 5–7
Bent-Leg Sit-Ups, 44
Bicycling, 64
Big toe:
  bunion of, 96–101 (*See also* Bunions)
  stiff, 91–92
  tendon, 101
Black toenail, 116–17
Blisters, 24, 119–21
  gauze for, 58
  prevention of, 63, 119–20
  Zonis Tape for, 58
Bone spurs, 115
  corns and, 123
  See also Heel spurs
Bunion bagel, 98, 101
Bunion pad, 98
Bunions, 83–84, 96–101
  big toe, 96–101
  latex jacket for, 98–99
  padding for, 98
  shoes and, 32, 84
  small toe (tailor's), 101
  surgery for, 100
Burning sensation between metatarsal heads, 107–9
Bursitis:
  anterior metatarsal, 105–7
  inferior calcaneal (heel), 129, 131, 134–36
Butterfly, 48

Calf muscles, 15, 17
  exercises for, 40–41, 46
  lower-leg pains and, 149, 150
  short bunchy, 84
  See also Leg pains

Calluses, 55
  on balls of feet, 104–5
  cracks on heels and, 126
  smoothing down, 59, 63
  See also Corns
Cavus foot, 82–83, 123
Children, 13, 14
  apophycitis of the heel in, 143–45
Chondromalacia of the patella, *see* Runner's knee
Clothes, 5–6
Colt, Ed, 70
Condyle, 123
Corn drops, 59, 121–23
Corn pads, 59, 121–23
Corns, 55
  doughnut pads for, 59
  hammer toes and, 102
  lamb's wool for, 59
  smoothing down, 59, 63
  on tips of toes, 123
  between toes (soft corns), 122–23
  on top and outer sides of toes, 121–22
Counter of shoe, 24, 26, 31
Cracks:
  on heels, 126–27
  between toes, 125–26
Cramps, 70
Cream, for heels, 63
Crest pads, 153
Cuboid pain, 114
Cushioning of shoes, 20–21, 31–32
  adhesive felt, 60
  heel pads, *see* Heel pads
  moleskin, 60